CU00802231

Blackness at the Intersection

Blackness at the Intersection

Edited by
Kimberlé Crenshaw, Kehinde Andrews
and Annabel Wilson

BLOOMSBURY ACADEMIC
LONDON • NEW YORK • OXFORD • NEW DELHI • SYDNEY

BLOOMSBURY ACADEMIC
Bloomsbury Publishing Plc
50 Bedford Square, London, WC1B 3DP, UK
1385 Broadway, New York, NY 10018, USA
29 Earlsfort Terrace, Dublin 2, Ireland

BLOOMSBURY, BLOOMSBURY ACADEMIC and the Diana logo are
trademarks of Bloomsbury Publishing Plc

First published in Great Britain 2024
Reprinted in 2024

A catalogue record for this book is available from the British Library.

A catalog record for this book is available from the Library of Congress.

ISBN: HB: 978-1-7869-9864-4
         PB: 978-1-7869-9865-1
         ePDF: 978-1-7869-9868-2
         eBook: 978-1-7869-9866-8

Series: Blackness in Britain

Typeset by Integra Software Services Pvt. Ltd.
Printed and bound in Great Britain

To find out more about our authors and books visit www.bloomsbury.com
and sign up for our newsletters.

Contents

Dedication: For Dr Nicole Andrews

by Kehinde Andrews

We started the Black Studies project in British higher education in 2013 but my career really started to take off in 2015 after I moved to Birmingham City University and started to institutionalize our research agenda. Launching Europe's first Black Studies degree in 2017 put the work on the map, generating a wealth of attention and plaudits. These years are ones I will always remember, but not because of work. They were the years my three sons with my late wife Nicole were born. Whilst my career was taking off, Nicole was giving birth to three children, pausing her own work for maternity leave. It is a testament to her talent and determinedness that she managed to complete her PhD and find a full-time academic job in between having three children. It should go without saying that I could not have achieved my professorship without the support of my wife, but I do not mean this in a paternalistic 'she took care of the household and kids' kind of way. Nicole was one of the most intellectually perceptive people I have met and everything I have created was done in conversation with her. Nicole's PhD, *Big Talk: An Exploration of Seldom Heard Discourses of Body Shape and Size from African Caribbean Women in the Context of Primary Care* was so good she passed with no corrections, something I did not realize was even possible. Her methodological approach was pioneering, researching in Black community spaces of hairdressers, church groups and talk radio. After finishing her PhD she worked as a health researcher at the University of Birmingham, before getting a full-time job in Health and Social Care in Newman University. It was only due to her maternity commitments that her career took a different shape to my own, a perfect example of how gendered inequalities lead to different outcomes. I don't want it to sound like I forced Nicole into being barefoot and pregnant, whilst I went out and conquered the world of work. We had many a conversation about what we wanted from life and she very much chose to devote more time to the kids. That choice was certainly influenced by the very real structural barriers that place childcare burdens disproportionately on women, not least the paltry paternity leave arrangements in place. When I took two weeks' paternity leave for our second child, I was shocked (and appalled) to find a huge dent in my pay cheque because my university only paid those two weeks at the statutory minimum level. There have since been changes to paternity leave, with the possibility of couples sharing the time off, but had that been an option I would have known better than to suggest this to Nicole. For the first two children she was a PhD student, and I wasn't earning enough to pay into a pension, so she went back to work before she would have liked. For our third child, Nicole was in a full-time job and enjoyed the extended maternity leave to the fullest. That was cherished time for her to recover and spend uninterrupted time with her babies, not something I was going to encroach on. Everyone is different and shared parental leave is a welcome development, but it wouldn't have worked in our household because there remain significant financial barriers. Legally, companies only have to pay 90% of pay for the parent who is off for the first six weeks. After that, statutory parental leave currently works out at just over £624 a month, which is less than half the minimum wage. Considering gendered inequalities, it remains likely the father's wage will be higher and therefore represent a larger loss of income for the family. Even if we had wanted to, we couldn't have afforded for me to take several weeks off and lose the difference in salary. So Nicole took three periods of maternity leave, but that doesn't even capture the amount of time lost in her career. Each time she was pregnant her hands swelled up from about halfway through the pregnancy and she had difficulty concentrating. When she did go back to work we still had kids to look after and that presented a whole lot of schedule juggling for the both of us. Despite dedicating such time to our family Nicole was promoted just before being diagnosed with breast cancer in the summer of 2020. She would not mind me sharing her illness with you. Her work was dedicated to health inequalities impacting Black women and her life was cut tragically short by triple negative breast cancer, which disproportionately kills women like her. Throughout her treatment she kept notes on what she was experiencing, which we hope to publish in the future. She was always engaged, always analysing. One of the most tragic aspects of being with her in her final months was that as the cancer spread to her brain it robbed her of the capacity to articulate her thoughts. I will forever be convinced she was still piecing it all together inside but was just unable to share her always invaluable insights.

As with every project I have been involved with for more than a decade, since I have known her, *Blackness at the Intersection* would have been impossible without Dr Nicole Andrews. As we explain in the book, we held two different workshops where we co-created the manuscript. These lasted multiple days and we had a growing family. As I was involved in running the workshops I had to be there, and Nicole mostly spent the time at work and looking after the children. She came to the beginning and end of both workshops but did not have the capacity to submit a paper to either. This really is a great loss to the book as she had some fascinating insights on intersectionality and greatly helped us in the editorial process. But in her time at the workshops, she was her usual ray of intellectual light. In the introduction we tell the story of Nicole piercing through a discussion to locate 'Blackness as the roundabout' in the intersection, the junction through which all identities must pass. This is one of the clearest articulations of Blackness and intersectionality that I have heard, and Nicole delivered it round a picnic table in between shouting over to the kids not to play too close to the car park. She had an incredible mind, but her life was cut too short for her to be truly appreciated. So you won't read a chapter by Nicole in the book but be rest assured that if it were dusted for prints the marks of her fingers would be found all over this project. We are all eternally grateful to have known her and for the legacy she has left behind. Dr Nicole Andrews is the roundabout through which all roads of this project passed.

Contributors

Kehinde Andrews is Professor of Black Studies at Birmingham City University, UK. He is author of *Back to Black: Retelling Black Radicalism for the 21st Century* (2018), *Resisting Racism: Race, Inequality and the Black Supplementary School Movement* (2013) and *The New Age of Empire* (2021).

Miranda Armstrong is a writer and sociologist at the University of York, a PhD candidate at Goldsmiths College and a Researcher in Residence at the Black Cultural Archives (BCA). Miranda held the prestigious Economic and Social Research Council PhD scholarship, and has taught sociology and criminology at Goldsmiths. Her scholarship has been published in *Feminist Review* and she is a contributing essayist to the pioneering anthology, *Motherhood Untold*. Miranda's writing has been published by *Black Ballad* and *The Voice* and she is author of the graphic pamphlet *Beyond the Myth: Single Black Mothers and Their Sons*, which is available for free download online. Her digital exhibition essay for the BCA, 'Black Mothers in the Forefront: Struggles and Resistance in the 1970s', launched in autumn 2022.

Katucha Bento is a Lecturer in Race and Decolonial Studies, Co-Director of Race.ED Network at the University of Edinburgh, UK, and the co-founder of the Free Afro-Brazilian University (UNAFRO). She is the associate editor of the journal *Identities: Global Studies in Culture and Power*. Her work focuses on quilombo communities' epistemologies and praxis, Black feminists and Queer subversive language.

Eddie Bruce-Jones is Professor of Law at SOAS, University of London, UK. He is author of *Race in the Shadow of Law: State Violence in Contemporary Europe* (Routledge, 2016) and writes and researches on human rights, migration, law & literature and legacies of colonial Indentureship.

Kimberlé W. Crenshaw is Isidor and Seville Sulzbacher Professor of Law at Columbia Law School, USA. She is a pioneering scholar of critical race theory, who coined the term 'intersectionality'.

Dr Constantino Dumangane Jr is a lecturer in the Department of Education at the University of York, and a member of the Centre for Research on Education and Social Justice (CRESJ). He is a member of the Steering and

Academic Advisory Group of The Network for Evaluating and Researching University Participation Interventions (NERUPI); a member of the board of ESRC Wales Doctoral Training Partnership (DTP) Management Board for Equality, Diversity and Inclusion; and a member of the operations team for the University of York's Staff Race Equality Steering Group and Forum. His research has been published in journals such as *Qualitative Research* and *British Educational Research Journal*.

Mary Igenoza is a Senior Associate researcher at the Equality and Human Rights Commission. She has a PhD in Sociology from the University of Sheffield.

Viji Kuppan completed his PhD in 2022 at Leeds Beckett University. His activism, research and scholarship focuses on thinking through the intersections of race, disability and gender in popular culture and society.

Kadian Pow is a lecturer in Sociology and Black Studies at Birmingham City University, UK. She holds a PhD in Sociology from Birmingham City University. Kadian's expertise in popular culture, feminism, representation and race has been featured in The Conversation, USA Today, BBC's Women's Hour, Ok Player Magazine, and Yahoo! Kadian is one of Canvas 8 Expert consultant in culture and an external researcher for a joint project between Birmingham Museums Trust and Beatfreeks on decolonising the museum. She is the author of Stories of *Black Female Identity in the Making* (2023).

Kelena Reid teaches history and psychology at Moses Brown School, USA. She has a Ph.D. in U.S. history and African American history from Rutgers University.

Francesca Sobande is a senior lecturer in digital media studies at Cardiff University. She is the author of *The Digital Lives of Black Women in Britain* (Palgrave Macmillan, 2020) and *Consuming Crisis: Commodifying Care and COVID-19* (Sage, 2022). Francesca is also co-editor with Akwugo Emejulu of *To Exist Is to Resist: Black Feminism in Europe* (Pluto Press, 2019), and is co-author with layla-roxanne hill of *Black Oot Here: Black Lives in Scotland* (Bloomsbury, 2022).

Dionne Taylor: Associate Professor in Sociology and Black Studies at Birmingham City University; MA Black Studies Course lead; Thesis entitled: '*I Wanna Love You': An Exploration into the Lived Experiences of Young Black British Women's Interpretation and Engagement with Representations* *of Black Womanhood*; SMaRteN funding award winner 2021 Pilot study of a Student-led Peer Support Wellbeing Programme Piloting the use of EEC™ and Healing Circles to improve Black student mental health.

Annabel Wilson is a sociologist. She has recently completed a PhD at Cardiff University. Annabel is a project manager and research associate on Surviving Storms: The Caribbean Cyclone Cartography project, which is based at Goldsmiths University.

Ajamu X is a photographic artist, scholar, archive curator and radical sex activist best known for his imagery that challenges dominant ideas around black masculinity, gender, sexuality, and representation of black LGBTQ people in the United Kingdom.

Introduction: Reframing intersectionality

Kimberlé Crenshaw, Kehinde Andrews and Annabel Wilson

Our project started when we convened a series of discussions about the myriad of issues with how intersectionality was being mobilized. As central as the concept had become in the everyday life of institutions we found that it was often being misused, thrown out as a buzzword by managers with no understanding of intersectionality's theoretical ground or intellectual framework. We set out to organize a workshop that brought together scholars interested in reframing intersectionality by producing work that re-engaged with the concept's intellectual roots and tradition. Over two workshops, spread across five days, and separated by two years, we co-produced the work presented here. *Blackness at the Intersection* is the product of endless hours of work, debate and socializing that went into developing the intellectual community around that initial premise. In order to reframe intersectionality we had to go back to the beginning to understand how it emerged, and why it became such a foundational concept underpinning how we understand the world.

Intersectionality is contingent on viewing the world through specific contexts. The theory emerged out of the struggles and experiences of African American women and therefore is rooted in a specific historical trajectory. Black women occupy particular locations within the American political economy, oppressed by both their race and gender. Their standpoints allow for a view of the oppressive social structure that is often occluded from different locations in the social pyramid. By seriously engaging with the standpoints of Black women, intersectionality has allowed us to see the way that racialized power operates through the intersections of different 'identities' in the system. Rather than locate identity politics within those oppressed by the system, intersectionality gives us the tools to understand that all politics is about identity; mobilizing resistance or oppression through a given subject position. This is no less true than with the White men who dominate the halls of power. What could be more an expression of 'identity politics' than the Alabama state senate seeking to control the bodies of women by trying to ban abortion; restricting voting rights; or Trump wrapping himself in the clothes of White nationalism to get elected? Intersectionality allows us to see beyond the supposed 'postracialism' of society that we were promised by the election of the first Black president, and to understand that the counter-reaction to that symbolic change was as violent as it was inevitable.

A Black feminist standpoint was essential to unlocking the promise of intersectionality because it demanded a re-articulation of not only how we understand the system but also how we conceive of resistance. The Civil Rights Movement was by some measures extremely successful, achieving reforms of the system that ended legalized segregation in the South and also gaining voting rights for African Americans. Affirmative action, something that is almost unimaginable in Britain, was also a result of tireless campaigning, as were victories in housing reforms and many other areas of social life. Unfortunately, embedded in much of the civil rights practice of the fifties and sixties was a deeply problematic patriarchy, which identified the root to Black equality as the reconstitution of the nuclear family headed by the male breadwinner. The oft-cited 1965 Moniyhan Report is the clearest example of this policy agenda, which argued that Black men needed to be given gainful employment in order that they could fulfil their role as the patriarch. The idea that the Black man is an endangered species, who has been neutered by the state has taken hold. There is certainly a reality to the oppression that Black men face: mass incarceration, police killings, murder, school exclusions and the list goes on. In fact, the situation is so bad that it is estimated that there are roughly 1.5 million Black men who are missing from American society, mostly either dead or in jail.[1] There is undoubtedly a war against Black men. But the focus of the narrative on Black men is harmful in two ways.

For one, it ignores the reality that there is equally a war against Black women who are also more likely to be incarcerated, killed by the police, excluded from school etc. In addition, Black women are also the ones who have to pick up the burden of the 'missing' Black men. Rather than seeking to support Black women, the dominant narrative not only ignores, but also demonizes them. It is Black women chasing away the men; getting pregnant so they can live off the state; and effeminizing the Black boys in their care. Within the dominant frame, supporting Black men comes at the expense of Black women who are struggling just as much. The twentieth-century version of Moynihan came from no other than Obama, whose response to the murder of Trayvon Martin was to launch his landmark 'My Brother's Keeper' (MBK), a mentoring programme funded mostly by the private sector to provide role models for those young Black men suffering from the absent father disease. That Trayvon was killed whilst he was visiting his father was apparently lost on Obama. It should come as no surprise that the programme was supported not only by right-wing Republicans but also incendiary figures like Bill O'Reilly. MBK was actually worse than Moynihan, which at least wanted to get Black men jobs. The economic piece has been replaced by attempting to stoke aspirations in Black boys to be better people than their single mothers could prepare them to be. MBK is problematic, not only because it neglects Black women and girls, but because it is a further attack against the boys it is supposed to help. It is telling that the only contemporary civil rights organization to come out against the programme was the African American Policy Forum (AAPF), founded by Kimberlé Crenshaw. That is the power of the intersectional world view.

Blackness at the Intersection comes out of a related but different historical context and political moment. Thousands of miles from the US, a group of scholars came together to discuss how intersectionality could be used in the context of work being done in Britain. The initial call for participants in the project was actually entitled *Reframing Intersectionality*, as we were responding to the ways that the term has been misappropriated. The most egregious of these was at a conference in Germany which invited Crenshaw, originally to mark twenty years since the publication 'Demarginalizing the Intersection of Race and Sex'[2] and included a panel called 'Celebrating Intersectionality'. Only when it came to the event the organizers had added an all-important question mark to the end, and ultimately critiqued the term, reducing it to a buzzword, an aberrant misreading of the racism drawn from the US context.[3] They argued that only by removing race from the foreground and applying a universalist framework could analysis be of any use. Of course, Europe was the perfect location to make these pronouncements given that the Enlightenment had given birth to the universalist understanding of rights, shattering the chains of bondage that dogged the old racial thinking. Rather than simply chuckle at the delusions of the legacies of colonial scholarship we wanted to use this reaction as a teachable moment.

Intersectionality offers a counter to the erasure of race, gender and other identities in all arenas. The Enlightenment is certainly not spared from this analysis. To see it as a coincidence that a group of White men from Western Europe and the United States developed an intellectual movement that guaranteed full rights only to White men with property, takes a special kind of myopia. The racism of figures like Kant, Locke, Rousseau and the assorted dead White men were not incidental to their ideas of freedom, but central in how they were produced. The founding fathers of the United States declaring that all men were created equal while they enslaved Africans contained no contradiction because Africans were thought of as less than human as the constitutional convention in 1787 made perfectly clear. Written into the founding principles of the nation was that the enslaved would only account for three-fifths of a White person when it came to representation in the new democracy. Make no mistake, this was just America applying the wider European 'universalist' framework. Kant, Germany's poster boy for the Enlightenment, not only justified African enslavement, he offered advice on the best way to beat the 'Negro' because apparently whipping us would not penetrate our thick skin.[4] A central tenet in his universalist philosophy was what he called 'moral geography', that due to climate Europeans were the only race capable of achieving the full capacity of humanity. So the supposed universalist basis upon which Western claims to objectivity are based are nothing more than White identity politics, a theory produced to prove the superiority of White men.[5] An intersectional analysis provides a basis to understand these claims for what they are.

When it came to reframing intersectionality the discussion was the need to reassert the theoretical basis of the concept, to reattach it to a critical understanding of racism in society. The power of intersectionality is that although it emerged from a specific context it can and has been applied across a vast array of different locations. For instance, Crenshaw's work presented in the United Nations 'Background Paper for the Expert Meeting on the Gender-Related Aspects of Race Discrimination' prepared for a meeting in Croatia in 2000 became a seminal tool for female activists across the globe.[6] This paper fed into the infamous 2001 UN Durban conference helping the women's movements around the world to find a common language. But in the widespread adoption of intersectionality there has also been the tendency to erase the foundation of the concept whilst appropriating its articulation.

Intersectionality was never simply about adding up the different axes of oppression that people faced. It was not about engaging in an oppression Olympics that placed Black + woman + queer + disabled in some rarefied position of oppression. In the same vein the concept is not an equation where you can replace the various axes in order to come to some special intersectional understanding. For instance, the position of woman + queer + disabled + poor will produce a fascinating standpoint, which is absolutely worth mining in order to understand social relations, but we should never see it as equivalent to the experiences of Black women. This is for two reasons. Firstly, to see intersectionality as a zero sum game, an equation of oppression widely misses the point. As such the notion strips the concept of its power, and any perceived axes can be added to the matrix: age, hair colour, accent, body type. Whilst these may all be relevant to a person's life experience the point of intersectionality is not to explore the infinite combinations of difference that shape people's lives. The point was always to use the differences that make a difference in order to see society through new eyes, which is directly related to the second problem of intersectionality as equation. The vantage point of

Black women made clear that race is an absolutely indispensable feature of societal oppression. Not only when there are Black people present, but at all times. If you were to put race into the equation we would have to see that woman + queer + disabled / (White) is the kind of sum that if you put it into your calculator you get the 'error' message.

When we held the first workshop we were keen to lay the theoretical foundations of intersectionality out from the start, in order to prompt meaningful discussions about how we could think through the concept in the present moment. Kimberlé Crenshaw and Devon Carbado led off the first two sessions, setting the scene and clearing the ground for the work that was to come. Black feminism was the first session we opened with for all of the reasons spelt out above. We felt it important to reassert the roots of the concept as a starting point for engagement. This was particularly important given the participants. Of the twenty-five participants at the first workshop, all but two were Black and the majority were women. All were well aware of Black feminism and had articulated it in our work. The second theoretical session was just as important but often overlooked as a theoretical root of intersectionality. Black feminism provided the standpoint through which to illuminate oppression, and it was Critical Race Theory (CRT) that provided the framework to understand systems of discrimination.

CRT emerged out of the disillusionment with critical legal studies, which had a strong class analysis but an absence of race; and also out of the failures of civil rights victories to secure meaningful changes. The battles to reshape the legal framework had been hard won, but racism continued to be reproduced. It was not just that issues like unemployment and poverty had hardly improved since the sixties, or even that new problems like mass incarceration had emerged. Some of the landmark legal cases so celebrated at the time and since actually worked to entrench racial disparities. Take for example the momentous *Brown v. Board of Education* so central to the folklore of civil rights. Often missed in the ceremony around the case is that Brown actually refers to a Black plaintiff Oliver Brown, father of Linda, who was refused entry to the White only school that was near her house. The Browns were protesting merely over the issue of convenience: travelling across town to the Black school was too much for a working family. But when the case went to court the issue of convenience was dropped and it became about the perceived deficits of the Black schools.

The case became notable not only for desegregating the schools but also for arguing that 'separate educational facilities are inherently unequal'[7] in direct rebuke to the established precedent in *Plessy v. Ferguson*. Black children were said to be missing out by not being able to socialize with White children in their run-down inferior schools. But the Browns were never imploring to be taught with White children because they thought that the education would be better, just closer and better funded. Segregation certainly had negative consequences but it also meant that there was a thriving sector of Black schools in the South. When the South finally integrated the schools they did so at the expense of the Black schools, closing down the supposedly 'inferior' institutions to integrate Black children into the White ones. As a result thousands of Black teachers, largely Black women, lost their jobs. At the NAACP fiftieth anniversary at the University of Michigan event to commemorate the decision, Linda Brown was the keynote speaker and read out part of the dismissal letter of Miss Buchanan, one of the Black female teachers who lost their jobs. The lack of representation in the teaching profession has never been recovered.

Not only did thousands of Black teachers lose their jobs, the problem as presented was never even solved. Seventy years after the decision the public schools in many parts of the US are more segregated today than they were before the gavel came down.[8] There is perhaps no better example than Derrick Bell's, one of the key founders of CRT, warning that 'what we designate as "racial progress" is not a solution to that problem. It is a regeneration of the problem in a particularly perverse form.'[9] Essential to CRT is the idea that racism is a *permanent* feature of society, in opposition to the classical liberal approach that sees the problem as something on the margins that can be reformed out of society. Once we understand racism as *the* system, then to articulate a position of intersectionality without race would be absurd. Precisely because we had all experienced this kind of usage of the concept, we felt it necessary to reframe how the concept was being mobilized.

One of the tools from CRT that we used in shaping the book was the idea of workshopping. We brought together the first group of participants for a three-day workshop, and the second time for two days, which we felt important not only to build a rapport but to substantively engage in discussions of the papers. We included a number of developing scholars and these kinds of workshops were essential in providing intellectual mentorship. We had to engage with the surprise at just how embedded racial oppression is as well as the trauma of that revelation. The workshops were extremely fruitful, as well as fun and emotional at times. There were tears, as there invariably are when the subject matter is so close to home. Intersectionality is a reminder that the personal is political, and therefore is a space that needs to be explored with delicacy. We were aiming to develop an academic community in the vein of CRT that could be strong enough to take root and spread branches out across academia. At the end of both retreats we took pictures of the group, which were eerily reminiscent of those taken at the initial meetings to found CRT.

CRT was the guiding intellectual framework for the workshops and this volume and if there is a founding text of the movement it is *Critical Race Theory: Key Writings That Formed the Movement* published in 1995. Tracing the emergence of CRT out of the legal context it emerged from the book outlines the key tenets that have remained vitally important almost thirty years later. The book explores how racism becomes a permanent feature in society through the law. A specific focus is on showing how race is socially constructed within the American legal framework to reproduce racism. In the American context the law is particularly important given that the Supreme Court has the final say on what is constitutionally allowable. One of the main reasons that so many social conservative, religious Republicans were able to mobilize behind the sacrilegious Trump was because of the battle to stack the Supreme Court with conservative justices. A wildly pro-choice House of Representatives, senate and president can only restrict abortion rights if the court votes that the constitution allows it.

Much more so than in Britain legal battles *are* policy ones. It is no coincidence that desegregation of schools in the South was a process started with a victory in court. So CRT's roots in the law should not be seen as a limitation. Laws are the mechanism through which policy is enforced, and the state is utterly essential in creating and maintaining racial systems of oppression. To interrogate the law is to understand the very nature of racialized oppression.

One of the key analyses from CRT is the notion that appeals to colour-blindness are in fact a tool to continue to maintain racial oppression. The figure of the lady of justice, Themis, standing with a blindfold is the perfect metaphor for the supposed fairness of law. Race supposedly does not matter, the law is dispensed fairly to all regardless of class, colour or creed. Obviously, this is nonsense but CRT has forensically analysed the absurdity of these claims. Worse still, by attempting to treat everyone the same, the law ends up reproducing racialized differences. An example in Britain would be the efforts to outlaw discrimination in terms of employment. There are strict rules about how long a job should be advertised for, and anonymization of the process so that a person's background should not be taken into account. These are noble gestures but for all of the legal and even institutional efforts to equalize the hiring process we still see the same patterns of racism in terms of hiring. Everyone is treated the same but it makes no difference, because the problems are far more entrenched that anonymizing a CV. Due to racism we are not starting off in the same position, so there are already huge imbalances in who has the access to qualifications, networks and general advantages in society. Not to mention that even if you get an interview this will be in front of the very people the rules do not trust to be impartial in the screening process. Treating everyone the same in this context is to legitimize racial inequality.

CRT's influence has spread widely outside of the field of legal studies because of the profound nature of its insights.[10] It is a testament to how durable and influential CRT has been and the intellectual movement provided the perfect framework for engaging the work in this collection.

Blackness in Britain

After the initial meeting we again invited participants to resubmit chapters for the proposed book. We were keen that the volume not just be an articulation of intersectional experiences, but do the theoretical work of re-engaging with the concept itself. This meant that each paper submitted had to be subject to rigorous engagement and the bulk of the editorial work was done within the preparation for the session and the events themselves. One of the strengths and weaknesses of the first workshop was that we had a wide range of disciplines and topics represented. From history to public health and everything in between the workshop showed the appeal of intersectionality. However, because of the breadth of subjects there was little theoretical agreement on how the concept could be mobilized. As we navigated our way through the papers and talked through the themes it became clear what underpinned the diverse collection of work we were discussing. The thread that held the work together was the diasporic experiences of Blackness.

All but two of the participants were of African descent but this included people from the Caribbean, Africa, United States and Brazil, and various generations of settlement in Britain from visitors to those of the third generation. The papers covered these varying experiences but what was obvious was how Blackness was the glue that held them together. For this reason when we brought people back for the second workshop we had changed the title of the project to *Blackness at the Intersection* to stress how pivotal Blackness was to our articulations of intersectionality. We again went through a process of workshopping, and some of the participants had changed with the new framing. For this second retreat we brought together twenty participants and we also invited early career scholars not involved in the book so that they could engage with the work. We were, and continue to be, keen to stress that we hope this book provides a framework for engaging the new dimensions in the way scholars utilize intersectionality and also build academic community.

Blackness as glue has two dimensions that will be explored when we introduce the chapters. The first is the external, how Blackness is used as a signifier in order for us to be oppressed. This is how we typically think of the concept, as a colour given to us by our oppressors. CRT being the frame for the work it is obvious to see how being of African descent presents a particular location in the racial status quo. When exploring the dynamics of this racialization we can clearly see how the law, policy and institutions are organized to marginalize us as Black people. In the British context, this discussion of Blackness becomes a little trickier because we have the concept of 'political blackness', which sees all those who are victims of racism (i.e. non-White) as being Black. This discussion also played out in the workshops and in this book as Viji Kuppan, one of the organizers, is South Asian, but identifies as 'black' because of the history of this term in some quarters in the UK.

Political blackness has been the subject of heated debate, with there being those who believe that we need to embrace the unity of all non-White groups, to those who shudder at the very notion of defining themselves in relation to their oppressor. Political blackness is defended because it rejects the European notion of race as something coded to biology and seeks to define blackness in the experience of racial oppression, which is not the sole possession of any one group. It is the 'strategic essentialism' bringing together all those facing oppression in a political identity to challenge the racial order.[11] But one of the reasons for the contemporary rejection of political blackness is precisely because racism does not apply equally across various different groups. In fact, intersectionality is the perfect tool to explore the inadequacies of the concept.

To be of African descent has meant being at the bottom of the racial totem pole since White supremacy became embedded into Western social thought. We were considered to be nothing more than the missing link, beasts of burden who could be used as cattle. Stereotypes of the hypersexual, hyperphysical and hypermasculine that derived from slavery are still read onto the Black body today. There is a reason we are so much more likely to be arrested and killed by the police. In the UK the criminal justice system is one of the easiest places to see how racism plays out differently.

If we were to look at racial inequalities across school achievement at sixteen we would find no disparities between Whites and non-Whites.[12] But if we look more closely we will see that those of African Caribbean, African, Pakistani and Bangladeshi descent all perform around or below the average. It is higher performing Indian and Chinese students who are bringing up the whole. These disparities also exist across genders where girls of different ethnic groups do better than boys but less well than their White counterparts. Racial discrimination simply does not work on a White/non-White axis.[13] Worse still, one of the reasons for the anger that comes with the idea of political blackness is that some non-White groups have also taken advantage of their relatively better position in the racial hierarchy.

In 2005 riots broke out in Birmingham over the rumour that a fourteen-year-old Jamaican girl had been gang raped by Pakistani workers in a hair care shop. It is likely that this never actually occurred. The girl never came forward and was said to have fled back to Jamaica in the aftermath. But the fact that the story was believed and that the Black community mobilized is testament to the longstanding tension between the two groups. South Asians dominate the local market for Black hair care and food items in some of the poorest areas of Europe. When Black unemployment is so high it is no surprise that there would be discomfort with Asians holding a near-monopoly over two industries that serve Black communities. Resentment is only highlighted by the lack of any attempt to employ Black people and the treatment that Black women often receive in the shops. The unrest was not solely about hair care shops but a general feeling that Black people were being exploited by Asians, and in many ways the riots were '30 years in the making'.[14] Again showing the parallels to the situation in the US, the dynamic is similar to how East Asians are often perceived in disadvantaged African American communities.

Hair shops are predominantly visited by Black women and staffed by South Asian men. There is nothing intrinsically wrong with this. Please avoid the temptation to pour fuel on the idea that South Asian men have some kind of predilection for sex crimes, as was the narrative with the child sexual exploitation scandal in Rotherham, where seven South Asian, Muslim men were convicted as part of a group who exploited young girls in the area. In another demonstration of the limits of political blackness, this panic is now being stoked by the second Indian female Home Secretary Suella Braverman. Most men in Britain involved in paedophile rings, and grooming circles, are White, so the fact that a grooming ring consisted of Pakistani men was incidental. In fact, often overlooked in that case was that the abusers took advantage of their positions as taxi drivers in order to get access to and facilitate child sex exploitation. Given the racism in the job market, Asian and other immigrant communities have been pushed into taxi driving in order to support their families. So it certainly is true that Asian men are far more likely to be taxi drivers and in this case abused their position. The same could be said for the overwhelming White and male Catholic priesthood who have such an appalling track record of abusing their position in relation to young boys. In the case of Asian male shop workers in Black hair care shops, they serve an overwhelmingly Black female clientele. There are consistent reports of women feeling treated rudely and subject to sexually inappropriate behaviour, which meant that when the rumour went round it was believable. But to pretend that the same environment could not exist with White (or even Black) male staff would be to ignore all the available historical precedent. Certain abuses are done by men *as* men to women *as* women. Intersectionality is not about adding layers of complexity to every individual case, but highlighting systems of power and oppression. What the Birmingham case tells us is that from the standpoint of Black women we can again see more clearly the issue of society once we look intersectionally. Male violence against women intersected with racialized, and localized, power to create a tipping point into conflict on the streets, which had been brewing for decades. In terms of political blackness the events shattered the delusion that non-White unity on that basis alone was a vehicle for change. There has been a backlash against political blackness in Black communities in Britain for this very reason, but objections to the concept also come from those who do not want to see the experiences of those of other than African descent erased.[15]

Britain is home to an extremely diverse set of migrant and migrant-descended communities, who represent almost every country on the globe. To imagine that there is any identity that everyone who is not White could buy in to ignores the realities that shape experiences on the ground. When people come into the nation they do not shed the ties that bind them. Diaspora is a vital and powerful bond that is not broken by being subject to racism from the British state. As much as political blackness has been, and remains, an organizing tool in specific contexts in Britain (usually in the professions where there are so few non-Whites that you have little choice), its legacy has been over theorized. This should not come as too much of a surprise given that theory emerges from the university, one of the Whitest of all professions. In reality, if we look back at how anti-racist activism has functioned in the UK it has mostly been through national diaspora organizations.

In the sixties groups like the West Indian Standing Conference and Indian Workers' Association collaborated on anti-racist campaigns, and in this supposed heyday of politically black activism there were in fact very few community-based politically black groups. We should not dismiss community formations like the British Black Panther Movement, Black Unity and Freedom Party, or the Black Liberation Front, which were all in principle politically black. But even these groups were dominated by those of African descent, if we are honest. It is one thing to theorize the global Third World struggle as that which unites all Black and Brown comrades, it is quite another to build a lasting coalition around the idea, given some of the issues we have addressed and more. Not being White is neither enough to mobilize, nor is it a solid foundation. There is little more disempowering than defining yourself in relation to the oppressor, normalizing Whiteness as inevitable and omnipresent. It is perhaps for this reason that the turn against political blackness has been so forceful as successive generations struggle with how to understand their position in Britain's racist political economy.

After rejecting political blackness and foregrounding the book firmly in Blackness defined as the African diaspora you would be right to question why we included Viji Kuppan's chapter in the book. At the workshops this discussion came up frequently and heatedly as you can probably imagine, with Viji staunchly embracing a politically black identity and he produces great work from this position. Importantly, we can reject the notion of political blackness without casting out those who embrace it. The point in anchoring the book in Blackness in the African diaspora is not to attempt to police the term or create fixed and rigid boundaries. Intersectionality came about through the standpoint of Black women, but these lessons can and have been applied across different concepts. Blackness in general is no different, as Professor William Cross so succinctly put it at a 2019 conference at Birmingham City University, 'Blackness is the discovery of the universal through the particular'. Different groups have mobilized through Blackness because of the understandings that the experience has illuminated. We should be no quicker to dismiss British political blackness than we would the Dalit, Aborigine or Israeli Black Panthers, who took up the mantle from the American originals. By seeing the world through Blackness, other experiences of oppression can be better understood, and the same is true of Viji's chapter. Blackness has always been a space defined by its African origins but accessible to all.

We also have to acknowledge that Blackness is not a fixed and stable identity, with historical origins baked into our DNA. Race as biology is the European version of difference. Blackness is, and always has been a choice, a possible way of understanding our place in the world. As we explained above part of that has been enforced, we have been treated as Negroes, enslaved, colonized, victimized through racial oppression, or as Malcolm X. put it 'we are all in the same boat'.[16] But those experiences do not necessarily mean a commitment to Blackness. As we have repeatedly seen there are many of us who will embrace individualism, conservatism and even racism to get ourselves a seat on the deck of the boat, rather than in the hold. Blackness is the commitment to the liberation of all those in the diaspora, it is a political identity and a choice. The diversity of experiences within the billion Africans on the continent and the 100 million plus in the diaspora is such that it is easy to see why people would not identify with the whole. Nation, tribe, language, location, individualism are all other prisms through which to view one's connection to both the world and its oppressions. Embracing Blackness does not mean erasing these differences but it does mean seeing them through the diasporic lens. This internal glue of Blackness is vital and what shapes the discussions throughout the volume.

As the colonizer-in-chief Britain has a large and diverse legacy of empire. Following the Second World War the Windrush generation[17] was the dominant frame for Black migrants who came from the Caribbean to rebuild the nation. Black people have a much longer historical presence in the nation but this was the first wave of mass migration. Caribbean migrants and their children so dominated the state's response and cultural understandings of Blackness that some African immigrants pretended to be from the Islands. When we think of the sixties, seventies and even into the eighties our image of Blackness is dominated by Caribbean experiences of racism in the schools and at the hands of the police, as well as cultural products like reggae and Rasta, and the rebellions against police brutality. This view misses the African presence, who were here during the period albeit in much smaller numbers. African migration started to rise in the eighties and today there are more Black people in Britain who define as African than Caribbean (although this is partly because of the longer settlement of Caribbeans many of whom no longer identify with the region).

It is fair to say that Caribbean and African (if not specific nation) identities were the strongest diasporic pull until relatively recently. Part of this was class related. Caribbean migrants tended to be from a wider class background when coming into the country pre-1990 and even if they were middle class on entry found themselves in below working-class conditions. African migration prior to the 1980s was largely led by students, a particular section of the African population who had a very different trajectory. Caribbean vs African beef was common in schools until well into the nineties, as Africans were seen as a 'model minority' as opposed to the underachieving, bad breed, and criminal Caribbean youth.[18] Dynamics from slavery did not help, with the formerly enslaved from the Caribbean being looked down on by those who 'had sold us' on the continent. In all honesty Blackness in Britain was largely a stand-in for 'Caribbean' pre-1990. With the growth of the African population and successive generations being born in Britain, and therefore subject to the same experiences of state racism, the Caribbean/African divide is less meaningful today. Culturally this is the easiest to see. If the Caribbean sound system dominated Black expression pre-1990, today it is the Grime and Drill scenes. Here you are just as likely to find those of direct African descent dominating as MCs whose families hail from the Caribbean. A truly emergent Blackness in Britain is transforming the nature of the diasporic connection to include all those of African descent more thoroughly. As such it should not be a surprise that Blackness is the tie that binds all the pieces in this collection together, both through their shared experiences of racism and struggles to overcome.

Blackness *in* Britain is important to emphasize because, as you will see in the volume, though these experiences happen on the island they are about much wider forces that are produced by the global nature of racism. Not only do we have contributors of African and Caribbean origins, but also African Americans, an Afro-Brazilian as well as various mixed heritage experiences. Just as with the broader lessons of the Black feminist standpoint, the specific setting in Britain is a tool through which to see the world, not a prism that limits the analysis.

Structure of the book

Deciding how to organize the book was a long and arduous process. Across the two different workshops we debated, shifted and re-organized the papers depending on the nature of the discussions. The benefit of such a dialogic and collaborative way of working is that it made us truly interrogate our choices and the frameworks we were using. One of the most important tools we used from CRT was the workshop format because it allowed us to co-construct the work in a way that would otherwise have been impossible. We eventually settled on having three sections to the book that highlighted the CRT dimensions of thinking intersectionally. As we explained this was essential to give a substantial theoretical standing to the concept; to reframe intersectionality in the context of the intellectual movement of CRT. Therefore, we split the book into sections addressing 'institutional oppressions'; 'marginalizing Black voices'; and 'counter-narratives'.

By engaging with the standpoint of Black women intersectionality was developed as a tool to shed light on the nature of institutional oppressions. It was only by going beyond the single-axis ideas of discrimination that we could appreciate just how deeply entwined oppression was within institutional settings. If it is *always* about race, gender, class, sexuality and ableism then there is no simple remedy through reform or policy change. This is one of the central components of the Critical Race Theory (CRT) framework that is so important to understanding intersectionality. Institutions are sites in reproducing the inequalities of the system and therefore it is essential that scholarship examines the ways in which oppressions are both mobilized and experienced within them. CRT started in law, but can be applied to any institutional setting to understand the mechanisms of discrimination. By examining institutions we are also always interrogating the social policy that underpins and shapes them.

In the first section of the book we have three pieces that interrogate the intersectional failures of institutions. These are written by Black women to explore in the different settings the forms of institutional and policy oppression. By engaging with the stories of Black women all of the chapters uncover the institutional narratives and practices that are so key in marginalization. All the chapters in the first section involve telling the stories of participants to understand the lived experiences and give voice to institutional oppressions. There is a range of approaches taken throughout the book from personal narratives to archival analysis. This is a central tenet of CRT that offers different routes into understanding the world. A major strength of this collection is the varied methodological approaches the authors have used.

We open with Annabel Wilson's herstory of her mother, Paulette's dealings with the state, diagnosed as she is with a mental illness. We are here reminded that the personal is deeply political and by exploring the abuse of her mother the account lays out clearly the systematic violence that is perpetuated against Black female bodies by the state. We can see beyond the narratives of care that the mental health system justifies itself with to see a brutally oppressive regime, which has devastating consequences for the individuals and families involved, but also for the wider communities subject to these mechanisms of surveillance and control.

We continue with Katucha Bento's herstories of two Afro-Brazilian migrants to Britain, Ceci and Gabriella. The intersection of being an immigrant comes through strongly in this chapter, where we can see how a hostile environment has been the default setting of the Home Office for decades. Through Ceci's and Gabriella's interactions with the state we can again see how the very processes that are meant to be supportive end up being the key sites of discrimination. The National Health Service (NHS) comes in again for particular scrutiny. This is particularly ironic given that the NHS has since its founding in 1948 has been a key source of employment for Black women. In fact, the NHS could never have started without labour from the Caribbean and the rest of the British Empire and still employs a significant proportion of both its doctors and nurses from the former colonies. Nevertheless, it continues to reproduce racist practice and as the biggest employer in the UK (and fourth largest in the world), its institutional inequalities have an outsize impact.

We then move to Francesca Sobande's exploration of the erasure of Black women in Scotland. As a nation Scotland imagines itself as a colonial subject to the despotic English who invaded across the border. This narrative does not allow for an understanding of Scotland's deep connections to the slave trade or colonialism, rendering any real acknowledgement of racism mute. Scotland the institution silences the histories of oppression and therefore in a myriad of ways erases the realities of its Black populations. The chapter explores how colour-blindness is used as a tool to mask the lack of representation in the media and civic life in general of Black women in the nation.

All of the papers make clear that the central tenet of CRT, that racism is permanent feature of society, applies directly to Britain. Hopefully, if you are reading this collection then this is not something you needed to be convinced of. We also opened with the chapters because they provide the route into intersectionality from which it emerged, the standpoint of Black women. Again, no reminder should be necessary but the conditions that produced intersectionality continue to exist and we should not divorce the concept from its Black feminist roots. We chose to open the book in this manner to establish both the tradition and important institutional analysis from which intersectionality arose. These powerful chapters outline what is at stake when institutions participate in intersectional failures.

Our workshops took place in a grade 2 listed Victorian mansion converted into a hotel, sprawling across seven acres of grounds. The story about finding a location that was not too difficult to get to, allowed us outdoor space and was not prohibitively expensive would be enough to fill a chapter. As nice as the hotel, the environment and the staff were, we couldn't help but feel a little out of place. This is no knock on the hotel who did everything they could to accommodate us. But when you are talking about the experiences of the oppression of Black people under the watchful eyes of various pictures of the dead White men who at one point laid claim to the space there is bound to be some discomfort. We were twenty-plus Black people taking over a space that was likely built at least in part off our ancestors' oppression. Small things, like the menu, made it clear that this was not a space designed with us in mind. We had a number of conversations, particularly at the first workshop, about the suitability of the location and whether we would have been better served in a Black-owned venue. But the space served up two useful reminders. The first is that due to the legacy of racial oppression there are no Black-owned venues that could offer the space, facilities and grounds. The idyllic surroundings of the countryside are those reserved by the exclusions of Whiteness, as is the wealth to own such property. Secondly, our presence in the space was a reminder of the marginalization of Black bodies more broadly within institutions. Even when we are welcomed in we never quite fit. Alongside this there are the institutional pressures to conform that further marginalize our experiences. We were using the space precisely to amplify the voices of Black scholars, but these kinds of institutional forms often work to silence those perspectives that we need to hear the most.

CRT has been mobilized in Britain predominantly through education studies because it draws attention to the way that Black bodies are marginalized within the system. Whiteness is the unacknowledged norm that dominates policy and practice, relegating Black students and staff to the margins.[19] A CRT lens has been increasingly applied to staffing higher education, where there are so few Black academics, and even fewer managers, that the situation can only be described as a crisis.[20] A result of institutional racism is to marginalize Black people and to silence our voices. A key tool of CRT, and particularly intersectionality, is to embrace the worldview of those struggling through oppression, making the marginalization of those voices epistemologically disempowering.

In the second section of the book we have brought together a collection of chapters that explore the marginalization of our experiences. Constantino Dumangane's chapter explores how Black men have to navigate the extreme Whiteness of the university space. For the uninitiated, the standpoint elucidated from the experiences of Black women also helps us to understand the challenges facing Black men. Gender intersects with racism in complicated ways that impact on the experience of Black men. Dumangane charts the efforts to conform and also to transgress the expectations laid down by the institutions. Universities do more than seek to erase the Blackness, they also try to transform the Black subject into an identity that the institution can understand, attempting to create a colourless subject so that the colour-blind ideal can thrive.

Kelena Reid's chapter presents a different form of marginalization, this time in the case of the Black women (of mixed heritage) who have been ignored in the archive of those who received compensation for owning enslaved Africans when the British abolished the practice. The chapter explores how understanding that a small number of Black women inherited enslaved Africans from their slaveholding parents provides different insights into abolition. Reid also explores how the Legacies of British Slave Ownership Project at University College London also excluded the voices of Black people in its team and ways of working. Again, highlighting the exclusions of the university the paper challenges academia and archives to embrace rather than marginalize Black perspectives. We cannot pretend that the background of the researchers makes no difference to the research.

Viji Kuppan highlights the extreme marginalization of those Black bodies who are also subject to what society constructs as disability. At this intersection the racialization of the disabled subject means increased jeopardy of discrimination. It is no coincidence that Kuppan uses a story from university to illustrate the dimensions of this marginalization given both his location as a doctoral student and the prevalence of racial marginalization within the sector. By exploring how people attempt to navigate these exclusions we can also see the efforts to provide a colour-blind framework to overcome.

In Mary Igenoza's chapter on femininity we are presented with a forensic examination of how Whiteness is placed as the basis of beauty. Worse still the perceived beauty of Whiteness is proven in contrast to the dark ugliness of Black women. In the chapter Igenoza explores how these historic manifestations are still alive and well and shape how Black women are marginalized in their personal and professional lives.

We end the section with Dionne Taylor's examination of how Black women bodies are used when they are mainstreamed. Through controlling images that limit the representational options, Black women can be simultaneously marginalized and centralized. Taylor uses the example of Dancehall and Hip Hop depictions of Black women to show how we can collude in such representations. The chapter also looks at how young Black women navigate through these representations, both with negative impacts and also by trying to reinterpret them as a basis of changing the narrative. Finding our voices whilst being marginalized has been a key tool of survival and resistance.

The collection of chapters highlights what is at stake when we are marginalized and silenced by institutions. In order to overcome racism we need the very voices that are being silenced to come to the fore and present new ways of understanding the world.

One of the best aspects about the two workshops was that they were both fun. We were doing serious work on deeply personal and traumatic experiences, trying to understand how oppression is manifest through intersectional lenses. But we also took the time to let loose, to connect and to socialize. Over a total of five nights we broke bread, shared stories and dusted off the party games. This was an absolutely essential element to the success of the workshops and the work that produced this volume. Blackness may exist in a context of oppression but it is defined by resistance. A key part of that resistance is to find beauty in struggle, to create joy and light even in darkness. The atmosphere created at the workshops allowed us to more honestly relate to each other and explore the issue we were dealing with. We also extended the conversations out into the breaks, over dinner and at the bar. By developing an immersed and supportive space we were able to rethink and challenge the ideas presented. By doing so we are able to create counter-narratives, different ways to understand the world which can disrupt the status quo.

Creating counter-narratives is a key tool in the arsenal of CRT because they let us imagine the world differently. If we can create a different story then we can hopefully bring people along in seeking social change. Narratives provide frameworks for our understanding, and therefore to tell the same story differently can lead to alternative responses and solutions.

In the final section of the book we bring together a collection of chapters that offer counter-narratives to the status quo. We open with Eddie Bruce-Jones who interviewed Black queer artist Ajamu X about the nature of his work. By exploring how Ajamu X's works creates new aesthetics of Blackness the chapter offers one way to produce new visions of society. Bruce-Jones does this, not simply by arguing that we need to include a wider variety of Black experiences but by showing how Ajamu's work offers a queering lens through which Blackness can be appreciated. To engage through the intersection of Blackness and queerness means shaking us out of our normative assumptions.

In Kadian Pow's chapter we are offered the social media space of Tumblr as a possible site for generating intersectional counter-narratives. By investigating how users have generated their Tumblr blogs, the chapter shows how resistance to racism is prevalent on the site as well as spaces to articulate alternative visions of Blackness. Spaces like Tumblr offer possibility but remain limited by the dimensions of the tools. But as a vehicle for exploring counter-narratives and how they are constructed they are a valuable space.

In Miranda Armstrong's chapter we see the object of state persecution, the Black single mother, in a new light. Rather than demonizing the failing welfare queen who inadequately raises her sons, Armstrong celebrates the relationship between Black single mothers and their boys. Such counter-narratives are absolutely essential because the demonization of Black single mothers goes to the heart of many of the intersectional failures of Black political responses to oppression. Far too often Black politics embraces the patriarchal view that the solutions to our problems is to reinstate the male breadwinner model in our families to produce strong and vibrant male children who can conquer the world. Not only is this a misreading of the structural nature of oppression but it places limits on the roles of Black women as well as blaming them for breaking up the family. We need far more progressive narratives of both the family and gender if we are to better struggle against our oppression.

Patriarchal framing of Black struggle also leads to other exclusions of Black women from the political imaginary. In his chapter Kehinde Andrews follows on from Kimberlé Crenshaw's presentation at the first workshop about the Say Her Name campaign, exploring why some Black activists rejected including the Black women who have been killed by the police in racial justice campaigns. By examining the complex interplay at the intersection of race and gender the chapter offers a counter-narrative of Blackness that can be an inclusive, rather than exclusive space.

In these counter-narratives we can see opportunities to reframe Blackness through an intersectional lens. This is vital if we are to imagine new possibilities in order to challenge the structural issues and their implications that we detail throughout the first two parts of the book. CRT and intersectionality are rooted in efforts to change the system as much as those to diagnose it. The pieces of counter-narrative that we have presented here are by no means meant to be an exhaustive list but fragments that can be built on in the future. Hopefully, the work within offers insights that can spark new intersectional visions of freedom.

Part One

Institutional Oppressions

Reframing intersectionality: A '*her*story' of my mother

By Annabel and Paulette Wilson[1]

Figure 1 Annabel Wilson with her mum.

In this chapter I share the biography of a mentally ill mother and her daughter's interactions with the British mental health system. I am doing this because 'the personal is political'[2] and sharing intimate stories which bind structural analysis with emotional realities can create accounts with the rhetorical power to mobilize others and engage collectivities.[3] My aim then is to share a story that any Black woman with experience of Euro-American mental health systems might relate to. It is a *herstory* as it acknowledges 'that women's lives, deeds, and participation in human affairs have been neglected or undervalued in standard histories'.[4] And so, I rewrite the authoritative 'history' presented in medical files, prescription papers and NHS ward reports, illustrating how intersectionality can be used as a micro-historiographic tool.[5] I argue that once intersectionality becomes ingrained in one's perception the past can be brought to new life as a heightened sense of consciousness is gained. I suggest that if the NHS is to deliver a mental health service that is safe for Black women it too must undergo a similar process of enlightenment to ensure that those working for NHS trusts provide treatment for Black women without undermining their humanity. I focus on the process through which I came to see the intersections of class, race, disability and gender in action and how their corresponding systems of domination – capitalism, White supremacy, ableism and patriarchy – stand as a barrier to equality, happiness and acceptance for many Black females.[6] By demonstrating how these systems of inequality damage the mental wellbeing of Black females and underpin services designed to help them, I hope to provide a methodology inspired by intersectionality that NHS professionals can learn from and use to improve their practice.

Herstory

Paulette is my mother. Her father Alfie came to England from Jamaica in the late 1950s and her mother, 'Miss Nicey', joined him shortly after he arrived, leaving five children behind. Her father was an alcoholic. She remembers him as not a nice person. She remembers her mother as a woman who rarely spoke. Paulette was the first in her family to be born in Britain and is one of seven children. She was raised in Bristol, a medium-sized city in the south-west of England between St Pauls and Easton, which at the time were the cities only 'multicultural' neighbourhoods (where post-war Caribbean and south Asian emigrants settled). Family members describe Paulette as a quiet and shy child who liked to be in control of her environment. Paulette says 'control' just happened: 'things need to be done and I became the one to do them'. Unlike her elder sister (two years her senior) who came to live in England when she was nine and soon became responsible for housekeeping and cooking, Paulette managed the household's limited finances and shopped for the family from a young age. Because of this, her siblings say she was 'spoilt'. In the family she is known for being 'different'. Marie, Paulette's younger cousin, describes how she looked up to my mother's creative flair whilst growing up and how this made her stand out from other friends and family members.

Following in Miss Nicey's footsteps, Paulette was a keen dressmaker. Art was her favourite school subject and 'Costume Design and Make Up' her first career pursuit. But, in her late teens, she was firmly directed by an aunt to get a 'real' career and become a nurse. Seven years after embarking on her nursing journey Paulette had to give up work due to mental ill health. In 1983, at age twenty-four she was 'sectioned'[7] for the first time. Looking back on this time in her life, my mother says she remembers feeling anxious, 'all of the time'. She says she went to work and woke up in a psychiatric ward. Reflecting, she notes how unaware she was of being unwell – something she has not since had the privilege of forgetting.

Diagnosed initially with bipolar depression, later with anorexia nervosa and borderline personality disorder, and most recently with emotional traumatic personality disorder, my mother has been in direct contact with mental health services for over thirty-five years – the majority of her life (she is sixty whilst I write this). In fact, she has spent the equivalent of eleven years in hospital during this time. Over these years, she has simultaneously battled herself, her illness and the mental health system. She has been detained under the mental health act[8] countless times and has been forced to have electric shock treatment (performed under general anaesthetic, where electrodes were attached to either side of her head and a series of high-voltage electric currents between 225v and 450v were passed through her brain with the intention of inducing a fit). Whilst the practice continues to be used by the NHS, it is not known how Electric Convolution Therapy (ECT) works. Yet, psychiatrists believe it to be an appropriate intervention in cases where people suffering with depression have not responded to other forms of treatment, such as anti-depressants. Its purported 'success' is often short-term or understood to be the result of a placebo effect.[9] Moreover, the long-term side effects such as memory loss, emotional suppression, difficulty learning new things paired with the violent nature of the treatment likely outweigh any supposed benefits of the treatment.[10] My mother attests to this, describing her experience of ECT as deeply traumatic and believing that it has caused irreversible damage to her memory. There is no public data to my knowledge on rates of ECT used on Black people in the UK. Nonetheless, the overall use of ECT has increased in recent years and it is allegedly being used more frequently now than ever before.[11]

Over the years my mother has been prescribed an inordinate amount of medication, often without care and attention. At its worst, this resulted in her being admitted to hospital to attend a rehabilitation programme to safely withdraw from the high dosage cocktail of drugs that had been prescribed to her. She described these prescriptions as,

> The chemical coshes they tried on me (sighs). And then they say I don't take my medication? But I know what suits my body from not. I'm not an expert but I refuse to have a chemical cosh that has me walking around like a zombie. And another thing, they've over-medicated me because they never reviewed my case, they just added things. That was the reason I was falling over, the reason I broke my leg. I have been in every aspect overlooked.

There is a recurrent lack of care inherent in the treatment my mother has received. On offer is a form of treatment that overlooks her subjecthood, instead focusing most directly on her diagnosis. This has had many physical and emotional consequences. For example, her experience of this system has led to an inability in others, often including me myself, to empathize with and relate to her. For my mother, this is what has been taken from her as a result of her medical and personal *history* being dictated by the NHS.

My mother characterized her journey through the system as one that began with feelings of shame and developed into a sense of loss,

> Paulette: All I know is when I first went in I was so ashamed
> Annabel: Are you still ashamed?
> Paulette: It's not so much ashamed – what it does – because I've been in it [the system] so long – other people with mental health I can talk to, sort of, but Jo Blogs, whether it's in the family or not, I have the feeling of being the odd one out … My history, is being treated in the mental health system. I haven't had that much, although I've tried, of normality. I feel very cut off from 'ordinary people', as John Legend would say, and that is why I don't sort of mix and things. Because, you know, I don't want to talk about it all the time. It just means I have lost so much really … through childhood trauma?

Paulette's experiences of the mental health system have become a barrier between herself and others. As she says, her history is so bound up with illness, treatment, stigma and being locked up. This then affects her relationships, as others often cannot see past her illness; and she has been so deeply changed by her experiences of treatment, that she struggles to form bonds with those unable to understand this part of her. This struggle occurs both within and beyond her family relationships. Paulette, for much of her life, has been left to fight a battle against the agents of the mental health system (psychiatrists, doctors and care coordinators) alone. She has been treated as less than human on so many occasions, her personhood degraded in countless interactions (in everyday exchanges and mental health review meetings). The sad truth is that my mum's illness stems from being sexually abused as a child. The misfortune of her childhood has been transformed into a long-lasting curse, that justifies her exploitation within a broken system.[12]

A lost voice: Being Black, 'disabled' and female

The context of silence is varied and multidimensional. Most obvious are the ways racism, sexism and class exploitation act to suppress and silence. Voices of oppressed peoples are seldom heard. These voices, when audible, challenge the status quo. Black women who raise their voices risk being labelled mad. Remembering her childhood in another Black Atlantic context to my mother's (the Southern US) yet during a similar era, bell hooks writes of how 'madness, not just physical abuse, was the punishment for too much talk if you were female'.[13]

For my mother, resisting forces intent on silencing her is a prerequisite for sanity.[14] And yet, too often her need to be heard is not acknowledged by practitioners who are unable see and therefore connect with her subjecthood when she is unwell. Loss of voice underpins my mother's understanding of mental health. To her,

> [it] is being locked up, sort of being in fear of going to the doctors for any little thing because something I say [may be taken] out of context, I use the word arrested because that's how I feel, like there's no communication. I think mental health for me, I don't know if it's a label or me per se but I feel, to me, it's like being locked up in an institution, whether you're inside or not. Not being able to voice an opinion because straight away it's like you've 'got mental health'. I listen to things about disability, mental health is not mentioned but it has such knock-on effects on myself and the family and everything. Mental health I feel is a curse I have had to bear.

Having poor mental health has left Paulette with a voice without credibility. A voice that others struggle to listen to. In this sense, she has been cursed. But her voice has also been her saviour. bell hooks writes,

For us [any oppressed marginalized group], true speaking is not solely an expression of creative power; it is an act of resistance, a political gesture that challenges politics of domination that would render us nameless and voiceless … Moving from silence into speech is for the oppressed, the colonized, the exploited, and those who stand and struggle side by side a gesture of defiance that heals, that makes new life and new growth possible. It is that act of speech, of "talking back", that is no mere gesture of empty words, that is the expression of our movement from object to subject – the liberated voice.[15]

My mother prides herself on her refusal to sit down and shut up, to be an easy patient, to not question, to follow the status quo. She believes that this is what stops her from giving up and enables her to defy being institutionalized, as through talking back she finds a sense of freedom despite the possibility of true liberation remaining out of reach. The deeper your marginalization, the more unlikely you are to be heard, regardless of how loud you shout. As a Black, working-class, disabled woman, my mother's voice often falls on deaf ears. Having an unheard voice is dangerous when you are locked into a system that misunderstands you. It continuously reinforces barriers that restrict the ability to move from psychiatric object to a sentient subject. Despite such barriers, voice and body is all she has, it is these resources she must draw upon in her fights to have her humanity acknowledged within a system that struggles to see and hear her. My mother discusses the consequence of this and how she draws upon these resources:

The one thing I did, I do, I always felt like a one-man army. Me against them. And I always say that. It's like they are not going to break me. They are not going to institutionalize me. And you know I wouldn't toe the line. It just felt I didn't have a voice – because 'I'm mad'. No matter what I say, that isn't being paranoid; that's just how it goes. It is like [I'm] a one-man army. When I go in, they call me into ward meetings, I say nothing. Doctors say they want to talk to you, I ain't saying nothing, you ain't getting inside my head. So, in a way it also makes me quite paranoid of actually saying anything. If they'd listen to me I wouldn't of had to have a full hysterectomy. I was in hospital, I kept telling them my womb was in between my legs; they did not believe me. I had to degrade myself by going into clinic, dropping my knickers, putting my arse in front of the staff which looked like a baboon (because of the prolapse) – oh they moved then! And I'm not the first person who has had physical things that they think is in your head. Another example, my new medication should have been taken on an empty stomach, but they didn't tell me that so I was throwing up a lot, going to the doctors throwing up, but they ignored me. I do I go in there now like 'I know you lot think I'm mad, however ...' and that's how I call it, and I keep myself to myself because I get anxious and everything. It's just robbed me, I'm not saying it's beaten me, it's just robbed me ...

Whilst Paulette acknowledges that her voice has kept her sane and granted her the power to resist on the one hand, she also reflects on how she is silenced. For her this silence is at times a choice, or at least a chosen reaction to being continuously misunderstood. Yet, she feels the consequences of this silence, just as she feels the consequences of raising her voice – as either way, she is ignored. It is this that leaves her feeling robbed.

Learning to fight alongside my mother

I too am guilty of not listening to my mother. Growing up, despite my mother's objections and hatred for the system which repeatedly detained her, I – influenced by the actions and explanations of others (my family, social worker and mental health professionals) – believed that these services were working in her best interests, that their job was to keep her safe and necessarily under control. Blinded by such logics and unfamiliar with the use of critical thought in everyday life I, like the rest of my family, sat in support of a system underpinned by structures of White supremacy, capitalism and patriarchy and believed they were doing their best.

As a quiet, 'cute' and well-mannered 'mixed-race' young girl my own life experiences did not afford an alternate way of making sense of this. There were, it seems, no obvious forms of empathy between my mother and myself at this point. I had not been abused, policed, surveyed or controlled in the same way that she had. I had not consciously experienced my position as a working-class mixed-race female as a disadvantage. Instead, I was always framed as the 'success story': the positive offspring of a 'broken woman', living proof that 'equality of opportunity' exists in modern 'multicultural' Britain – a myth that mixed-race bodies are often positioned as evidence of.[16]

Central to my coming-of-age story was the process of coming into consciousness. Through the sociological imagination I had developed during my undergraduate studies, I acquired tools that enabled me make sense of the world around me beyond the level of the individual; instead, situating myself in relation to a social context. Until this point I had been somewhat, and arguably rightfully, consumed with feelings of being let down by my mother, who could not care for me at many points throughout my childhood.

People often become stuck in their own perspective, shaped mostly by their own life experiences, and they are unable to see beyond them. However, as time passed, I began to understand my mother's perspective more (especially her objection to the mental health system), seeing as she saw and getting glimpses of the power dynamics she was up against. I then saw clearly how her social position had shaped her attitude toward authority figures and why it differed from other family members and NHS staff.

I started to fight alongside her. I came to understand how I too was positioned and reacted to by those who worked closely with my mum. I found mental health professionals reacted to me in varying ways, dependent upon their knowledge of me. Those who were aware of my educational and employment achievements granted me the privilege of being heard. With those who were less familiar, being heard was not given but had to be fought for. Now, using acquired forms of 'cultural capital'[17] I attempt to 'speak the right language' to access a voice my mother is denied. These experiences have made me aware of the implicit and explicit ways my mother and I are classed and racialized. My lighter complexion, performed 'middle-classness' and perceived 'mental wellness' provides me the opportunity to challenge medical professionals and convince them, if only for a moment, that I am worthy of listening to. But my mother remains a victim of tacitly held discriminatory attitudes, which lead to her silencing.

Although my mother and I are always responding to these dynamics and fighting to be heard, the professionals we encounter remain unaware of how they are responding to the colour of our skin, our perceived class position, our health and gender. In the next section I highlight how having an awareness of the structural positions we inhabit shapes our interactions across mental health services. I illustrate how re-imagining these experiences through an intersectional lens has enabled me to re-vision and write my mother's *her*story.

Bringing it back to intersectionality: Unpicking misconceptions that underpin NHS interventions and 'treatment' of Black bodies

In Britain, women are more likely to encounter mental health services than men.[18] Black people are over-represented in mental health services and most likely to be subjected to the harshest interventions.[19] Black people are significantly more likely to be admitted to hospital compared to the population overall as their illness is more likely to be diagnosed whilst in crisis. Thus, Black Britons are 44% more likely to be sectioned than White

Britons.[20] Black people's prevalence in the mental health system continues to rise: it is estimated that detentions increased by 2.4% between 2016/17 and 2017/18 alone.[21] In addition, those from working-class backgrounds are five times more likely to have a mental health illness than those above the poverty line.[22] Given these patterns, it makes statistical sense for women in my mother's social position to be labelled 'mad' and thus treated as if they are deficient. Like many others, my mother's womanhood, working-classness and Blackness place her in an inferior position that frames her way of being as 'wrong'. As bell hooks states,

> As far back as slavery, White people established a social hierarchy based on race and sex that ranked White men first, White women second, though sometimes equal to Black men, who are ranked third, and Black women last[23]

Intersectionality as a tool enables us to both disaggregate and show the collective traces that systems of power leave on Black women's bodies.[24] Using this tool, we can begin to unpick the construction of madness and its relationship to Black female bodies. There has long been an association between women and madness. Women have for much of history been considered 'over-emotional' and vulnerable to extreme cases of hysteria – thought to be a condition experienced solely by women for over 4,000 years.[25] Slavery as a White supremacist system of domination invested slave holders with the authority to define sanity and madness amongst the enslaved. In the colonial era slavery as a system of control was thought to be essential to the maintenance of sanity.[26] During the enslavement era, this notion helped to legitimatize claims that freedom was not in the best interests of enslaved Africans as this put them at risk of developing 'Drapteomania' – a pseudo-psychiatric illness invented to explain enslaved people's attempts to flee captivity.[27] Post-emancipation this same logic supported the institutionalization of Black people, and the reproduction of colonial structures within mental asylums.[28] Moreover, as Du Bois has argued time and time again, throughout history many (such as eugenicists, social reformers, early twentieth-century biological anthropologists) have endeavoured to find a scientific basis that links one's race to one's ability and, ultimately, one's location in a biological hierarchy.[29] This is a legacy that lives on. It is evident in the disproportional number of ethnic minorities diagnosed with some form of learning or intellectual disability.[30] Being disabled and Black then furthers marginalization and legitimates subhuman treatment.

Bruce explains that 'Black womanhood is double-crossed by myths of female hysteria and myths of Black savagery and sub-rationality'.[31] Such an understanding of Black women has been encapsulated in fictional characters such as the 'Mad woman in the attic', first mentioned in Charlotte Brontë's *Jane Eyre*[32] and further explored in Jean Rhys's *Wide Sargasso Sea*,[33] who succumbs to madness once her plantation-managing British husband lays claim to her family estate and moves on from his initial erotic attraction to this Dominican (West Indian) woman. Such images depict Black women as incapable of reason; they constructed them as lost beyond help. The only hope for these women comes when they are subjugated to control and structure regardless of their objection to this – because they are far too mad to speak and to know for themselves what is best. It is this imagery that informs the dominant perceptions of Black bodies who appear mentally unwell and the treatment designed to help them.

As there has yet to be an anti-racist reckoning through which the extremely biased conceptions that inform psychiatric practice has been acknowledged and resolved, we must question how madness is assigned to those who inhabit Black bodies. Questioning the assumptions bound up in madness as a concept, Bruce[34] writes,

I contend that madness entails four overlapping entities … First is phenomenal madness: a severe unwieldiness or chaos of mind – producing fundamental crises of perception, emotion, meaning, and self-hood – as experienced in the consciousness of the "mad" subject. Second is clinical madness: an informal shorthand for any range of psychotic, psychopathic, or severely neurotic disorders (as diagnosed or misdiagnosed by clinicians) that may or may not coincide with phenomenal madness. Third, madness as anger: an affective state of intense and aggressive displeasure (which is surely phenomenal, but is here set apart for its analytic specificity). Fourth, and most capacious of these categories, is psychosocial alterity: radical divergence from the 'normal' within a given psychosocial context … any person, idea, or behaviour that perplexes and vexes dominant psychosocial logics is vulnerable to the ascription of 'crazy'. In this fourth category, madness is less a measure of a 'mad' mind than it is an index of the limits of a 'reasonable' majority in processing radical difference.[35]

Whilst from the outside my mother is seen by so many as embodying phenomenal madness and she has been given several 'clinical' labels that formalize such perceptions, Paulette displays deep-seated levels of rightful anger, especially in the presence of professionals who forever overlook her subjectivity. However, in truth she is a victim of psychosocial alterity because she is not like others. She is disabled by the world around her as her way of being diverges from the norm and is considered unacceptable. This in turn places her in a position where, despite the gross systemic flaws she has been subjected to, she must remain forever grateful for the treatment she has received and labels that have been placed on her, for these ensure she is eligible for state support (housing and income). Given that her way of being is misrecognized and there is no place for her in this world, maintaining this eligibility is essential to her material survival.

Conclusion

The system

In summary, through my acquisition of an intersectional lens I am now able to make sense of and witness the social relations underpinning my mother's experience as she moves through phases of her illness, encountering different professionals and services. When my mother is 'manic', with lower-status health professionals (like community workers and nurses who are mainly female) she may attempt to stand up for herself. But because in this world Black women's voices should not be heard, her outspokenness causes others to fear her and perceive her as 'difficult to manage'.[36] She is constructed as the 'angry Black women',[37] as unintelligent,[38] as having transgressed what is considered acceptable feminine behaviour[39] – and so they believe she needs to be controlled. In these moments, White males (or occasionally Asian males) in high-status medical professions are brought in to shut her down. Their 'authoritative knowledge' disempowers her faith in her understanding of herself.[40] As they waltz in carrying both the implicit power of their Whiteness, and explicit statutory power to restrain, sedate and electrocute, their presence muffles my mother's voice. She knows that it is only when she has been silenced that they are happy she is 'well' ready to go home.

The curse

Whilst Stephen Fry, a poster boy for bipolar awareness, is positively described as a 'refined eccentric',[41] my mother's 'unconventional' nature symbolizes madness. Unlike a White middle-class man, my mother's working-class roots, skin colour and gender together mean that her creativity must be stifled and her right to an eccentric persona denied. Lisa Simone says her mother, Nina Simone, was 'too creative', too large a presence – too 'dangerously free', as Toni Morrison once put it – for this world. This is also true of my mother. My point here is not to argue that my mum's or anyone else's illness is wholly imagined. My mother is at times truly unwell. The issue is that the treatment she has received when she has been at her most vulnerable has often been counterproductive, either exaggerating her mental illness or leading her to experience physical pain and trauma. And so, the point of this chapter is to highlight the ways in which the acknowledgement of Black women's humanity is at risk of being overlooked within current mental health services. This is especially worrying considering the new push across Western societies to encourage Black women to access mental health services.[42] These systems are not ready for these women. There is much work to be done before Black women can safely turn to the state and ask for help. This fact is known by Black communities and underpins their rightful reluctance to proactively engage with mental health services. Until this is resolved women like my mother will continue to be subjected to the harshest forms of interventions during times of crisis. It is essential, then, that the power dynamics within these systems, which threaten to suppress Black women and amplify any illness they may have, are understood, acknowledged and challenged. Whilst my mother suggests an increase in community resources, more peer support workers and 'just being treated like a human being and not a diagnosis', may improve this system, we both agree that what needs to be changed is, as Paulette puts it, 'the whole bloody system really, if the truth be known, the whole bloody system!'

The solution

This paper encapsulates my challenge to NHS mental health services. My hope is that by sharing this personal and intimate story, and through re-centring my mother's humanity in her *her*story of the British mental health system, the providers of these services will see and begin to address the dangerous flaws in their system. I have demonstrated how applying an intersectional lens to one's *her*story enables the past to be revisited, for new meanings to emerge, and perceptions to be altered. Intersectionality provides the critical consciousness needed to interrogate the latent power dynamics that underpin the experiences of people like Paulette; it highlights the subtle ways that Black women's continued devaluation in society is manifested, in this case, within a system that disproportionally diagnoses Black people with severe mental health illnesses and controls them excessively through their care.[43] So, whilst I was once unable to empathize with my mother, reframing her experiences through an intersectional lens has produced an intimacy between us that previously did not exist. This process, I believe, can be replicated by NHS professionals who have not yet come into an enlightened consciousness, giving them the ability to acknowledge their power, misconceptions of Blackness and re-imagine how they interact with and treat patients they encounter.

Herstories: Black Brazilian women narrating intersectional oppressions in the United Kingdom

Katucha Bento

This chapter begins from a perspective that intersectional oppressions and racialization are issues present in Black women's diasporic lives.[1] That is, the diasporic element impacts Black women's lives in a particular way when institutions reproduce the politics of racialization by using nationality as one of the justifications for exclusion, injustice and oppression. The experiences of Black Brazilian women with institutional discrimination in the UK happen in multiple and overlapping ways that affect our possibilities of being and extend to and through society, culture and the political economy.

Looking intersectionally at how multiple identities of Blackness, oppressions and agency are being validated on the ground of diaspora are intrinsically related with the coloniality of power. The relationship with coloniality here indicates on one hand the cosmology, knowledge and societal organization based on restricted European colonial references that represents the pillar of power relations, system of production and exclusion in a modern society.[2] On the other hand, intersectionality is present in relationship with possible decolonizing ways of self-representations and redescriptions.[3] Here, intersectionality is not a contradiction of the prior as opposite binaries, but as a process of transformation in which possible strategies for individual and collective identity happen.[4]

Centring Black women's voices in my work is a way to first recognize the importance and need of politicizing racialized bodies, moving away from the neoliberal framework of Whiteness. Such neoliberal approaches either understand intersectionality as part of a common ground for all Feminist Studies[5] or 'kidnap' the understanding of intersectionality from Critical Race Theory, suggesting that it was part of White feminist history.[6] These attempts are problematic because they tend to universalize particular struggles by questioning standpoints or not recognizing the position of privilege that White feminists occupy in the debate. The result is the depoliticization of struggles, engaging in hegemonic agendas that smash the concept of intersectionality in CRT as a methodological and analytical tool. Consequently, such theories mislead the understanding of intersectional oppressions, blurring the effects of institutional racism, ableism and classism in the analysis. My intention in using intersectionality as an analytical tool is, therefore, to make an 'analysis-in-progress'.[7] Instead of exhausting the articulations of oppressions, I will delimit the intersections according to the narrative of a Black Brazilian woman about her experiences in the UK, acknowledging my provisional and incomplete approach to all possible intersections. The limitations allow my analysis to be focused on dismantling specific structures of White-Wo/Man-Western-Euro-centric power.

These intersections are not present as additive to my work, but as analytical categories to understand Black Brazilian women's emotions about our multiple and conflicting dimensions and experiences with diaspora. Engaging with some of these intersections also opens paths to further research and debates on CRT, Black and psychoanalytical feminism, decolonial studies and critical discourse analysis to demonstrate how institutionalized notions of nation and race constructs and redefines social categories.[8]

Djamila Ribeiro argues for an intersectional gaze towards oppressions suffered by women and men of colour, pointing to the dynamic of intersectionality and the constant negotiation that it requires to understand both oppressed and privileged positionalities according to situated discrimination.[9] Here I would like to make a pause to consider how the gaze of the normalized White, able, Western, European, heteronormative, rich, gathering categories make the body of racialized as non-White people a constant 'Other'.

Therefore, the intersectional location of Black Brazilian women cannot be represented by the binary opposition between oppressed and privileged, White and non-White, rich and poor. Rather, this reflection considers the 'in betweenness' or multi-dimensioned pyramids of privileges that change their prisms according to the violence experienced by the 'norm'. This is why the *lugar de fala* allows an efficient way to voice how oppressions are perceived and felt by situated marginalized knowers.[10]

Lugar de fala has an important analytical foundation for a standpoint that reassures the sense of agency and the dynamic processes of collective meaning-making.[11] Situating the *lugar de fala* with an intersectional analysis, more importantly, allows one to point out the restrictions of colonial identifications of being and non-being. The social construction of 'Othering' takes away the possibility of humanity, complexity, depth and mobility that is grounded on the shackles of colonialism.[12] Here I am referring to the coloniality of being in which 'identity' is inscribed on the language that defines what human beings are. Since this knowledge of 'being' is normalized by White-Wo/Man-Western-Euro-centric perspective, the racialized 'Other' becomes to *be* as a *non-being*. 'Look, a Negro!' is the point at which Fanon explains the source of finding meaning in being racialized, imbued with the definition of an object, taken out of the world and restored into it as non-being.[13]

Engaging with affect from the lenses of intersectionality

It is from understanding *lugar de fala* that I centralize the voices of Black Brazilian women in the process of a legitimation of their discourse. From this point, I develop the methods of talk in order to explore narratives and herstories in a weaving process of (dis)identifications and feelings of how affect politics is present in the experience of being migrant in the UK. Finally, *lugar de fala* allows me to analyse the discourses, contemplating the continuity of the dialogue that is constantly negotiated (in)forming a variety of possible positionings, different from crystallized ideas of Blackness.[14]

Lugar de fala, therefore, situates how affect politics is being translated in the discourse about experiences of migration of Black Brazilian women. The central aspect of language in this research is for use as translation practices of multiple identities across/within/through intersections of race, gender, nationality, disability that are centralized or marginalized in the conversation according to how affect economy is playing a role in the situation narrated to me.

I define affect economy as an implication with relationality in the spaces of contact, circulating in our spaces of encounters and mutually (re)creating bonds, (dis)attachments 'moving us to act, driving us to think, developing relationality in our daily practices and encounters'.[15] Affect circulates, involving orientations towards others considering potential translations of relationality within a larger social sphere.[16] It is important to understand how affect operates through language, recreating and renegotiating meanings and positionality. Black feminism helps us to focus on and understand articulations of coloniality of power in the way race, gender, sexuality, nationality, and ableism are experienced in/through/with the intersections of identifications and oppressions. Lélia González suggests an authentically Amefricanista perspective that starts by centring the *lugar de fala* from the intersections of marginalized identities, confronting the limitations imposed by patriarchal language in existing paradigms of White-Wo/Man-Western-Euro-centric discourse.[17] Translating conversations about experiences of Black Brazilian women in the diaspora takes me to the task of unfolding the concept of affect as part of the languages that are explored in this research in the form of talk. Affective politics can be understood as a form of action, permeating the language as expression. Black Brazilian women's narratives about their intersectional selves and oppressions weave multiple ways of how Blackness can be affected by and affect the settings of where they live, the policies, the media, and other uses of language to locate difference, power and agency. Therefore the historical ways of portraying racialized and gendered migrants with brutality, stereotypical representations, inferior humanity, are provoked by new possibilities of identification, resistance, agency, and liberation when offered different uses of language. It is an intertwining of individual life, geographical site, institutionalized scene, shared experiences that produce and are produced by social positions. Intersectionality is a relational interaction that 'make[s] visible the multiple positioning that constitutes everyday life and the power relations that are central to it'.[18] Affect is circulating intersectionally evolving within a racializing and gendering script of power, prescribed by the British hostile immigration environment, coloniality of power and politics of othering in the UK. These feelings form a part of what Encarnación Gutiérrez Rodríguez calls 'structure of feeling' inscribed in less tangible parts of our human existence than semantic or cognitive structure.[19]

What affects the participants of this research also affects me, becoming the 'ontology of the present' that is presented in the body and verbal language at the moment we are weaving the meanings of Blackness within the intersections that facilitate our identities.[20] The *lugar de fala* of the participants results in a space where our standpoints have an affective relational integration of race, gender, class and nationality. Relationality here is part of the affect economy in which Black Brazilian women participating in the research, including me, are in constant negotiation in order to make sense of ourselves.

Herstories: Narratives of intersectional oppressions in the diaspora

Herstories being approached through the lenses of intersectionality raises the issue of politicization of the participants *lugar de fala*. Politicizing these locations transforms the logic of 'the Mask', the colonial object that implements a sense of speechlessness and fear, a brutal regime of silencing naturalized in the everyday lives of the so-called 'Other'.[21] The transformation into the possibility of enunciation is the act of negotiating the moment of being listened to, weaving the meanings of being in the centre of validated narratives. This is why the herstories in this chapter are presented in the first person, as if the participants are taking over the narrative, sharing with me the space of writing. It also enables a particular process of translation and reflexivity from the participants' local meaning and coherence at the same time that my subjectivity has a dual meaning of 'authoring the self'.[22] Authoring the self from a Black feminist perspective is a way of promoting a counter-movement to idiomatic homogenization, respecting Black Brazilian women's idiomatic articulations and forms of speech.

Ceci and Gabriela present cases that are related within British institutions such as Government Legal Service (more specifically with official solicitors and judges), police forces, Welfare Centres (work and pensions), the National Health Service (nurses) and Immigration and Asylum Support. The frame in which power works in the British context affects Black Brazilian women with oppressions, as the intersectionality present in this group's experiences with violence and discrimination conveys the articulations of race, class, gender, disability, language and nationality that are part of the harm suffered through institutionalized actions. I will answer two key questions: how do intersectional oppressions affect Black Brazilian women's use of British institutions? And how are these experiences in relationality with the everyday negotiations of domination and resistance?

First I present Ceci's herstory,[23] which talks about the implications of the variety of oppressions (in)forming her diasporic experiences of difficult obstacles to find work; divorce; and an acquired disability due to an accident and depression. Secondly, Gabriela's herstory[24] talks about the solitude of Black women during pregnancy, obstetric violence and living in poverty. I finish by analysing aspects of British coloniality that articulate race politics as a way to institutionalize discourses and practices of othering (dominance), affecting the realities and sense of self of Black Brazilian women (possibilities of resistance). I am interested in showing the way affect circulates in the power relations with agents of the state, enabling a variety of relationalities where oppressions against/the agency of Black Brazilian women are manifested in the context of diaspora.

Ceci: At the crossroads of acquired disability and domestic violence

I am 41 years old, from Rio de Janeiro. My only family is my mamma … She is a domestic worker in Brazil. She works for the same family since I was born, so the couple who hired her are my godfather and godmother. That's why I had good education. They paid for my private school. Today I see that's why I had a kind of double notions of my status of class and race. I only to 'find out' I was Black when I was around twelve or thirteen years old! Well ... I grew up and tried to go to a university and besides not feeling myself ... Not seeing myself there – everything was so White – I couldn't afford it. I started exploring my artistic abilities, going to drama classes, afro dance and samba. I danced samba as a 'mulata' for a few years in a famous samba club in Brazil, with a few promises of going abroad to dance ... promises of glamour that never happened. So, I left Brazil very frustrated with the lack of job opportunities. I was sure that abroad I would make it!

I came straight to England in 2001, to a friend's house who hosted me on my arrival. This friend is also Brazilian, a single mother, and at that time she was struggling with problems in her personal life, so I had to leave after a few months. I had to go back to Brazil because of my visa situation but ... By the time I left I was dating a guy. He went to Brazil to meet me and we got married in May of 2004. That was the dream, like ... having a married life and all, but I was completely dependable on him because I didn't speak English, didn't have a job or any money ... No friends who I could go talk to or visit. Eventually, I started cleaning offices and houses in a big city of England. I cleaned this entire city, already!!! At the same time, I felt lonely. I felt like I had to strip off my Brazilianess. I had to change my dressing code, the physical contact I was used to ... No more hugs or kisses as we are used to in Brazil, you know? Like that I felt I was more respected or respectable. So, I had, I still have a sense of being enclosed in a social paradigm, which was also what I was living at home.

My husband sometimes wouldn't come back home at night, he was very absent. Sometimes I picked up the phone and it was his lovers' calling our home. The relationship with him was abusive. He had a son during our relationship, and even then, his mother supported him. She said that I should be a good wife and I would not receive any support if I walked away. One day I called the police because one of his girlfriends came to my door asking for my husband. I told her I was not going to accept that. She hit me! When the police arrived, I couldn't express myself. I used a dictionary to say that she was threatening me and then they ... The officers just left. They didn't register the occurrence. So the police are not .... prepared to give this support. I couldn't say anything about what was happening. I suffered the domestic abuse of physical and psychological violence in silence.

Eventually, I started the process of separation and divorce alleging domestic abuse which one of the grounds of the violence were adultery from my husband. It would help to lead the argument for 'unreasonable behaviour' (one of the grounds for divorce in English law) in order to enable a quicker lawsuit and the possibility to continue with my visa procedures for permanent status in the country. The judge dismissed him of the accusations of abuser and adultery – even with the *proof that he had a son during our marriage. The police call was also not taken into consideration ... Of course! A migrant, non-White woman making a call to the police with limited fluency in English! The judge decision left me in a difficult position to process my residence permission. I lost the dispute.*

It's a strange thing the way the judiciary, or even the police itself ... They are not prepared to deal with this thing of domestic violence, of domestic abuse, of ... When the girl hit me, if the police were prepared, they would understand the situation ... The court is also not prepared for this kind of situation, you know? Nor the solicitors. Because as it was the legal aid solicitor, the solicitor is for free, so they do a basic job ... This is serious. I was completely alone.

After this decision I had a terrible car accident on a way to a concert with a few friends that left me with a permanent disability that reduced my mobility. At this point I learned how to be resourceful! I learned how to speak English. I had to be able to explain my pain and understand what was happening to my body. I had to plea a negotiation with my ex-husband, I received a compensation by the Welfare Centre, but I wasn't covered by the insurance company for accident. I started to contact doctors who were experts in my disability in Brazil to be able to talk to someone.

I met a few Brazilians who needed someone who knew a bit of English to help them to rent a house, so I managed to find a place to live. At the same time, all this process was lonely. I didn't want anyone in Brazil to know about my failed marriage, my accident, my disability, my lacking money, any of this. I was ashamed. You know this thing ... This pressure of being a woman that holds a marriage and everything? Only my mom knew what was happening. I started getting really depressive. I learned what unhappiness is here in the UK.

My solicitor helped her to get an agreement with my ex-husband, which helped me to survive financially for a while. What comes with bad vibes, just disappears. The money disappeared really fast. He paid that and it was OVER. We never spoke ever again. I don't hold any anger or grudge. It's all over now. Slowly I restarted to work. I still have a dream to become a mother. For the past few years I live with my partner. Our union is the reason my visa situation was legalized here. Nowadays I drive an adapted car, maintain my cleaning jobs according to the limitation of my mobility. Today I feel like I am an accomplished woman. I have some happy days.

Ceci: Herstory overcoming intersectional oppressions

Ceci's herstory presents the failure of British institutions in understanding the nuances of domestic abuse, migratory situations and women's experiences when trying to leave a toxic relationship. As Ceci was telling me her story, she was reflecting about the lack of preparation of the police force and the legal system. We were speaking in Portuguese, a language that points to the gendered classifications of each professional involved in herstory: the police officer, the judge, and the solicitor. The translation to English does not allow the same gendering politics. I find important to highlight that they were all men, the normative of masculine voices authorized in the *lugar de fala* validated to establish what is just, legal, correct and fair. The gender of these professionals shows how masculinity is normalized in the process of decision- and police-making, holding power not only over people's lives, but in the institutional practices that can be followed by other genders in the same position, unless it is – and must be – contested. The particularity of Ceci's herstory in the British setting is in terms of how the divorce was processed, putting in risk her 'leave to remain' in the UK. The gap between law (police and legal system) and justice did not recognize her as a victim of domestic violence, which then turned her into a victim of the system that should be able to understand and protect her. Ceci was harmed in different ways in respect to her humanity, ripped into nationalized, raced, gendered, abled oppressions.

Ceci eventually encounters her *lugar de fala* that negates the location of marginalization that the institutions involved in her experience tried to allocate to her, what Lélia González calls 'Amefricaladina'.[25] It is about an alternative psychoanalytical grammar for the language that Black people negate to remain at the margin. González suggests that each marginalized person of colour find liberation by putting geography, consciousness, racialized and nationalized aspects to create resistance, claiming for a decolonial positionality of constant 'negation' of the place that racism reserves to racialized peoples.[26]

Ceci's herstory is one example on how the White-Wo/Man-Western-Euro-centric colonial voice has been centred in the production of the meaning of justice and violence in institutional instances. It is not a coincidence that the agents of the state did not assist Ceci's needs. As a non-European migrant, the limitations to access justice and benefits in the UK created a particular subjectivity that historically averted recognizing the White European male centrism in the construction of institutions. The result forged a rhetoric of neutrality and colour-blind meritocracy that made it difficult to dialogue about politicized bodies or make claims about discriminatory treatments.[27]

Contesting meaning is to understand relationality as a way to enact multiple intersecting subjects' positionings within the work context, such as the judge, the solicitor, the police officer, and many other public servants whom Ceci met in her crossroads of intersectional oppressions.

According to Hunter, 'the enactment of an identity connects governing subjects to any one idea in complex ways, and it is this set of complex and potentially contradictory affective connections which are constitutive of the idea's variable and contested meanings'.[28] Hunter is calling attention to the emotional investments that agents of the state use to build a sense of equality, when their own positions are ontologically/biographically related with such contradictory ways to create meanings.

The diasporic experience present in Ceci's narrative shows the emotion-laden phenomenon that intersectional oppressions represent on an everyday basis for marginalized groups in the UK. The condition of migrant is a first condition to put Ceci at the sideline to access the labour market, rights and services in the UK. According to the *Report on Latin Americans Migrating from Europe to the UK*, the low resources in public services provision and welfare restrictions for migrants create barriers for vulnerable migrants, reducing outreach and information services to new arrivals, which results in 'practical exclusion' of migrants from public services, affecting women particularly due to the position of being the main carers for children and family.[29] This means not only that Ceci's story meets at the crossroads of intersectional barriers due to her nationalized, racialized, gendered and classed position, but also that an entire community is systematically targeted to be in isolation, exclusion and emotional overload. The implications of such systematic harm will be also explored in Gabriela's herstory, which follows this section.

Gabriela: Herstory of giving birth and building community

My name is Gabriela, I am thirty-eight years old, from Central Brazil. Since early childhood my parents were divorced, which became a landmark in my upbringing. They both came from a poor background. My mother was uneducated and used to be a cook, selling cakes on demand. My dad started working when he was seven years old to provide for his family, so they would eat in the charity refectory of the church, sometimes the same sweet corn pudding (canjica) for several days. The stories of his extreme deprivation make me tearful to this day. He managed to graduate in business from a good university, which improved my family's social class position.

My parents' relationship was very conflictive. My dad was a proper womanizer and my mom was very jealous and scandalous. After their divorce, my mom started to be overprotective and very restrictive towards my sister and me.

When I finished high school, I left my mother's house and went to live with my father and his wife. He is evangelical and took me to the church, and now, so am I. There were a few ups and downs in my social relationships, but it was a public humiliation by an ex-boyfriend in the university that gave me the boost to leave Brazil. A friend told me about London, how fancy it was to speak English, and I said, 'That's where I'm going!' In less than two months after that idea, I arrived in London. It was in January, I arrived wearing a t-shirt and high heels, had only a few pounds in my pocket and one phone number to call, so a guy I didn't know would pick me up at the airport. It was a proper confusion of hours waiting in that cold, hungry and lost.

After my third day of arrival, I had to move to another house with a new host because the girlfriend of one of my housemates was jealous, but I couldn't understand anything. I didn't speak nobody's language and I was always left without food, I was shy to ask for bread or something. I shared the apartment with many other Brazilians, nobody had papers at that time, including me. Nowadays things have changed, and everyone is legalized. I didn't speak English, so what helped me the most was to get to know more people in the Brazilian community. That opened the doors for me to start selling handicraft work every week, in a Brazilian market. About the same time, I met a guy with whom I felt in love. I am not really sure where he was from, but he wasn't Brazilian. He had some strange attitudes, sometimes he would disappear for a month, and then reappearing as if nothing had happened, and then he got to the point to ask me for money ... I thought to myself 'I am here, in this situation, making crafts for a living, working, to give money to men? I don't want this!'

Short after I broke up with him, I found out I was pregnant. At this point I was living in the UK for two years, but still undocumented. My flatmates and friends from the Brazilian community started to reject me, everyone! It was the worst moment of my life. My friends said that it was impossible to have a child here because I was illegalized, alone, they would say it was not worth it. They offered me £600 to make an abortion.

I called him [the progenitor of the child] *to break the news, but his response was very negative. He said that he didn't want children; called me all sorts of names, accusing me that it was just because of his passport. I then found out he had a long-term relationship with another woman, who at first was angry at him because of our relationship. She told me that he was a gambler, addicted in playing cards so she was supporting him financially. After his failed attempt to make me have an abortion, I tried to call once more to ask for help. I understood he was back with his girlfriend, because she was the one who finally picked up the phone. She told me that he threatened to call the immigration on me to denounce that I was illegalized in case I didn't disappear. I couldn't afford to take the risk. So, with months pregnancy, with the big belly, I had to move out from where I was living. My new room was unfurnished, no bed, no mattress, nothing! I slept on the floor for a few nights. It was horrible.*

As I was being rejected from my Brazilian friends because I decided to keep the baby, the ones from the Brazilian church helped me with some financial support, furniture and baby layette ... However, nothing was for free. I worked hard throughout my entire pregnancy, I showed up, it wasn't easy. In the beginning, I didn't have the guts to tell my folks in Brazil about this situation. I was so embarrassed. I used to cry for everything, desperately ...

Eventually I told my parents, but they wanted me to go back to Brazil. I wanted to stay and be a winner. I did all the prenatal check-ups in the same hospital, and at some point, I felt like I was building trust with the nurse. So, I decided to tell her that I was illegalized. A few weeks before giving birth, I had to take a vaccination and I saw that nurse talking to another one about something like 'poli ...'. When I was entering the room, one of the nurses told me not to. She pointed to another waiting room saying that I had to check something else before the vaccination. I thought it was a lie and they were calling the police on me, so I decided to run away from the hospital!

Later on, they called me from the hospital explaining that they were not going to call the police, but in my situation at that time, I had to pay for the cost of this vaccine. They told me that the administrative procedure for the vaccination is completely different from the police, but if I didn't go back there to take the vaccine, they would report me for mistreating my baby. I went back, took the vaccine and managed to negotiate to pay in instalments.

Towards the end of my pregnancy, I would spend days without electricity or phone credits to call for help, which led me to ask for help of strangers, who took me to the hospital when my water broke. When I finally went to give birth, it was a shocking experience. After I had my second child and I was legalized I could see the difference of treatment from the first delivery.

If I could ever say I suffered racism in my life, it would be THAT moment. They put their hands inside me ... They didn't even tell me what was going on, I just felt hands going into my body! I was screaming with pain, I asked ... I begged for an injection and they didn't give it to me. I felt being teared apart from inside. After, when they saw the damage, they put me in a special bed to give me the injection of epidural anaesthesia. I stayed for 22 days in observation, I think I lost a lot of blood. After that the nurse told me that she asked, I don't know if she did. Maybe they could have given me the injection before ...

After having my baby, I continued working. The baby was two weeks old when I received a call from the organizer of the Brazilian fair saying that I didn't need to go anymore. I was breastfeeding when the guy said I was dismissed because I didn't have the documents. My room was full of my handcrafts, ready to be sold. I cried and prayed.

A friend of a friend knew about a couple who was organizing a party and needed handmade decoration. They bought all the things I had to sell. From

that point on I started working for them as a domestic worker during that year.
After that the couple moved out of the country, but they promised to send one
thousand pounds every month until my baby completed three years old. That
helped me to study, learn English, establish myself and move on with my life. It
was a relief. Nowadays I am happily married, have two children and work in
something I like. I feel like a winner.

Enduring the solitude of the Black woman

The herstory of Gabriela offers many nuances to analyse the presence of
coloniality in White-Wo/Man-Western-Euro-centric patriarchy. Gabriela's
family structure was negatively affected by the conflicts among her parents,
which were aggravated when her father left, shirking his emotional and
material responsibility to the family for a while. Her mother started selling
the furniture to make money. Gabriela's mother's overprotection was
mediated by the use of alcohol and the physical abuse, translating into the
psychosocial effects of systematic abandonment and solitude among Black
women. Gabriela's mother, Gabriela as a child and the next generation that
is part of the intergenerational harm present in Herstory. Ana Claudia
Lemos Pacheco explains the solitude of the Black woman as part of the social
tensions in the Brazilian setting that excludes and marginalizes Black men,
relegating Black women to the 'solitude' and the arduous task of fighting for
the survival of their children.[30]

The conflicts in Gabriela's family sets the context to her experience
with the abandonment by the progenitor of her baby informing that these
interactions are naturalised intersectional harm in social and institutional
practices gender roles show power imbalances that allow the father to
show up in herstory as a solution, the saviour who took her into his house
and the church. I am not trying to detach the figure of the father from
the positive impact that Gabriela describes. Instead, I want to point out
the relational aspect of coloniality and the formation of toxic masculinity
that leads the father to incorporate the dangerous epitomes of manhood:
heteronormative womanizer, neglecting his family while he was pursuing
his career; resolute.[31]

Furthermore, solitude is beyond the aspect of not having a partner, but
the lack of support for survival that Black women endure, a social location
that is systematically neglected. The projenitor of Gabriela's baby is a direct
example of naturalized White-Wo/Man-Western-Euro-centric patriarchy,
leaving her to experience solitude after getting pregnant. This solitude is the
progenitor's attempt to make her to have an abortion; in the rejection of her

friends when she decided to keep the baby while she was illegalized in the country; the threat that the hospital makes for her to go back and get the vaccination; the delivery of her baby; and being laid off after giving birth. I understand that the process of solitude is relational with the different levels of social experience, roots of coloniality and institutionalized actions that are imbricated in this reproduction of exclusion.

When Gabriella is called by the nurse, she is convinced to go back to the hospital under the pressure of having the police called on her for mistreating the baby. Studies on British health care demonstrate that Black women have more likelihood of suffering an independent risk factor for severe maternal morbidity and mortality.[32] That is due to a possible role of inadequate access and utilization of healthcare services among the Black ethnic groups.

While Gabriela was asking for an 'injection' – translated from Portuguese, 'injeção' – the nurse allegedly did not understand that she was in pain. She only received anaesthesia (in Portuguese the word is 'anestesia') after giving birth, in order to be stitched. In 2008, when Gabriela gave birth, the average length of stay after giving birth in a UK hospital was 1.9 days.[33] It is clear that the twenty-two days that Gabriela had to remain in the hospital was much longer than this figure. This is the case of possible postpartum severe morbidity, which Black women are twice as likely than White women to suffer; they are also five times more likely than White women to die during the postnatal period.[34] This data shows that it was not an issue of being lost in translation from the Portuguese language to the English language. Gabriela and the institution who received her were lost in translation of universal values and norms to the local level. Gabriela was speaking from her belief of *being* human. The (people in the) British institutions have another meaning for Gabriela's life, locating her in the zone of non-being, Othered by the language that authorizes practices that develop in such obstetric violence. There is a need for policy-makers, health professionals and service managers to have practical national guidance for women with multiple vulnerabilities, including emotional and psychological. I would add that the intersection with nationality and legal status may increase the vulnerability and dangerous consequences to the mothers' and babies' lives. Gabriela told me that she was not aware of the reason why she remained in the hospital, but she thinks she lost a lot of blood. In any case, this is a call for improving obstetrician care of women with sensitive attention to the intersections that may cause harm if neglected.

The inequality that affects Black women who are not nationals has worse consequences in case of abandonment by the baby's progenitor. Due to Gabriela's immigration status, she was unable to claim benefits, nor could she request the social services to take action against the progenitor to compel him to shoulder his responsibilities toward the newborn. The British system is racist, sexist and xenophobic, including unaffordable charges and taxes to make life impossible in an environment that has been hostile since even before Theresa May coined the term to set up a draconian immigration policy secured by the British 'hostile environment'.[35]

It is fundamental to understand how affect and solitude circulate as part of the racism and sexism in which Black Brazilian women grow up. It is, then, permissible that Black Brazilian women suffer harms from British institutions, where patriarchal language has been crystallized in existing paradigms of White-European-Male-Hetero-centric discourse. Gabriela's *lugar de fala* is also in the negation of being recognized as 'Othered' in the context of her diasporic experiences. Her agency of limited decision making must be acknowledged not only to understand the dialogue between multidimensional expressions of harm, hope and power, but also to understand her diasporic movement that was embodied with her resolutions of keeping the baby, not going back to Brazil, finding ways to continue working and accomplish her aspirations in life. The paths that lead Ceci and Gabriela to possibilities of resistance while enduring institutional oppression are interplaying with the intricate and contradictory categories of raced, gendered, abled, classed, nationalized dis/identifications. In this relationality of categories, there is a possibility to go beyond the binaries of victimhood and agency to illustrate a possibility of analysing Black Brazilian women's diasporic experiences, as presented in the next section.

Speaking through Black Brazilian women's intersections: The affect economy of colonial discourses in experiences of diaspora

Dealing with challenges and concerns about how to build up a sense of belonging outside the home country has been an important topic of discussions in Diasporic and Migration Studies.[36] In the cases of Ceci and Gabriela, there is an utterance flowing towards a process of finding belongings and strength. Ceci says that her encounter with 'happy days' was through her discovery of pain and sadness. Gabriela values her feeling of winning in life because she followed her decisions. The agency, resistance, oppressions are not in opposition, but rather imbricated and creating counter-narratives in the dominant [British] language. I stress the importance of these counter-narratives assuming that language has a key importance to (in)form dis/identifications and positionalities that result in the constructions of meanings and practices that are part of the everyday. When negotiated, meanings and practices may gain a different movement that 'resonates with legacies of a racist colonial and imperial past, new border and migration regimes, heteronormativity and the current world order'.[37] The use of language, therefore, is a practice of marking the presence of Black Brazilian women in the triangular space of the Black Atlantic in which those dehumanized claim their humanity through their authentically *lugar de fala* Amefricanista.

Ceci and Gabriela did not speak English well in order to explain their pain, domestic violence or emotional traumas. In this regard, the question of their agency reflects the relevance of translation: their presence was located in the semantics of 'Othered', producing an ever-same in the politics of differentiation of raced, gendered, abled, nationalized individuals that systematically silences, neglects and ostracizes those who are located as non-beings. Gutiérrez Rodríguez talks about the question of being lost in translation when using a uniform market logic without noting the specific grammar and semantics of the context: 'this act of translation aims to transfer one single dominant idea into a variety of languages without experiencing any transformation/alteration through the specific context of reception'.[38] Ceci and Gabriela offer a counter-movement to this effect, with the limitations that encompasses the dialogical relation with the White-Wo/Man-Western-Euro-centric patriarchy.

Self-location as a Black woman in the world is an act of resistance (*Amefricaladina*). This movement opens interstices in the normative, interacting with the language game that situates Black Brazilian women's 'place' and our subjectivity in the ongoing condition of being/becoming subject. It dislocates the homogenizing politics of coloniality of power, unfolding a mission that requires words 'as they lead us out to the re-presentational where the subject commences its journey in the looking glass of the symbolic'.[39] Words form a textile of discovering where the Black Brazilian woman is at the standpoint and the *lugar de fala* that will be in transit with self-interrogation, reflexivity on how agency is weaved transiting through/against/with the intersectional oppressions reproduced by British institutions.

Looking at intersectional oppressions *through* Ceci's and Gabriela's language, positionality and perspectives helps us to draw on particular ways of experiencing oppressions as part of systemic inequality rooted in colonial constructions of racialization and the depoliticization of these bodies. The use of herstories are indicatives that illustrate the biographical/ontological way to *speak through* intersections. According to Hunter, *speaking through* intersections 'implies the ongoing affective relational integration of intersections into personal biographies', avoiding the denial of personal (ontological) involvement in institutional reproductions.[40]

Affect economy is also circulating in the policymaking of the Government Legal Service, the police force, Welfare Centre, and Immigration and Asylum Support in Ceci's experience of being victimized *through* intersections. The same is the case in the healthcare system and social service that failed in providing care for Gabriela. I insist on stressing the word 'victim' as a strategy to denounce the harm produced by British institutions. It does not mean that Ceci's and Gabriela's images should be frozen as such; however, these institutions do not make them 'survivors' of the harm they suffered. They are survivors due to the dynamic of power imbalances that also reflects on their agency to be. Further research on the treatment of Black Brazilian women by British institutions is relevant, especially in ongoing changes during Brexit and more open institutional racist, xenophobic social policies represented by the discourse for a hostile environment. More importantly, a more accurate form of training should be given to public servants to understand the impact of such authorization of intersectional oppressions in the lives of people who are located in the unhuman 'Othered'.

The hostile positionality of British institutions *affect* how Ceci lived with her emotions, often described as *sad, depressive, desperate* along with feelings of isolation and solitude. In Gabriela's case, she also used the word *desperate* to describe the situation during her pregnancy. The socioeconomic status of the Latin American community in England has so many features of neglect and exclusion from public services, which creates a sense of the invisibility of this targeted group.

The emotional investments that Ceci and Gabriela need to put forward are the burden of being victimized by a system that does not consider their ontological/biographical self as a possible subject to access what public institutions are calling equality, rights and services. However, overlapping layers of contradictions and oppositions complicate this oppressive configuration through the alternative ways used by Ceci and Gabriela to remake themselves as 'with some happy days' and a 'winner'. It is not simple or little, but way beyond what is expected by a racialized, gendered, classed, heteronormative, nationalized politics of othering.

Ceci and Gabriela herstories are also the repeating histories produced by African, Asian, European and Indigenous people as they became entangled in the confluence of the Caribbean Sea and Atlantic Ocean.

If grounded in a violent penetration of and command over human and non-human life, this meeting point also laid the ground for modes of becoming otherwise.[41]

Black women's narratives, the location of our voices, the validation of our erased and marginalized truths are places to start gathering the deconstruction of what makes diasporic experiences so harmful. Through our language we survive and perhaps open different paths to find new crossroads (*Laroyê!*) where narratives of herstories can mark the radical decolonial presence of *being*.

> *they wanted us colonized*
> *but when a Black woman revolutionizes her word*
> *feeds the freedom of all Black people in diaspora*
>
> *they wanted us between the devil and the deep sea*
> *but when a Black woman intercrosses her word*
> *– Laroyê! –*
> *brings inner peace in the path of all Black people in diaspora.*[42]

(In)visible Black women (be)longing in Scotland

Francesca Sobande

Black women in Scotland exist: those who were born there; those who found themselves in Scotland at other points in their lives; those who are Muslim; those who identify as Black and mixed race; and those whose self-preservation is dependent upon their presence there going unnoticed. This is far from being a definitive list of the different realities of Black women in Scotland, as no two are the same. Among these are experiences at the intersections of racism and sexism, as well as entwined structural discrimination connected to issues regarding ableism, classism, and Islamophobia. Associated challenges that Black women encounter can involve complex similarities and differences between their experiences, which are often obscured by the dominance of aggregated data on Black, Asian and Minority Ethnic (BAME) people in Scotland. It is also crucial to observe that as long as discussions of the lives of Black women in Britain are predicated on the interchangeability of 'Britain' and 'England', both the nuances of their lives, and those of British regional relations, will be overlooked.

Further still, although there is a record of some of the isolation and frustration that has ignited the collective organizing of Black women in Scotland, of the accounts in existence, the term 'Black' often encompasses Black women and all women of colour who face racist and sexist discrimination.[1] For this reason, my work focuses on Black women who are of African and Caribbean descent specifically, and which includes those who also identify as mixed. Reflection on their encounters, via an intersectional framework, sheds light on how such Black women's lives take shape in relation to structural dynamics tied to their identities, systemic oppression, and 'the legacy of Scotland's place in the British Empire'.[2] Making Black women in Scotland the focus of this work provides an opportunity to expand understandings of how their experiences of 'multiply-burdened' oppression are impacted by the particularities of the Scottish context, including its positioning within Britain.[3]

Crenshaw's foundational research outlines the need for intersectionality to sufficiently account for Black women's experiences of structural subjugation. The intersectional approach to my work involves recognition of how overlapping articulations of systemic oppression, such as racism and sexism,[4] can be mediated by geo-cultural location; including relations between Scotland and England within Britain. In turn, this chapter considers under-explored issues pertaining to the influence of regional location and national identity, in intersectional understandings of life in Britain for Black women. This involves discussion of the intricacies of Black women's experiences of misogynoir in Scotland – which refers to 'both an historical anti-Black misogyny and a problematic interracial gender dynamic'.[5] My writing is embedded in the narratives of Black and mixed women in (and from) Scotland, myself included. As such, it draws on interviews with individuals who participated in my broader research on Black women's media experiences, and whose self-selected pseudonyms feature in this chapter.[6]

Blackness in Scotland

While Britain's role in the transatlantic enslavement of Black people is increasingly the subject of scrutiny, Scotland's inclusion in, and collusion with this, has received comparatively less attention. Yet, this is gradually changing, as is suggested by the University of Glasgow publishing a report on the institution's historical links with slavery.[7] Throughout history 'constructions of Blackness within the Western imperialistic framework' have positioned Black people in Britain as 'belonging' to 'homes' elsewhere in the world.[8] Still, the term 'Black British' is one that has become more commonplace over the last several decades. That said, the concept of being 'Black Scottish' or a 'Black Scot' remains much less taken up as part of public discourse about Black lives in Britain; as does a focus on the perspectives of Black people in Scotland.

The topic of 'political blackness', which refers to forms of solidarity and unified organizing between ethnic minority groups,[9] is not the focus of this chapter. Nevertheless, it is relevant to recognize that this concept, and its potential to overshadow the experiences of Black African and Caribbean people, has not received as much critique in Scotland as it has south of the border. What all of this means for Black women in Scotland is that they can face a steep uphill struggle to be regarded as authorities on their own experiences, which are often diluted within Scottish discourse to do with race and gender, as well as commentary concerning Black British experiences.[10] In fact, it was only recently that I found myself in conversation with somebody under the impression that Black women frequently led Scottish spaces dedicated to anti-racist and anti-sexist issues. It took a few seconds for me to realize that their understanding of 'Black' was one which encompasses the identities of a broad range of ethnic minority groups, not just those of African and Caribbean people. It seems important to acknowledge these different aspects of the Scottish context, before commenting on how Black women in Scotland are both (in)visible and hyper-visible; in ways linked to the intersections of racism and sexism, and the relative obscurity of present-day Scotland in relation to commentary concerning Black Britain.

My writing is stimulated by records of the lives of Black women in Britain[11] and extant discussions of matters to do with the intersections of racism and sexism.[12] One case in point is Hirsch's work on the liminality, hybridity and marginality of Black Britishness, resulting in the potency of the word 'Brit(ish)'.[13] Its bracketed component mirrors the tentativeness with which some Black people in Britain may perceive themselves as British, if at all. This chapter builds upon scrutiny of the 'ishness' of being Black in Britain. Aligned with the underpinnings of intersectional praxis, which stem from the work of critical race legal theorists, it centres the lives of Black women. This writing includes discussion of their limited representation in British public spheres, and changes to their representation in Scotland. Such work unpacks associated issues to do with how Scottishness is entangled with matters regarding identity, (be)longing, (in)visibility, hypervisibility and Black women's lives.

The isolation, mixed-ness and hyper-sexualization of Black women in (and from) Scotland

A sense of isolation can be a hallmark of the lives of Black women in Scotland, due to the intersections of racism and sexism, as well as a sense of (dis)connect between being Black women there and elsewhere in Britain. My interview with a participant named Lucy is indicative of these issues. Lucy, who is twenty-three years old, said:

> … of course there are some [Black] communities here, but it's not like we're all living on one block and looking out for each other … that sisterhood and brotherhood. I just don't feel like that has really ever existed here … I mean, here is so White, that sometimes it can be a bit isolating … you know, looking at it factually, it's all to do with patterns of immigration. Let's talk about West Indian migration first of all, the sort of Windrush era that did not happen in Scotland … so the way

that they settled in places like London and Manchester and Liverpool, all these communities became cross-generational, and they're still there and they made a massive impact on those cities and that simply hasn't happened here … so we … have processed being mixed race or Black in very different ways than people in these other cities, because it has been such an *individual* experience.

(Lucy, twenty-three years old)

As Lucy also stressed, being a Black woman in Scotland does not simply equate to being regarded as Scottish. If anything, it is only ever a bracketed form of Scott(ish)ness which seems within grasp: 'To what extent do I feel Scottish? It fluctuates because … my authenticity as *that* is constantly called out and questioned, so a part of me always feels uncomfortable'. Lucy spoke of feeling a conflicted sense of (be)longing when living in Inner London at another point in her life, which has a significantly higher percentage of Black people (16.8%) than Scotland (< 1%).[14] The word '(be)longing' captures the fluid and fraught nature of feelings regarding a sense of belonging (in Scotland and to a collective Black experience), as well as a form of longing to be somewhere (else), and for Black women's existence in Scotland to be less questioned. Lucy's remarks echo the Afro-Caribbean Women's Association, who in 1990 wrote of their being 'a lack of cohesion' between Black people in Scotland.[15] This is punctuated by the paucity of visible community leaders who are Black African and Caribbean women, because of the combined effects of racism and sexism.

Other participants also spoke of their interest in moving 'down south' because of the prospect of living among larger populations of Black people. Therefore, participants conveyed both critiques of the hegemony of 'Englishness', and expressions of wistful inclinations to move to parts of England where 'being a Black woman is different, because you're less likely to be the *only* one'. They also commented on being aware of groups and spaces in England established by Black women, and which place them at the forefront in ways that Scotland seems yet to embrace. My own experience of previously co-founding a Black-led collective of women of colour in Scotland made me particularly conscious of how often Black women (t)here are expected to assist, help, support and offer their opinions when called upon, without being provided with the opportunity to lead the very conversations and communities that concern them. This is far from being an occurrence that is specific to Scotland. However, the burden of visibility is pronounced in this setting, given its distinct scarcity of known and supported collective organizing led by Black women.

Among the various themes that emerged across interviews with Black women in (and from) Scotland were experiences of isolation, as well as interactions that involved their hyper-sexualization. Lucy spoke of how the mixed nature of her Blackness seemed to be responded to differently in London than in Scotland, when reflecting on how the 'mixed-race "thing" was not something that I had ever really encountered before, because there really aren't enough mixed-race people in [Scottish city] for that to be a prevalent stereotype' of its own. Such reflections suggest that the relative scarcity of Black women in Scotland can result in less of a societal focus on the differences between their identities, than in certain parts of Britain such as London; where Lucy's mixed-ness may be acknowledged more than her Blackness per se. Comparably to Lucy, Mamanyigma hinted at there being a lack of recognition in Scotland of the specificity of mixed Black women's experiences, because of the scant population of Black people; mixed and otherwise. Mamanyigma is twenty-five years old and said:

> ... for me when I grew up abroad [in Africa], Black wasn't really a thing because everyone is Black. When I moved to Scotland it was very much a thing. Like, I was Black ... whereas growing up in West Africa I was never Black. In fact, I was more White because I had a White dad, while when I came to Scotland you were just branded 'Black', so it was something that I found quite interesting and it kind of made me think about my relationship with my culture and my skin colour.
>
> (Mamanyigma, twenty-five years old)

Both Lucy and Mamanyigma discussed how in certain contexts, including in Africa and in London, their light-skinned complexions result in more of a focus on their mixed identity and perceptions of their closeness to Whiteness than to Blackness. The intrigue that some people seemed to exhibit towards Lucy when she lived in London appears to have been to do with how her gender identity intersects with her Scottishness, Blackness, *and* mixedness; the combination of which Lucy said resulted in 'this sort of quick fascination' conveyed by 'a lot of men, especially a lot of Black men'. Lucy recalled comments such as 'oh, you're not like the *others* because you're Scottish!', which hint at the potential fetishization of Black Scottish women, including outside of Scotland.

Lucy's experience exemplifies how the otherness that is often ascribed to Black women in Britain is connected to their multifaceted positionality and links to intersecting elements of oppression. In Lucy's case, this relates to her social location outside of normative perceptions of White *and*

Black British identity; which are impacted by the systemic othering of Blackness, and the hegemonic status of both Englishness and Britishness in comparison to Scottishness in Britain. Furthermore, this is complicated by the spectacularization of Lucy's embodiment as a Black and mixed woman, and which is rooted in the combined effects of racism, sexism, misogyny, and colourism which results in the societal oppression of dark-skinned Black women and the comparatively favourable treatment of light-skinned Black and mixed women such as Lucy. While Lucy spoke of experiences of her fetishization in London, she also reflected on how despite her Scottish accent contributing to her hypervisibility there, she felt that her Blackness was much less of a source of scrutiny:

> London was this bittersweet thing of feeling so relaxed, because no one was ever going to question why I looked the way I did or where I was from … so I didn't feel this sense of responsibility to explain 'aw, I look this way because …' no one cared … you're just another brown face, in a really nice way … but on the other hand, whenever anyone spoke to me, obviously they can hear my accent … so the way that I had to answer in Scotland for the way that I *look* constantly, I had to answer for the way that I *speak*, my accent, in London … I felt like I belonged, but in another way, not belonged.
>
> (Lucy, twenty-three years old)

As participants, including Sasha-Barrow, also mentioned, with the simultaneous (in)visibility and hypervisibility of Black women in Scotland, often comes their exoticization. For example, even a Google search of terms such as 'Black women in Scotland' more quickly returns results to do with interracial 'swirl' dating which fetishizes Black women, than information about their lives, or content created from their perspectives. The same cannot be said to do with searching 'Black women in Britain'. However, both internet searches return many disparaging and stereotypical results.

Comments from Sasha-Barrow's interview present a perspective that is similar to Lucy's. Sasha-Barrow, who is 36 years-old, spoke in detail about her awareness of how her Black and mixed embodiment in Scotland is interpreted differently than when she lived in an English city with a larger population of Black people. Sasha-Barrow discussed arriving in Scotland after moving from England, where she had been since leaving Barbados as a small child:

> It [Scotland] was really White [we both laugh] because you know, Barbados is a very small island but as I identify as being Black, I always

felt part of the majority … and [English city previously based in] is very multicultural. It was a bit of a shock moving to Scotland. All the ways in which there were certain expectations of me that I really wasn't prepared for … and the way in which my body was read in certain ways. My body was very *very* public. People wanted to touch my hair. My hair was a very big focus. People wanted to touch my hair and grab it as I walked down on a Friday or Saturday night, but also there was this very particular sexualization of my body and of me, without me really doing anything, and which has in kind of subtle ways really impacted how I comport myself. Whereas before, if I felt like wearing something quite sexy I might go for it in Barbados and in [English city]. Here? I *never* would, because I just feel [sighs], I just feel a bit too fetishized ….

(Sasha-Barrow, thirty-six years old)

The realities of misogynoir, which Sasha-Barrow's remarks reflect, run throughout Britain. Misogynoir 'is particular and has to do with the ways that anti-Blackness and misogyny combine to malign Black women in our world' including via their objectification and street harassment.[16] Both Sasha-Barrow and Lucy recognized how the pervasiveness of colourist ideologies is enmeshed with how their Black and mixed embodiment is read by others in Scotland and England. This connects to the structural privileging of light-skinned Black women, including among Black communities, due to their proximity to Whiteness, and in contrast with the more acute degradation, discrimination, and dehumanization of dark-skinned Black women. To reiterate, the hyper-sexualization of Black women is not something that is solely situated in Scotland. However, as the experiences of Lucy and Sasha-Barrow indicate, the curiosity and exoticization that can surround the embodiment of Black women in Britain is shaped by different regional contexts they find themselves in. It is also influenced by the degree to which the intersections of their perceived national and racial identity appear to differ to those around them.

On one level, Black women in Scotland continue to be treated as exoticized and hyper-visible, but on another, their existence there is continually erased in media and public domains. The extent to which Black women's experiences of discrimination and spectacularization in Scotland differ from those of individuals in England is up for debate. Nevertheless, all fourteen of my interview participants based in Scotland commented on feeling as though this is the case. This, in itself, signals the need for increased critical engagement with the role of regional factors in the lives and oppression faced by Black women in Britain, especially those of individuals who may be theoretically erased as long as 'Britain' is used in the place of 'England', and specific cities within it.

Black women in Scotland and the media

In 2013, Emma Dabiri rightfully called out the paucity of representation of Black women in British media in an incisive article for Media Diversified – a social enterprise dedicated to challenging and changing the British media landscape by furthering the representation of Black communities, as well as those of people of colour.[16] When accounting for the limited depiction of Black women in British media at that time, it is apparent that of those images available, very few portray the experiences and identities of Black women outside of England. Recognizing inequalities bound to the nexus of race, gender, ethnicity, as well as regional and national relations, can contribute to rich intersectional observations of the specificity of Black women's lives in different parts of Britain, and beyond. Even interview participants of mine based in England commented on how hierarchical regional dynamics affect the uneven media depiction of the experiences of Black women in Britain:

> … what kind of voices dominate? … so like, Black British people … I feel even then, it will be dominated by English voices … it would be nice to see people who are Black and in Wales … and you never hear about their experience, or what it's like to live in [Northern] Ireland or Scotland.
>
> (Rachel, twenty-one years old)

Hence, an intersectional understanding of the lives of Black women in Scotland, including their limited media depiction, requires acknowledging the dominance of England in relation to Scotland amidst British media, politics and public life, but without overlooking Scotland's role in British colonialism.

The relative lack of media representations of Black women in Scotland, in British media, was commented on by an interview participant named Temi – a postgraduate research student who is twenty-six years old. Temi said:

> … sometimes you're even happy to see any Black people [on TV]. You're like, 'Wow! There's a Black lady on TV' … that's a good example actually! My mum … was watching the news and I was getting ready to go to uni and she was like, 'Aw Temi, come through, come through, come through!' … I was like, 'Oh, what is it?', and she was like, 'There's a Black presenter on Scottish national news!' [laugh together]. I remember seeing it and being like, 'Oh my gosh this is groundbreaking' … it's history! … for me. I know it seems like it's sad, but for me it was

massive ... especially being born and brought up in Scotland you *never* see it[.] [E]specially Black *women* news presenters ... not actually seeing anyone who looks like you on TV ... it's a massive thing when you actually *do* see someone.

(Temi, twenty-six years old)

It is worth noting that shortly after Temi's interview, the news presenter that she evocatively spoke of was no longer featured, and Scotland's broadcasting landscape returned to appearing to exclude the voices and presence of Black women.[17]

The experiences of another participant, named Miss Africa, raised issues to do with the intersections of ableism, racism and sexism, which can manifest as part of the media experiences of Black women in Scotland, and elsewhere. Miss Africa, who is twenty-seven years old, is visually impaired, involved in activist work and plans to train as a counsellor. She spoke of the stigma that surrounds Black people in Scotland with disabilities. Miss Africa also laughed off preconceptions of the life of a Black woman with visual impairments, when speaking of people's surprise in response to her independence and her choice to wear high heels, at times. Over the course of her interview, Miss Africa shared experiences which reveal how the oppressive media representation of Black women can take many forms, including non-visual ones.

When discussing how she listens to audio descriptions of media content in Scotland, Miss Africa expressed frustration at hearing a Black woman's hair described as 'bush' style. Her experience brings attention to the multi-layered nature of racist and sexist media constructions of Black women, which even take the form of audio descriptions intended to ensure the accessibility of content. Miss Africa emphasized that Black women in Scotland do not simply need access to increased media representation. Instead, they should be able to engage with representations that depart from tired and pervasive stereotypes, in both visual and audio forms. An intersectional analysis of the perspectives of Temi and Miss Africa, paired with scrutiny of the representation of Black women in Britain, illuminates how media experiences (un)available to Black women in Scotland are the by-product of overlapping structural issues to do with race, gender, dis/ability, as well as the hegemony of England within British public life.

As the experiences of interview participants such as Poppy suggest, the marginalization of Black women in Scotland is heightened when they are Muslim. Throughout her interview, Poppy continually referenced her Muslim and African identity, as well as her Blackness. She discussed how regardless of feeling Scottish, she knows that she will never fully be accepted as such. Poppy reflected on being asked to feature in a media project about the lives of Black people in Scotland. Despite her passion for media, Poppy decided not to participate because of her hypervisibility as a Black Muslim woman:

> You know, it's just the system, it makes you … people want to bend … to almost not want to be yourself anymore to fit in. … there's just *that* feeling of you not wanting to be too … you still don't want to be too … too … yourself but not *too* Black, to be accepted, you know? … and you know, the funny thing is I really never got to know all of this, until I came here [Scotland]. I wasn't quite comfortable [with the idea of featuring in a media project] because of my accent, and thought my accent might put people off … I thought, they [Black people] are the silent minority, nobody knows them, why don't we celebrate them? I didn't know if I'd be accepted and I wear the hijab and I just thought … are they ready for a Muslim woman on the screen? She's Black, she's [laughs] she's got an accent, she's got a hijab on, she's this and that.

As Johnson asserts, the experiences of Black Muslims are commonly overlooked as part of the discussion of Black lives, Muslim ones and women's experiences; which are often treated as existing separately from one another.[18] However, as Poppy alludes to, markers of her religious and gender identity (hijab), as well as those related to her Black African identity (accent), result in people societally positioning her outside of a sense of Scottishness. Poppy also referred to the limited media opportunities for Black women in Scotland, in contrast with those that can be available in England, where there are considerably more media hubs and jobs available. She highlighted how the salience of her identity as a Black African Muslim woman specifically, and potential negative responses to it, is what dissuaded her from featuring in a televised media project that she was encouraged to pursue. In doing so, Poppy hints at the strategic (in)visibility of some Black women in Scotland, who may walk a tightrope between seeking greater representation and wanting to avoid scrutiny at the intersections of racism, sexism and other systems of oppression, including Islamophobia.

Black women's current and changing representation in Scotland

The representation of Black people in Scottish public spheres is notably limited. For example, the Scottish political landscape includes a small number of BAME members of the Scottish Parliament (MSPs) and local councillors.

Yet, Black women of African and Caribbean descent are constantly absent from such arenas. Black men in Scotland face myriad issues related to racism and intersecting inequalities, but they are also more commonly at the helm of race-related organizing than Black women. Moreover, organizations based on issues of gender in Scotland tend to be led by White women and non-Black women of colour, much more so than Black women of African and Caribbean heritage. In highlighting this, I am not suggesting that such issues are absent elsewhere in Britain. Rather, although Scotland has a history of anti-racist and anti-sexist organizing that includes Black women, it is imperative to account for how it contrasts with the stronger mobilization of Black women-led groups and activities in England.

Despite the scarce representation of Black women in Scotland in mainstream media, various public arenas, and discussions of Black British identity, there are still numerous examples of their self-documentation, activism and creative practice throughout history. Among these are the ruminations of artist, writer and cultural historian Maud Sulter, whose first volume of poems was titled *As a Blackwoman*.[19] Through the story of tracing her birth parents, Jackie Kay's *Red Dust Road*[20] brings to life issues regarding race, gender, self-identity and Blackness in Scotland. In recent years, writers and activists including layla-roxanne hill have facilitated key relevant conversations, including a public panel on Women of Colour, the Media and (Mis)Representation – National Union of Journalists Scotland, Glasgow in October 2016.[21]

In addition to both hill and myself contributing to the aforementioned event, it brought together Samantha Asumadu (Director of Media Diversified) and Briana Pegado (Founder and Director of the Edinburgh Student Arts Festival). This panel, along with the first annual Black Feminism, Womanism and the Politics of Women of Colour in Europe Conference (WoC Europe) at the University of Edinburgh (September 2016), which Akwugo Emejulu invited me to be on the organizing committee for,[22] catalysed the development of Yon Afro Collective (YAC) – a Black-led collective of women of colour in Scotland. As a co-founder of YAC, who is no longer involved since leaving Scotland, witnessing how it stirred dialogue about Black women in Scotland was exhilarating and daunting. The experience also reminded me that it is not enough for Black women to be represented in a collective capacity in Scotland; as representational change is nothing without transformational politics and structural shifts. To put it briefly, future efforts to address the (in)visibility and oppression of Black women in Scotland require a positioning that decentres the perspectives of relatively privileged, middle-class and cis-gender Black women.

Increasingly, exhibitions, artwork, workshops and events provide a platform for the voices, visions and visual creations of Black women in

Scotland. Such activities include: Yon Afro Collective in Our Own Words (at the Centre for Contemporary Arts, Glasgow (August–September 2017)), LUX Scotland and Mother Tongue present AfroScots (at Glasgow School of Art (February 2018)), as well as (Re)imagining Self and Raising Consciousness of Existence through Alternative Space and (Re)imagined Place (at Govanhill Baths in Glasgow (April and May 2018)). The (in)visibility of Black women in Scotland may be shifting to some degree, partly enabled by digital technologies that can help them to reach vast and global audiences, and which can help them to connect with a collective sense of Black womanhood. However, while the representation of Black women in Scotland may slowly be changing, it is vital that a broad spectrum of identities and experiences are foregrounded, including those of women outside of the nation's largest cities, and who are among the most marginalized by society.

My writing explores experiences of living in Scotland, via a lens that centres Blackness and the perspectives of Black women. It analyses (dis)connections between what it means to be a Black woman, in (and from) Scotland. Consequently, this work yields insight into the challenges that these individuals can face, including those influenced by Islamophobia, as well as racism and sexism. This writing also highlights the power of intersectional approaches in deepening understanding of how issues to do with geo-cultural location and sense of national identity are caught up in the lives of Black women in Britain. While the experiences of Black women in Scotland involve clear commonalities concerning those of Black women elsewhere in Britain, their (in)visibility in various public settings still significantly relates to hierarchical dynamics between Scotland and England; the common way that Britishness is equated with Englishness, in addition to the combined effects of racism and sexism.

Adopting an intersectional approach to analysis of the lives of Black women in Britain can effectively emphasize difficulties and encounters that are particular to their experiences. Unpacking intra-national dynamics as part of this helps to unearth how the hegemony of England influences the lives of Black women in Scotland, as well as affecting which experiences tend to be at the forefront of conversations and media depictions concerning Black lives in Britain.

The presence of Black women in Scotland is still often more of a question than observed as being a fact. It is in the moment when a Scottish accent leaves a Black woman's mouth and sparks confused facial expressions. It is in the surprised silence that follows when a Black woman refers to Scotland as 'home'. It is precisely because Black women's location in and relation to Scotland is frequently called into question, that much is to be gained from turning to their words and work in an attempt to understand the intricacies of their lives. This chapter conveys a snapshot of what life can be like for Black women in Scotland in the early twenty-first century. A rich body of writing by Black women around the world illuminates much about their experiences of discrimination and misogynoir. However, efforts to understand how these issues unfold in a Scottish setting are still in their relative infancy, as are those based on an interrogation of tensions between the notions of Scottishness and Black Britishness. It is my hope that this chapter serves as kindling for future research that foregrounds the (in)visible, hyper-visible and varied experiences of Black women in (and from) Scotland.

Part Two

Marginalizing Black voices

Freshwater fish in saltwater: Black men's accounts navigating discriminatory waters in UK higher education

Constantino Dumangane

Black British men have often been represented in stigmatized and exploitative manners in educational research, suggesting that they have higher rates of behavioural issues and are less educationally capable or more inclined to have anti-learning dispositions.[1] Despite these negative ascriptions Black British men have attended university at higher rates as a percentage of their ethnic group than White students for over a decade.[2] However, within the UK's elite higher education Russell Group institutions (which are often considered the equivalent of US Ivy League and Public Ivies), representation of Black students remains low. The twenty-four Russell Group institutions are understood to represent the UK gold standard in higher education, as all twenty-four are ranked within the top 205 universities in the world. In 2015, Black students were least likely to study at a Russell Group university, with only 7% of them being admitted compared to 11% of White students and 13% of Asian students.[3] Yet Black and minority ethnic students are more likely to be represented in the 'new' MillionPlus institutions where they make up over 30% of the student body, and have lower levels of attainment and poorer graduate prospects than White graduates of the elite Russell Group.[4] Using a Critical Race Theory lens, this chapter examines techniques participants performed in order to manage their verbal and physical feelings to discriminatory offences to 'get on' and 'get through' elite education in order to reduce being 'othered' and stereotyped as angry Black men. Black men's accounts as Black 'freshwater fish' trying to succeed through the appearance of seamlessly swimming in elite saltwater higher education environments surrounded by a '*school*' of White, saltwater fish are explored. Applying an intersectional 'race', gender and class lens, this chapter explores multiple ways that race and gender interact with class in UK elite higher education and some of the ways Black men chose to challenge, manage or be complicit in their Blackness in situations where they experienced discrimination.

The metamorphosing guise of discrimination and racism

Many discriminatory occurrences that Black and minority ethnic people experience are not necessarily egregious conspicuous acts of racism. In this chapter, counter-narratives – a Critical Race Theory tool – are used to expose, analyse and challenge the majoritarian stories of racial privilege through Black men's discussions of their university journeys. Although overt racism still exists in society, subtle strands of discrimination are more prevalent in everyday UK society represented in mini-assaults or microaggressions directed toward people of colour, 'often automatically or unconsciously'.[5] I contend that my participants' accounts are representations of their efforts to manage the stigma associated with challenging everyday racism that they experienced.

Stigma, bodily hexis, gender and hypermasculinity stereotypes

Students and academics of colour, both females and males, struggle to survive academically while battling against racism, and it is well acknowledged that discrimination is prevalent within UK higher education, yet universities are complacent in its existence.[6] Black male students are often the mark of verbal and racially influenced offences and often confront negative stereotypes about their intelligence and must excel academically despite racially biased course content and racially insensitive educators.[7] How Black men's bodies and Blackness are perceived has a routine effect on academic power dynamics and discrimination they experience as well as the tools they utilize in order to get through and get on with attaining their academic goals. It is useful to acknowledge the effects that intersectional axes of gender, race and class have, when overlapped with stigma bodily hexis and hypermasculine stereotypes about Black men, to understand the effect these have within higher education power dynamics, which are discussed in this section. Stigma is most commonly experienced as an assault on one's worth and operates to maintain dominance over 'others' in society.[8] To call racism by its name can result in the stigmatic discriminatory preconceptions being racialized by the majority population (for example being viewed by White people as the angry Black man or woman, for calling something out as racist). Stigma management involves people adopting strategies that enable them to avoid, manage, ameliorate, or escape feeling that they are the victim of discrimination.[9]

Bodily hexis is a useful tool for understanding the positions of some Black men's bodies. It is concerned with 'clothing, jewellery and makeup, but also posture, facial expressions, ways of moving, gait, accent and gestures'.[10] Bodily hexis processes can also be ontologically complicit such as 'automatic gestures or the apparently most insignificant techniques of the body – ways of walking or blowing one's nose, ways of eating or talking'.[11] In my participants' accounts most are merely performing and doing what they need to 'in order to be what they have to be …', in order to 'fit in' and succeed in their educational fields.[12] However, there were a few outlying participants who made conscious efforts *not* to conform to an educational field's expected ways of fitting in. For over sixty years Black male hypermasculinity has been utilized as a hegemonic tool to reinforce negative stereotypes about Black men through television, film, internet, radio and other media outlets.

I contend that Black males have intersectionally raced, gendered and sometimes classed preconceived hyper-masculinized experiences at all stages of their educational pathways due to majoritarian society's ingrained discriminatory judgements of them, which are often yet detrimental to their educational aspirations and achievement. As a result of their bodily hexis or performativity, Black youth are often stigmatized as 'others' who are dangerous, troublemakers, and non-academically inclined or focused. This occurs, for example, in primary and secondary schooling, where Black boys are more likely to be excluded from primary and secondary school often for a bodily hexis that does not 'fit' within schools' habituses.[13] Teachers may perceive Black boys as having too much masculinity because some enact a type of racialized hegemonic masculinity[14] in school that emphasizes swagger, coolness, hipness 'and a sense of being an ordinary bloke with no pretensions'.[15] Teachers may misread these boys' bodily hexeis (or 'behavioural attitude') as challenging authority and disrupting the dominant middle-class normative school habitus, resulting in some teachers perceiving these boys as unintelligent and aggressive violent threats to their schools. My participants' accounts suggest that presuppositions and misrecognitions continue into elite higher education where White students and faculty members, who are the dominant group in elite university fields, often misperceive Black males' bodily hexis in a similar way to some teachers working in primary and secondary education. However, instead of being perceived as troublemakers, Black men are often perceived and stereotyped as 'others' in the forms of exotic, dangerous or unfamiliar 'space invaders' with devalued capital, which positions them as less educationally and 'intellectually' capable.[16] When Black men are confronted with possibilities of discrimination, racism or microaggressions, many engage in 'race work' involving code-switching[17] and moderate Blackness strategies to navigate and manage racial, gender and class expectations by producing positive, restrained emotions to avoid confrontation while not acknowledging everyday racisms in order to reduce or dis-identify conflict and/or avoid stigma and victimization.[18]

Analytical approach

Fifteen Black male UK domiciled participants were recruited from ten Russell Group institutions in England and Wales. Four participants attended Oxbridge. Participants were invited to talk about their experiences as Black men transitioning to and through elite predominantly White UK universities. Participants discussed resource capitals in the forms of family support, after-school tutoring and faith as examples of factors that were beneficial to their successful acceptance and transitions to elite higher education. Discrimination and how it was managed was merely one aspect of these men's accounts, yet it is the focus of this chapter.

In an effort to elicit discussions on discrimination, participants watched a satirical video called *Shit White Girls Say to Black Girls* that exposed some of the everyday offences that African American women experience during discussions with White people. I chose to use this video as a CRT tool to engage my participants in discussions about racist issues in a gendered and racial space somewhat different from their own: they are Black British men and the video was about Black women. But when racist offences occur, often conscious and unconscious decisions have been made to silence or shift racism's centrality from one's own life experiences, because to acknowledge its presence is to acknowledge being a victim, which is painful. However, to acknowledge discrimination in relation to a group (i.e. race) to which they belong – but are not the specific focus of the stigmatization – is easier to acknowledge and discuss because it is indirect and is *not* about them. Utilizing a video that focused on African-American women's experiences with discrimination enabled my participants to comfortably discuss issues of racism as they were not specifically focused on them. However, the video was beneficial in enhancing my ability to get my participants to unearth and share their personal accounts with discrimination in ways that did not emerge as easily with semi-structured interview questions about racism. Black men's accounts of whether and how they recognize, respond to, manage and in some cases dis-identify, resist or silence everyday discriminatory offences follow.

Bewilderment yet reluctant acceptance of offensiveness: Exercises in restraint

I think it's bizarre that I don't seem to have a clear memory of having to deal with a situation like that [points to the video] because I know I've heard statements like that my entire life and I suspect that, like with most things I try and talk through them, I think I do call them out, like 'don't be so stupid'.

(Alex, middle class, British African, Russell Group graduate)

[When White students say offensive things] … I guess it would depend on the person who's doing it, like if they are saying it … unknowingly and they're not truly aware of what they are saying, then I will try and explain it to them, 'You don't say this because for these reasons'. But then if it seems like they've made up their mind and they have a fear of Black people or whatever, then it'll usually be … like, drop it, sort of by saying, 'You can say that to your friends in a corner when I'm not there but don't say it around me. Don't try and disrespect me by doing it'. But I think for the most part you're always going to get that. Like, they're not Black, they're not us, they'll never really understand. It's just one of those things.

(Allen, middle class, British African, Oxbridge graduate)

Alex's and Allen's accounts suggest that discrimination is a routine experience of their lives that they tend to respond to in measured ways. In most participant accounts, as reflected here, the use of the word 'racist' or 'discriminatory' is seldom if ever mentioned by participants when discussing offensive accounts. Allen in particular appears to accept these offences as a normalized part of Black people's every day that he must deal with in a constrained manner. During participants' conversations I explored how they felt they were perceived by other White students at their institutions:

Dwayne: … I recall one thing. One of my friends … said that the first time he met me he thought I was going to stab him … He's from [name of town]. It's down south. I think there's very few Black people there … I think that's one thing I've learned. Just in terms of the ignorance that people can have. And I think I'm somebody who would never kind of blame people for that position. If anything I would try to teach them and show them or help them to kind of see how ridiculous they are (laughs).

Researcher: So would you say that's more ignorance than racism?

Dwayne: Yes. I think it's very unlikely that anyone would be the victim of kind of what's the word I'm looking for, just overt direct racism, like in today's day and age.

Researcher: What do you equate as being direct racism? Can you give me an example?

Dwayne: For someone to call you nigger or something.

(Dwayne, working class, British Caribbean, Oxbridge graduate)

Franco: I never felt that there were any real race things at [university name]. The real issue was class. ... But when I went to [university name], it was incredible. You know, this one girl I went out with her very briefly and it ended. And I felt really weird about it actually. I did not fit into her world. ... She was incredibly good-looking. ... Do you know what she asked me once? I'll say this loud for the tape. When we were going out with each other she actually asked me if I had ever killed anyone. She asked me that and then I realized she was serious.

(Franco, working class, British African, Russell Group graduate)

Alex: I had a uni housemate who called me a monkey once. But he didn't see what the problem was and I obviously went for him – but in a calm manner! Sometimes things come out and people think it's ok to say that, but it's hard when you're on your own, constantly fighting everybody all the time and then guess what? Then, you're the stereotypical Black man, so you need to make a choice ... Because White people see Black men as angry and I don't want to use the word dangerous but certainly a little bit shady. ... See this is the best thing about Britain. In Britain we are repressed a little bit like that, [yet] we're more open than we used to be. ... We are racially tolerant, etcetera. I don't say we are multi-cultural. We are tolerant of other people, but I'm still very aware that as a Black man I'm not part of the club.

(Alex, middle class, British African, Russell Group graduate)

These accounts reaffirm many stereotypically racist assumptions that the majority of my participants shared regarding what White students presumed Black men were like. Neither Dwayne nor Franco identify their experiences as racist. Franco categorizes his situation as classist. Dwayne understands his friend's perception of him as someone who might stab him of ignorance rather than racism. There are major risks of isolation, exclusion and being perceived as a complainer or troublemaker when challenging a possible racist action. However, not naming racism and allowing it to go unchecked and unmentioned is also dangerous, because it shifts racism from the foreground 'to less formal domains … [where it is] embedded in structures, without being explicitly named'.[19] Racist accounts are often denied when the recipient of the experience has a friendship or regular interaction with the perpetrator. The recipient may not want to accept what the action could construe: that a mate or partner actually harbours racist perspectives of him. Hence for Dwayne, for an offence to be labelled as discriminatory, a person would have to use a racial slur.

In contrast to Dwayne and Franco, Alex acknowledges his encounter as racist and has made a conscious decision to respond to the offence in a measured manner. He has moderated his Blackness to prevent being perceived as the 'angry Black' man by Whites, even when he would be justified when someone has called him a 'monkey'. Alex concludes his account by saying that he is aware of his status as a tolerated 'other' in British society who is not accepted as 'part of the club'. My participants' accounts also elucidate the intersectionally gendered and raced nature of racism – regardless of the students' social class background as is evident in Alex's account. As a middle-class Black student Alex is aware that how he may present himself in reaction to an offensive discriminatory assault may place him in the category of a dangerous, angry Black man. Most of my participants minimized their experiences with discrimination. It is suggested that for an offensive racist act to be called out as such it usually had to be exceptionally blatant to be identified and challenged as racist. In terms of understanding Blackness at the intersections, my participants' accounts suggest that although we do not live in a post-racial society, challenges to racist behaviour are often only addressed in the most egregious and blatant of instances. This is problematic as it enables the promotion and acceptance of lower-level racist offences, mini-assaults and microaggressions to passively go unchecked and to be considered acceptable and non-racially offensive within society.

Feeling Black: Isolation and exhaustion with being other

> At times I felt isolated. It's definitely a lot less diverse here. You see a lot more White people than where I'm from … and even within the White people here there's a lot less diversity … just look at their names and it's all like Smith and Wood, you know. You wouldn't even really see any Italian Whites, or Spanish Whites, or eastern European Whites. It's just like a lot of English Whites. So you get less diversity in terms of race here. … you'll just be excluded socially or something. They see you and

they immediately see that you're different to them and it's like they'll go for the safe option and go for someone who looks more like them and speaks like them. … I think that's just the way it is here … You're always in the situation of like – you're the one who always has to initiate the conversation and everything. They come here and they've lived such a sheltered lifestyle. They are literally scared of people like me.

(Duncan, working class, British Caribbean, Oxbridge graduate)

Alex: I read an excerpt from [Condoleezza Rice's] book where she was complaining to her father that she'd been racially abused at school and she wasn't doing very well. And he said, 'It doesn't matter: you're Black, you've got to deal with it; you've got to be better regardless'. I like the sentiment, it's pragmatic. I'm a pragmatist. I'm loathe to be as glib as to say I was Black and they were White, but the fact is, I didn't feel like I belonged at [university name]. I was the anomaly. I'm always the 'Black guy in the room' and you can see people's faces when they come in the room they're like 'oh right' … and I could see their faces in the room and it's not until I open my mouth to *speak* [participant's emphasis] [Received Pronunciation (RP) English] that they're like, 'Oh right … wow, well done you!' But having to do that, starting from a deficit most of the time, is frankly exhausting and many times I wish … and I can't believe I'm telling you this, I just wanted to be part of the group. I've got to be honest, I just wanted to disappear.
Researcher: Sometimes you wished to be White?
Alex: Yes, absolutely, I just wanted to be part of the group and get on with it and not be different because it's exhausting being different. But that, as I've said, it is what it is and as I've grown older that's the approach I've taken.

(Alex, middle class, British African, Russell Group graduate)

Duncan and Alex's accounts of 'otherness', isolation and exclusion at university were common amongst many participants. In Alex's account the feeling of being singled out as different is occasionally exhausting and makes him wish he were 'White' so that he could seamlessly 'fit in' without being 'other', instead of being a Black freshwater fish trying to swim unnoticed with a school of White saltwater fish.[20] These Black students experienced confidence-deficit feelings even after they succeeded at being accepted and whilst attending elite institutions. Their accounts also reflect the reality of the intersections of 'race' through Blackness, gender and class where 'race' ascends the other axes and feels like a more significant marker of their 'otherness' in routine discriminatory situations that they encountered.

Being the 'right' and acceptable kind of Black man: Performative techniques utilized to moderate one's Blackness to minimize racism

During my second interview with Allen he acknowledged discrimination from White students as an 'inevitable part' of his university experience. Consequently, he discussed techniques he believes are beneficial to prevent them from making 'negative assumptions' about the type of Black person he is:

> I dress in an appropriate style that people at [Oxbridge college] wear here. I think I'm around good reasonable people and that I behave in a way that is also good and reasonable so that people are not given additional (pause) are not given any random opportunity to make negative assumptions about Black people based on how I behave.
>
> (Allen, middle class, British African, Oxbridge graduate)

Allen appears to suggest that as a consequence of dressing and behaving in an appropriate and acceptable manner that is conducive to the habitus of his elite university and socializing 'around good and reasonable people', 'White' people are unlikely to think of him as a certain type of Black male (i.e. the angry or aggressive Black man). Due to his dress and performative representations he suggests that White people are not given any reason to think of him as anything other than a positive, normal and good Black man. Allen's account is an example of what is referred to as 'rules of racial standing'[21] and 'unspoken rules of racial engagement'.[22] Allen is presenting a form of acceptable 'respectable' middle-class White performativity, which he believes prevents White people at his elite university from perceiving him in any sort of dangerous, racist or ignorant 'other' way. For centuries during colonialism, 'shape-shifting' practices occurred as a response to the performative expectations that the dominant, privileged and implicit field of Whiteness required Black people to perform in a subtly restrained civility-coded manner.[23] This prevents Black men from being perceived as possessing an inappropriate temperament and prevents stereotypes that range from the lazy to the mean or angry Black man.

Becoming hyper-aware and paranoid of one's Blackness

> I feel I definitely stood out more at (Russell Group). I just felt excluded. I just didn't fit in. I feel I definitely stood out more. I had this moment actually in my second year where I became really self-conscious of being

Black. I feel like saying I became Black in a certain way. I used to go for drinks with one of my friends. So we're in the pub and she just out of the blue says to me, 'Bob isn't weird, do you ever feel weird like being the only Black person in this place or in this pub?' Which is something that, even though I'd obviously been in [Russell Group] for about a year and a bit and I'd noticed you know, that was true in a very sort of limited way, but when she said that I kind of looked up and thought, 'Is this actually true?' first. I looked around and I was like, 'Hold on a second, yeah you're right', and I noticed like a handful of people actually staring at me. That realization and noticing eyes actually looking at me, something in that moment just changed. Suddenly I'm sort of like looking around everywhere. When I'm walking down the road at night I'm looking 100 paces ahead of me. Looking behind me. 'Oh God what does she think?' Does she think I'm going to mug her or did she think I was going to burst into this sort of violent stranger rapist person? Like you just wonder what people are thinking, like, 'How are they're perceiving me?' I just became very paranoid in the sphere of visibility.

(Bob, working class, British African, Russell Group graduate)

Bob's depiction of his experience in an all-White university town pub has made him consciously aware of his Blackness. Consequently, he is now particularly hyper-aware of his 'otherness' in the evenings when he walks around campus, as he now feels and fears that his Black body may be perceived as that of a 'rapist' or someone dangerous to White people, which until his discussion with his 'friend' he had never considered himself to be. Bob's account suggests that he has experienced paranoia, stress and hurt in the form of a microaggression as a result of the comments. In his counter-story owing to the intersections of class, race, ethnicity and gender, Bob finds himself in a space where he feels he does not belong. His otherness is representative of hysteresis, or 'fish out of water' syndrome, whereby his body is not perceived by the dominant group at his university as an appropriate fit.[5]

Unlike high school, Bob's university experiences have shed a new reality about how some people may perceive him, his 'race' and his body as threatening to them. His habitus does not align smoothly with the university's frame. He is unable to seamlessly swim through the educational system and instead feels like a 'fish out of water'. Many of my participants expressed experiences similar to Bob's, where White students feared them or were apprehensive about engaging with Black students, which led many to feel 'excluded', isolated and like 'space invaders', with an out-of-place body on campus.

Things White staff said to Black students: Faculty as perpetrators of discrimination

White students were not the only perpetrators of offences that made Black students feel 'othered'. Faculty at these institutions also appeared to be unconscious of their positions of privilege and misrecognized offences that they directed at Black students. The following account is Edmund's experience of being 'othered' by a lecturer.

> Edmund: Like one of my lecturers in front of like 500 students, he called me Tiny Tempah.
>
> Researcher: Tiny Tempah the rapper? Why was that?
>
> Edmund: Yeah. Basically he was doing an economics equation. I think it was C plus I plus G minus E X. So he wanted us to memorize that … And then he said, 'Oh can we try and rap this'. And then he said, 'Edmund, Tiny Tempah, you do it', and everybody was like 'Oooooohhhh'.
>
> Researcher: Why do you think he took licence to do that?
>
> Edmund: I don't know. He thought that – I don't know – 'You're one of the only Black guys in the class. You can probably rap'. He did [say] … he was very sorry.
>
> Researcher: How did that make you feel at the time?
>
> Edmund: I was like cool. Like there are jokes, I mean, but it really wasn't really necessary. I just walked out of the class.
>
> Researcher: Did you ever confront him on it?
>
> Edmund: No. I'm not the confrontational type. Anyway he apologized and said that he told his wife that he thought one of his students was going to take him to court.
>
> Researcher: Did you think about doing that or following up with the university's administration?
>
> Edmund: No. I haven't got time. I'm trying to get a degree.
>
> (Edmund, working class, British African, Russell Group graduate)

Edmund's account of being racially insulted in front a full lecture hall is indicative of the way most of my participants discussed their reactions to discriminatory incidents – as forms of ignorance or banter, but not racism. Dis-identification is a tool used to tune out or disengage from the experience of racism to avoid being angered or hurt by a racial experience.[24] Edmund's statement that his focus was 'trying to get a degree' was a recurrent theme in several participants' accounts of discrimination. In a university speaking engagement Toni Morrison[25] stated:

> It's important … to know the very serious function of racism, which is distraction. It keeps you from doing your work. It keeps you explaining over and over again, your reason for being. Somebody says you have no language … [that] your head isn't shaped properly … [that you have] no art … no kingdoms and so you spend twenty years proving that you do. None of that is necessary.

In accord with Morrison, Edmund and many of my participants saw racism as a distraction that might prevent them from achieving their academic goals and as such chose to dis-identify or not engage with those who tried to distract them from their goals. Furthermore, resistance to the institutional and lecturer's habitus status quo comes with risks. The recipient and identifier may be labelled a complainer or troublemaker and may be ostracized by others at university where they are seeking to have a sense of belonging. I suggest that Edmund conducted his own cost-benefit analysis of his experience and determined that it was not beneficial to exhaust copious amounts of energy to challenge a racial microaggression. This, coupled with the lecturer's apology, appears to be a sufficient remedy for Edmund. It does not excuse the lecturer's actions but appears to reduce his level of anger over the situation. Edmund has made a conscious decision to adopt coping strategies to deal with the stigma of discrimination – unless he can find a very compelling argument to challenge a discriminatory act. In accordance with the majority of my other participants, these participants chose strategies to help them 'keep calm and carry on' in order to avoid confrontation while simultaneously keeping their minds intently focused on attaining their goal: their degrees. Furthermore, there is a faculty–student power dimension that occurs at university whereby students may be apprehensive about interacting with and/or challenging a staff member's offensive actions.[26]

Choosing the road less travelled: Resisting moderate Blackness and 'switching up'

The majority of the participants routinely exercise moderate Blackness techniques at their universities. However, three participants were resistant to implementing these tactics. In the following account Damien reflects on his observation of Black students from backgrounds similar to his own who moderated their culture and bodily performativity at his institution:

> I've seen one of the dudes who I was speaking to, you know, when he was with me he was just like a normal one of my friends at home. And then when a couple of White dudes from uni came along, right then he was completely stiff … this dude's body language changed. I'm saying he *switched up* [participant's emphasis]. It's the way he was talking and some of his views slightly changed, and the way he was expressing it … It wasn't until after uni that I dropped the whole baseball cap and hoodlum type of thing. Because at uni the way I looked at it is this is who I am and I refuse to arbitrarily posit somebody else's culture above and beyond my own. I refuse to.
>
> (Damien, working class, British Caribbean, Russell Group graduate)

Damien emphasizes that there is an expectation or practice by some Black students to adjust their culture and performativity in university settings. It is suggested that Black students are aware that they are engaging in 'double consciousness' by performing two different mind-sets in an effort to conform and be more accepted in their educational and social environments.[27] Damien expresses a moral opinion of how he feels about people who engage in this practice. He sees it as a mark of dishonesty. He also elucidates the dangers associated with 'switching up'. Although this 'dude' may be 'passing' due to his conformity and adoption of middle-class university habitus that may be accepted by White students at his institution, he is judged by Damien and perhaps by others from his local community as a fraud for 'selling out' his original embodied habitus in order to 'fit' within the habitus of the university. Damien's ability to choose the 'road less travelled' with respect to maintaining his own culture over 'switching up' to someone else's made him one of the refreshing outliers in my study. He acknowledges that his dress style may have been perceived as 'hoodlum' in style but this represents maintenance of his culture and respect by remaining true to his authentic self.

This chapter has provided an overview of my participants' accounts of managing offensive and discriminatory experiences from both White students and faculty at elite UK universities. Black men's experiences with 'othering' in the form of misrecognitions and discrimination led some students to endure racial microaggressions. When the majority of participants did respond to discriminatory experiences, their actions often took the guise of bodily hexis, code-switching and other moderate Blackness techniques that these young Black men equipped themselves with to represent themselves as being reasonable, measured and moderate in the face of offences. Even when the assaults appeared to hurt their feelings, most did not directly confront their offenders. Instead, these Black men usually worked to moderate their Blackness because they did not want to be perceived as stereotypical angry Black men. This performative behaviour involved emotional 'race work' to present themselves in ways that would make them seem calm and acceptable 'fish in water' in order to manage a less combative way through their universities. I was surprised and frustrated by hearing the experiences: it remains true that 'many students, especially students of color, may not feel at all "safe" in what appears to be a neutral setting … the politics of domination are often reproduced in the educational setting'.[28]

Educational settings are supposed to be safe, supportive and welcoming learning environments where students of all backgrounds fit in. Many institutions believe they provide such a habitus, yet two decades after hooks' comments on the minority experiences in education, they appear to remain an unfortunate reality for many Black students in elite UK higher education. However, without more resistance from participants to challenge discrimination at institutions, change is slow. Contemporaneously, White students are not scrutinized in the same way as Black students and most do not have to endure the emotional work and strain involved in moderating their disposition that many of my participants felt the need to perform. White students are able to perform along a performative spectrum without being questioned about their legitimacy within elite university fields.

'A sweaty concept': Decolonizing the legacies of British slave ownership and archival space

Kelena Reid

Judith Philip is identified within the digital database as a 'Claimant or Beneficiary'. She was born to French baker turned planter Honore Philip and his wife Jeanette, who had been enslaved before the birth of Judith and whose status became unclear because of her relation with planter Philip and 'claimant' Judith on the Island of Carriacou. This record has no additional mention of Jeanette. Judith was one of eight siblings who inherited property worth approximately 400,000 livres upon the death of their father in 1779, when Judith was approximately nineteen years old. She inherited and lived on the Grand Ance plantation, which indicates that her property included people enslaved, like her mother. What is overshadowed in this record is the social and economic magnitude of the Atlantic slave trade and plantation slavery in the Caribbean and the complex positioning of Judith whose wealth derived from the capture, enslavement, and forced labor of people with whom she shared a physical and racial identity, whose bodies were related to her own.

Judith began a relationship with 'Englishman Edmund Thornton' sometime in the 1770s and they moved together to London in 1794. Judith purchased a home at 33 Great Coram Street but lived apart from Edmund, who married a wealthy White woman two years after they had moved to London. After having several more children with Edmund and fourteen years in London, Judith Philip returned to Carriacou where she remained until her death. The archival narrative of Judith states that 'she remained a prominent and respected part of the Grenadian plantocracy', and owned 'property' in Grenada and London. As I read this record, I am shattered by the silences. Am I to assume, for example, that Judith's life was no different from that of her 'White French uncles' who are mentioned? How *did* she live her life? What is the metaphysical meaning of her experience? Was she at home in her world?

In this chapter I will investigate and interrogate digitized archival spaces of the Atlantic slave trade, and of British slave ownership using methods and frameworks of intersectionality and Critical Race Theory. The questions I am asking of the archive arise from the theoretical work of women of color and Black feminism. In an attempt to understand the impact of the slave trade on the experiences of Black Britons, my focus is on one collection: Legacies of British Slave Ownership, a database that has been well funded and constructed to aid the process of 'rethinking British history through the lens of empire'.[1] My intention is to describe my response to the archival space and to flush out the meaning of the slave trade for Black women of mixed racial descent who are captured in the database due to their problematic positioning as property owners and slave owners. The women I am looking at and thinking about are inheritors of property that gave them some physical mobility but very limited social stability and immeasurable complexity. They embody what I have come to understand as the 'conundrum' as articulated by Critical Race Theorist Patricia Williams.

My process draws from decolonization studies but does not fully replicate them. I am privileging the stories of women who were caught between intersections of the institutions of slavery, the slave trade, and colonization. Mine is a process of bringing awareness, observations, and new questions to the archival space. How does this alter the efforts and intentions of the archive? Who is invisible? Why is it acceptable within the norms of 'research' and 'scholarship' to devote abundant resources to a project that is devoted to an understanding of the legacies of slavery and in which the actual slave experience is buried, and those who have digitally organized and categorized the materials are all identified as White? Is *that* not in itself a 'legacy' of slave ownership and the system of inequality it created? What intersectional frameworks must we begin to employ in our interactions with newly digitized archives, records, and 'databases' of enslavement? How does Critical Race Theory help? I believe that the absence of adequate, individualized representation, focus, and discussion of Black people and Black *bodies* is an example of what Crenshaw has recently referred to as an intersectional failure. I am also making flush a small and awkwardly positioned set of records of women of mixed race, whose status was tenuous, tricky, problematic, and real. I will attempt to describe these entries and my sensibility toward them as I think through the theoretical foundations of intersectionality and Black feminism. As Crenshaw has stated, 'because of their intersectional identity as both women and of color within discourses that are shaped to respond to one or the other, women of color are marginalized in both'. She goes on to urge us to account for the 'multiple grounds of identity when considering how the social world is constructed'.[2] The women of mixed race who are 'othered' in the collection were traversing these 'multiple grounds of identity' during the slavery period and its aftermath.

In her writing on feminism, Sara Ahmed helps us to understand the implications of applying feminist frameworks. She calls them 'sweaty concepts' because the work is both intellectual and emotional. She describes it as 'another way of being pulled out from a shattering experience'.[3] Ahmed admits to feeling 'rebellious' by asking questions and questioning authorities: 'I think that the more difficult questions, the harder questions, are posed by those feminists concerned with explaining violence, inequality, injustice'.[4]

> By using sweaty concepts for descriptive work, I am trying to say at least two things. First, I was suggesting that too often conceptual work is understood as distinct from describing a situation: and I am thinking here of a situation as something that comes to demand a response. A situation can refer to a combination of circumstances of a given moment but also to a critical, problematic, or striking set of circumstances.[5]

Ahmed states that 'a sweaty concept is one that comes out of a description of a body that is not at home in the world'. Ahmed's solution is to stay in the process 'of exploring and exposing this difficulty', and to 'reveal the struggle we have in getting somewhere'. It is an experience that is felt in the body. In this chapter, I will ask sweaty, rebellious questions of the digital archive of slave ownership. In asking tough questions I attempt to uncover the inadequacies of typical and institutionalized frameworks and assumptions to adequately organize, present, and describe the lives of the Black/mixed/othered women in the collection. As Crenshaw has stated, in order to reveal the layered and complex relationship between marginalized people and systems of power, we must employ 'the dynamic and contextual orientation of intersectional research', and avoid an orientation that is 'static and fixed'.[6] It is not to argue that the work that has been done to create the Legacies database is not valuable. Indeed it is invaluable. But it is also deserving of response. I offer a difficult perspective that is informed by my own identity, and my experience of working through the available records. Black feminist theorist, Brittney Cooper, argues for a return to the past that 'reminds us that we have a foundation that is both broad and deep in terms of the kinds of questions Black feminist theory has always asked and that it should be asking today', such as do we need our own metaphysics?[7] What would a metaphysics of the slave trade look like? I am arguing that digitized and archival spaces that foreground the White experience of the slave trade re-institutionalize the enslaved, and cannot account for the multidimensionality of women of color who appear within them. Their life experiences are so complex, painful, and confounding that only an authentic accounting can help us understand something fundamental and real about the experience of enslavement.

One main point that I am making here is that the history and experience of slave-ownership is tied to and derived from the metaphysics of enslavement. Mixed-race women who inherited property (but not stability) from the trade were inheritors on both ends. They were descendants of the enslaved as well as inheritors of wealth derived from the bodies of people they were directly related to. Treating the experience of slavery and the wealth generated from the trade as separate, as the Legacies of British slave-ownership database does, is a 'single axis' framework. The women of color in the collection experienced the Atlantic world in multidimensional ways. The property they inherited gave them elements of mobility and pockets of wealth, but not true freedom as experienced by wealthy Whites. Theirs was not the experience of White women or men. They *must* have deeply understood their relative and unequal position. How were their identities informed by the institution of slavery? How did their identities shift when they travelled across the Atlantic and lived in London, as Judith Philip did? My questions are additionally informed by Crenshaw's articulation of 'intersectional subordination' and intersectional failure. As Crenshaw explains, 'intersectional subordination need not be intentionally produced; in fact, it is frequently the consequence of the imposition of one burden that interacts with pre-existing vulnerabilities to create another dimension of disempowerment'.[8] This is not accounted for within the archival space and therefore alters and informs my experience with the records and the way that the material is understood, referenced, and used by the public.

How were these women of color more vulnerable within the transactions of the slave trade and how are they more powerful? What was their ambiguity and relationship to power and property? How can digital archives be reconfigured to account for the multidimensional, intersectional, and metaphysical experience of the trade and the ways that race was transcribed on Black/mixed/othered bodies on both sides of it? Why is this difficult process important? I have been asked the confounding question of why even look at, of all things, mixed-race women who inherited slave property? As if it is *my* questions that somehow made them exist. The concern stems from those who would not want to displace blame for the full weight of the institution of slavery on the marginally few descendants of the enslaved who sought or accumulated profit.

Just to be clear, enslaved Africans and their descendants did not build the institution of slavery or the empire-building trade that fed it. Black people of the African diaspora are not the inheritors of multigenerational, life-altering wealth from the trade. This is not our legacy. *We,* and they, were caught up *in* it in ways that are tangled, complex, and intersectional. To ignore or not adequately address the real lives of women of color who bended and shifted their identities, relationships, and transactions to just exist in this world is to dishonor the true legacies, and does not help us understand the very real and deeply felt repercussions of the institution for Black people. However, to apply colonizing 'single-axis' frameworks and limiting, boxed understandings to these records is an equally shattering experience.

Critical Race Theorist Patricia Williams has provided a useful explanation of the global repercussions of the institution of slavery. Her articulation proves a fuller accounting of its legacy. Williams is concerned with the concept of self-possession:

> Ownership of the self still vacillates for its reference between a Lockean paradigm of radical individualism assuming a dualism between the body as commodity and the person as transactor and an older paradigm in which ownership of the self is understood in terms of the ability to defend one's inalienable corporeal integrity against oppression and abuse.[9]

In a sense, women of colour who owned property in this world experienced elements of *both* 'the body as commodity' and the 'person as transactor'. This was neither simplistic nor safe terrain to exist between. They experienced directly 'the uniquely dislocating magnitude' of the transatlantic slave trade. Theirs was the disturbing metaphysics of the trade.

> At the center of the resolution of any of this, I think, is the conundrum posed by the slave who doesn't own her body, but at the same time owns nothing but her body. The uniquely dislocating magnitude of the actual eighteenth- and nineteenth-century slave trade, viewed as a kind of forced migration that created a domino effect of worldwide uprootedness, set in motion the social forces of a kind of global grief that has colored the question of self-possession with excruciating literalism ever since.[10]

In this analysis, Williams is able to distinguish between the multiple understandings of self-possession described here. Ideally, to be self-possessed affords one protection from 'oppression and abuse'. This, however, was not the case for enslaved people of the African diaspora trapped within capitalist systems and industrial expansion. Her articulation of the 'conundrum' is key to any understanding of slavery. As she states, slaves owned *nothing but their bodies*. They also had limited power over transactions made over their bodies. Black bodies were the most prized commodity of the nineteenth century, and Black female bodies even more so for their ability to reproduce capital and wealth for the slave owner. How were partnering, mothering, and maintaining property and inheritance complicated and vulnerable scenarios for the women of mixed race contained in the Legacies database?

In order to fully account for their experiences we must employ intersectional and feminist frameworks. In other words, I argue that the lives of women such as Judith Philip, Ann Eliza French, and her mother 'said Jane Charlotte Beckford Mulatto' are better understood using Patricia Williams's theoretical framework employed for the enslaved, rather than those used to explain White slaveholders.

Ann Eliza French's mother, Jane Charlotte Beckford, is among the small group of women I encountered in the database who were legally given, 'with certain restrictions', the status of White people.[11] The fact that this was necessary to do signals quite clearly that their position was unstable, unsuitable, and unsafe as anything other than White. Ann Eliza French, like Judith Philip, appears in the records because she was a 'Claimant or Beneficiary'. The Legacies database was created to trace the legacy of slave ownership and the social and economic implications it has had on Britain. Those who have constructed the archival space have justified it by stating that 'slave-owners were one very important means by which the fruits of slavery were transmitted to metropolitan Britain'.[12] The database was constructed by collecting and digitizing records that were generated by the compensation for slave ownership that occurred in Britain following the banning of the institution in the nineteenth century. Ann Eliza French, whose mother was a 'Mulatto' and who was also of mixed race, put forward a compensation claim during this period, and therefore show up in the otherwise overwhelmingly White database. Her entry is a particularly tangled web of ambiguity and personal frustration. Here is my attempt to pull meaning from it.

Ann Eliza French, who was baptized in Jamaica in 1790 at three years old, along with her older brother and younger half-sister, lived a full and complicated life in Jamaica. Her life is interconnected with that of her mother, Jane Charlotte, and with those of her five children. Jane Charlotte, Ann's mother, was born in Jamaica on 11 July 1763. She was the owner of a lodging house in Spanish Town, Jamaica. It was Jane, along with two of her elder sons, who were granted, 'with certain restrictions', the rights and privileges of a White person in 1784. Her two sons were then sent to England to be educated 'in such manner as to make them useful to the community'.

Jane Beckford was unmarried and the man with whom she had children married another woman, Ann Elizabeth Jackson, and left to her and his 'legitimate' child his estate.

Ann Eliza was the executor of her mother's estate, which included belongings associated with the lodging house. It was Ann Eliza who acquired property more directly tied to slave ownership, who had owned and was compensated for '52 enslaved people and the values of their subsequent apprenticeships'. The records are silent as to how she acquired this property. Like her mother, she was not married to either of the men with whom she had children. They either could not, or simply did not marry. Like her mother, several of Ann's children relocated to England and established lives there. In 1832, one of her children, Marie Antoinette Swaby, was removed from her care and sent to England because Ann Eliza was living in 'a state of concubinage' with the child's father, Anthony Britton. It appears that both Ann and her mother were in relationships that were unable to provide them with social and economic stability. I do have legitimate questions that are unanswered from the database about why and how Ann acquired human property and what that meant for her.

What appears from a close reading of these entries is that Judith, Jane, and Ann each made multiple and varied attempts to gain footing in their environment. There certainly did and does exist a complex history of race, color, and social class in Jamaica and other Caribbean islands as a result of colonization, the slave trade, and plantation slavery. These women socially benefited in some ways from their mixed-race heritage. But theirs was not a simple life nor was it neatly equivalent to that of White slave owners, which is how they are treated within the records. I also believe that if an adequate accounting for the full ramifications of slavery were part of the 'context' provided by the scholars who constructed the database, it would clarify the complex intersectional space that these women inhabited. Additionally, the fact that the team of scholars is entirely White, and the complete void of any records, context, or meaningful mention of enslaved African people, from whose bodies the empire-building wealth was produced, makes it feel frustrating and emotional to encounter. It is a sweaty concept to reconcile. As Sarah Ahmed states, living a feminist life might 'mean asking ethical questions about how to live better in an unjust and unequal world (in a not-feminist and anti-feminist world)'. To live as a feminist is to support those who find themselves in the face of 'histories that have become concrete, histories that have become as solid as walls'.[13] How can we use intersectional research methodologies to dismantle the single-axis historical walls that diminish the complex experiences, negotiations, relationships, and inheritances of Black women?

Any attempt to quiet or diminish the value of the Black body in any conversation about the institution of slavery is indefensible and replicates institutions of power and oppression. It is an odd and dislocating experience to encounter. The multiple identities included within the collection require that we ask new questions of it. As Stuart Hall has masterfully informed us, 'no archive arises out of thin air. Each archive has a "pre-history", in the sense of prior conditions of existence'.[14] According to Hall,

> Constituting an archive represents a significant moment, on which we need to reflect with care. It occurs at that moment when a relatively random collection of works, whose movement appears simply to be propelled from one creative production to the next, is at the point of becoming something more ordered and considered: an object of reflection and debate. Archives are not inert historical collections. They always stand in an active, dialogic, relation to the questions which the present puts to the past; and the present always puts its questions differently from one generation to another.[15]

The Legacies of British Slave-ownership archive has a very specific purpose. The collection documents and attempts to account for the scope and legacy of slave ownership and the way in which the institution has contributed to the British Empire.

> The slave-owners were one very important means by which the fruits of slavery were transmitted to metropolitan Britain. We believe that research and analysis of this group are key to understanding the extent and the limits of slavery's role in shaping British history and leaving lasting legacies that reach into the present.[16]

The clear focus is on 'ownership' and 'legacy'. They openly acknowledge that the stories of those who were enslaved are not recorded in the collection. The framers of the database hope that somehow the stories of enslaved men and women will emerge and that the records will 'provide information of value to those researching enslaved people'. Yet, enslaved people of the African diaspora are invisible within the archive. The only identity that is explicit is property owner. Specificities of race and gender are not fully explored and in some cases are diminished. How does this problematic and striking framing impact a thoughtful reading of the materials? It is stated that 'the compensation records are rich in evidence on the enslaved but our focus in the first project was on the myriad Britons who benefited directly from the fruits of slavery'. From this wording, it is unclear what and where the 'evidence on the enslaved' exists. Additionally, that the project team was all White has been raised as a concern 'both in the UK and the Caribbean'. Their response to this is:

> That the history of slavery concerns White people as well as Black. Our particular subject is slave-ownership and its relation to British society, rather than the experience of the enslaved. At the same time, we greatly regret the paucity of Afro-Caribbean students choosing to do research in history. This is related to the ways in which history has been taught in schools and universities and is part of what we, together with many others, are trying to change.

This explanation is not adequate, in particular that the researchers 'regret the paucity of Afro-Caribbean students choosing to do research in history'. It is inadequate and frustrating because it replicates institutional racism and a colonizing perspective. If there is indeed a lowered representation of Afro-Caribbean scholars and historians it is worth considering what forms of systemic racism and inequality are in place. Academic institutions are majority White because they are created by and supported within systems of racial inequalities. Majority White academic programmes and scholarship are in themselves legacies of slavery and slave ownership. This statement is concerning additionally because it collapses the identities of appropriate scholars of colour to Afro-Caribbean and does not account for expertise within the wider African diaspora, including Black scholars within the UK.

The project records are valuable and more work and new questions must be asked to account for the multiple grounds of identity, and the interconnectedness of slave ownership with the lives of the people who were enslaved. To isolate slave ownership from the records and experience of the enslaved is historically inaccurate and misleading. It removes and erases the bodies on which the legacy itself is dependent. The underlying assumption from the current framing of the database is that the slave owners are all White and equally positioned. Women of colour appear in the collection because of their status of 'beneficiary', yet are not mentioned in the 'context' or recognized as problematically positioned inheritors of the legacy. Additionally, the 'rich evidence of the enslaved' is yet to be revealed. My experience interacting with and pulling information from the collection is burdened by this contextualization of the material and the justifications of an all-White international team of scholars.

The women of mixed race who owned property and appear in the records are positioned awkwardly. The full complexity of their identity and experiences are not accounted for. Margaret Dunbar is recorded in her first child's baptismal record as being a 'free Quadroon woman', and having resided in Kingston, Jamaica. She appears in the database, like Judith and Ann, as a 'Claimant or Beneficiary', which indicates that she did have or believed she had property associated with slavery. It is unclear from this record exactly what that property was. Margaret was granted, as a descendant of the deceased planter Nicholas Blake of St Elizabeth, 'with certain restrictions' the privileges of Whites later in her life and after she had worked as a domestic in the home of prominent White barrister and had one child with him. What the meaning of this was for Margaret and her descendants is not fully clear and warrants much deeper investigation and analyses. What was the social and racial space that she inhabited? Her eldest child, Sabina, was born in 1784, the same year that the barrister died and left Margaret property including 1,000 pounds, household items and 'one of my horses which she may choose for herself'. Three years later Margaret was in a relationship with another man, Ebenezer Robertson of Scotland, with whom she would have ten children, all baptized in Kingston, and in each record Margaret is recorded as 'a free Quadroon woman'. Her sons and daughters lived their lives in the Atlantic world and were tied to major institutions associated with the British crown such as the Royal Highland Society of London and the East India Company. Her eldest daughter, Sabina, maintained a close relationship with at least one of her half siblings, as indicated by her will of 7 November 1844, in which she left the property she had inherited from her mother to her half-brother Ebenezer Robertson Jr. Margaret's record, like that of Judith and Ann, is ambiguous.

I am burdened by questions about her record and about her life. To what extent was Margaret limited by her sexual relationships with White European men? To what extent was she liberated by them? The persistence of the term 'free Quadroon woman' in each of her ten children's baptisms says something about the liminal space of freedom that existed for her as she lived among the enslaved. She was not a slave, but she was not fully White either. How did her racial identity and sexual partnerships influence her transactions?

My questions about the life of Margaret Dunbar are unanswered by the database. In their chapter on the work of creating a community archive, Andrew Flinn and Mary Stevens acknowledge the work that is being done to rethink and meaningfully engage with archival materials. 'Archivists and others concerned with exploring archives and their power are beginning to examine the significance that engaging with archival materials – and the history created from them – can have for individuals'.[17] Given the increasing access and engagement that is available through the digital materials and archival spaces it is increasingly critical that we rethink the framing process and thoughtfully consider the interactions we have with historical records, especially those that carry a legacy of violence and dislocation. Other scholars, such as Marisa Fuentes, have dug deeply into the meaning of archival materials. Fuentes has asked important questions of the archival material of free woman of colour, Rachael Pringle Polgreen,

> What language should we use to describe the economy of forced labour? How do we write against historical scholarship that too often relies upon the discourses of will, agency, choice and volunteerism, which reproduce a troubling archive that cements enslaved and free(d) women of colour in representations of 'their willingness to become mistresses of White men'? If 'freedom' meant free from bondage but not from social, economic and political degradation what does it mean to survive under such conditions?[18]

Fuentes admits that it is difficult to write a narrative of the life of Polgreen that allows her human complexity and her 'inner self' to emerge when using documents that are produced within a slave society and 'limited by capitalist and elite perspectives'.[19] A true accounting of the lives of women of colour caught up in the slave system, whether free, semi-free, or enslaved, requires a sensitive, liberated perspective, and intersectional frameworks. Crenshaw's ground-breaking paradigm is essential to the process. The concept of intersectionality functions in ways that free Black women from the hard spaces of history and research. Intersectionality does do this difficult work.

Black crip killjoys: Dissident voices and neglected stories from the margins

Viji Kuppan

I have been hurt to the point of abysmal pain, hurt to the point of invisibility

(Ralph Ellison[1])

Without frames that allow us to see how social problems impact all members of a targeted group, many will fall through the cracks of our movements, left to suffer in virtual isolation

(Kimberlé Crenshaw[2])

As a new century awoke and began to stir, the African American sociologist W. E. B. Du Bois foresaw that the 'problem of the twentieth century' would become 'the problem of the colour line'. Writing towards the century's end, Stuart Hall, the Black British Cultural Studies scholar, re-interpreted and clarified Du Bois's original insight for changing times. Hall argued that the coming question of the twenty-first century would be 'the capacity to live with difference'.[2] His conjunctural analysis that grappled with the problems and possibilities of *new ethnicities* owes a debt of gratitude to the work of Du Bois and scholars like him. Similarly, Kimberlé Crenshaw's[3] ability to develop a framework, for what she specified as intersectionality, emerged from the struggle and contribution of Sojourner Truth, Anna Julia Cooper, Savitribai Phule and the Combahee River Collective, women of colour, who thought with an intersectional perspective without ever employing the phrase 'intersectionality'.[4] This work venerates the aforementioned Black activists/ scholars and others – whether living, dead, emerging, established or erased, as the citational chords that connect us to a deep history of revolutionary praxis

In this chapter, I foreground the material, discursive and affective realties of the often-forgotten or erased Black *disabled* subject. Audre Lorde poignantly wrote of how 'it hurts when even my sisters look at me in the street with cold and silent eyes. I'm defined as other in every group I'm part of'.[5] Lorde was speaking not only from her position as a Black woman, mother, lesbian, poet and feminist scholar, but as someone who had the intimate knowledge of living with a chronic and life-threatening illness. She provided us with a portal into what social and cultural life sometimes feels like for those who inhabit 'the liminal alterity of disablement'.[6] Ayesha Vernon, another disabled activist-scholar of colour, echoes Lorde's experience by telling us that she too often feels like a 'stranger in many camps'.[7] This chapter takes such affects seriously and will place them in a wider material and discursive context exposing the veiled operations of power at work in society. Blackness at the intersection in what follows will focus on entangled racialized, disabled and gendered dynamics.

To understand these complex moments and situations of multiple and simultaneous oppression I will interrogate social and cultural life in its spectacular (including spectacularly violent) and many mundane forms. The stories that unfold in this chapter are about Black crip killjoys, a term inspired by both Disability Studies scholars and in particular from Sara Ahmed's figure of the 'feminist killjoy'.[8] The Black crip killjoy works with the feminist killjoy not only to expose the important moments of racism and sexism that occur in everyday life, but re-orientates us to think about how disablism works alongside these other debilitating processes. The Black crip killjoy is a 'sweaty concept' (see also Chapter 6 in this volume, by Kelena Reid) as it comes out of a body/mind that is not made to feel at home in the world.[9] These Black crip body/minds reveal the complexities of representation, domination and subordination, and in this chapter trace the intersections of Blackness and disability in neoliberal times.

As anti-Black racism continues to travel across borders and nations, and is also perpetuated by communities of colour, a primary concern for me is that other people of colour (PoC) are heard speaking back to disabuse and reject these false notions of racial superiority and inferiority. I In this chapter, I strategically position myself as a *Brown* brother, who stands and fights (writes) in solidarity with and for Black lives. In what follows, I begin by discussing the academy's hallowed 'ivory tower' through the 'intersectional failures' of White Disability Studies, and its uneven ability to think critically about Blackness and race in relationship to disability. From here, I move to consider the mega-event pop concert, alongside tales of homes, shopping and travel as imagined places of escape, refuge and pleasure, but which are, concomitantly, frequently scenes of racialized and disabled censure and criticism, and more cataclysmically of systemic and institutional failures that render Black people abandoned, imprisoned and terrorized.

There are so many unspeakable things that communities of colour have had to endure; these histories of alienation and elimination could push us further into the abyss of individual despair, or unify and align our struggles, finding strength and solidarity in our shared, sinuous stories of suffering and survival. And yet the task at hand is so much more than fine words and rhetoric and demands the quality of our attention and intervention. It is about bearing witness to the lives of PoC that are too easily dismissed, of developing feelings for all Black lives including disabled ones. I therefore conclude this chapter by challenging critical race scholars to take more account of disability in their analyses of social processes. I argue that we should be jolted to action by the plaintive cry of the African-Caribbean disability scholar Ossie Stuart, who asks: 'Am I Black or disabled?'[10] His lugubrious question reaches back to touch Lorde's suffering, in which her Black 'sisters' disregard her with their 'cold and silent eyes', rendering her as 'other'. These 'wailing' voices of anger, pain and frustration evoke the Jamaican patois 'mi vex', mobilized so powerfully by Shirley Anne Tate.[11] But, whereas Tate uses this feeling of vexation to communicate Black women's experiences of being out of place in the White academy, I also see how it functions to inform and charge Black communities with their own disavowal of Black disabled others. The depth of these emotions urgently suggests another reason why an intersectional Black politics, which takes account of the multiplicity of Black lives, is so necessary.

Decolonizing Disability Studies and thinking Black

The lecture theatre was packed and buzzing with excitement. The assembled audience had gathered to hear the disabled White professor, a renowned international scholar and 'media celebrity' in the field of Disability Studies, speak about his research in Africa. The professor spoke. He told stories about his Black disabled participants, their struggles and their successes. The audience murmured with appreciation at his disquisition. He told jokes and the audience laughed. He cried, and the audience fell silent, supportive in their hush, and anxious that he should recover. He did recover and continued. The talk ended and the disabled White professor received a rapturous ovation. Was I the only one who felt uncomfortable with his analysis? I put my hand up to ask a question. Too late, he was out of time.

The ubiquitous wine reception follows. I notice him on the far side of the room with his coterie of admirers. I walk over, breaking the seal of their reverence. 'Hello', I say. 'I wanted to ask you a couple of questions if I may?' 'Of course', he replies. 'Well firstly I wanted to say that I was disappointed with the racial and ethnic scholar who introduced your presentation, and failed to make any kind of intersectional linkage, between race and disability in Africa'. He looked pleased. 'But', I say, 'I'm interested in why you didn't think it was important to address issues of empire, colonialism, violence and dispossession within your lecture? And also why you didn't acknowledge your own positionality and privilege as a White man, albeit disabled, with high social rank and economic capital in your research?' He now looks glum. 'I only had an hour', he replies, 'you cannot deal with everything …' He also tells me that his mother is South Asian. I am somewhat taken aback. I had not asked him to deal 'with everything', and secondly, what did privately introducing his Asian heritage offer his previous discussion? In his talk, he had connected himself to a White history but not spoken of his Brown one. Moreover, his Brown heritage could have been used to articulate the complexities of race: for example, that, notwithstanding that Asians were oppressed in colonial Africa, they were also oppressors and overwhelmingly occupied a superior position to Black Africans.

We make a conscious choice about what we say, and what we omit to say, in a presentation. As much as anything, this is a political decision. To refrain from speaking about empire when discussing Black lives is to conceal the violence of colonial conquest and its equally brutal repercussions. A White female academic comes between the now not so White disabled male professor, and myself. 'I think that is quite enough', she says curtly, as she ushers him away to 'safety'. I (the disabled PoC) was deemed too 'aggressive and angry'. I had unsettled the narrative of the 'White saviour'. I was a *Brown crip killjoy* who had spoilt the promise of happiness that was to be so much a part of this occasion.

This vignette is designed to highlight the intersectional failures that often happen in dominant expositions of Disability Studies in Britain. The failure shows up as an absence in the ideas of race as they converge with disability and of the critical role that White supremacy plays in generating and maintaining impairments. On the surface, the issue of disability rights that the disabled professor was discussing can appear laudable. He highlighted the struggle for access and acceptance within several African countries, providing the audience with an understanding of some of the barriers, accomplishments and resistance shown by Black disabled people living in the African 'elsewhere'. Yet it was a deracinated account, denuded of White culpability, and missing *any analysis* of imperial projects in creating and sustaining war, poverty and famine. What continues to silently stalk the rapacious regimes of neoliberal/neocolonial political economy, and is often unremarked upon, is their centrality to the production of disability and disabled bodies of colour. In my piece 'Crippin' Blackness: Disabled People of Colour from Slavery to Trump', I trace this deep and dismembering history of the Black Atlantic, following its brutal course from the Middle

Passage, arguing that the violent imbrication of racialized subjects becoming racialized *and* disabled subjects is intrinsic to understanding the continuities of race and disability in 'post-racial' America.[12]

In her explosive and searing examination of the invisibility of disabled bodies of colour, Jasbir Puar makes a powerful intervention to explain further the silences that exist around race within Disability Studies and the Disabled People's Movement.[13] In order to unpack these elisions, she takes us from Black Ferguson to Brown Palestine, from the White, capacitated and privileged metropolitan centres of America to the global peripheries of lives lived in the tourniquet of precarity. Her central argument is that there are certain bodies that do not matter; these are bodies that can be killed, *maimed*, *debilitated* and disabled: where those maimed and debilitated do not enjoy the same privileges or capacity as those who are disabled. These are the bodies of PoC. The maiming and debilitation that take place in the global elsewhere are of bodies already *pre-ordained* as expendable, marked out for their 'backward' and 'bestial' natures. Therefore, the ability to kill, maim and debilitate are strategies 'mobilized to make power visible on the body'.[14] At the same time that certain bodies are being incapacitated, other bodies who also experience trauma, invariably White bodies, are capacitated by being granted futurity. This White imagination is endowed with the preparedness of material resources – financial compensation, physical and psychological therapies, rehabilitation and assistive technologies. These material possibilities exist within affective and discursive economies that operationalize care, listening, support, rights, freedom, access and justice. As Puar argues in her own words:

> Assemblages of disability, capacity and debility are elements of the biopolitical control of populations that foreground risk, prognosis, life chances, settler colonialism, war, impairment and capitalist exploitation … Disability rights [become] a capacitating frame that recognizes some disabilities at the expense of other disabilities that do not fit the respectability and empowerment models of disability.[15]

Tales of debility and disability from the margins

I want to utilize Crenshaw's and Puar's conceptual framing as a basis to interrogate the Ariana Grande pop concert terrorist attack and place this event alongside the glocalized predicament of the Grenfell Tower residents who were left displaced and homeless in the aftermath of a terrible fire that engulfed and destroyed the building in June 2017. The incidents speak to the differing structural and institutional provisions that are made available to some bodies but not others.

On 22 May 2017 Salman Ramadan Abedi, a twenty-two-year-old British citizen of Libyan descent, detonated a device packed with nuts and bolts. Twenty-three people including Abedi himself were killed. The number of people now reported to be experiencing physical and or psychological injury has increased from 159 to 800.[16] The victims and survivors of the incident were overwhelmingly White children/young people and their parents/guardians.

On the first anniversary of the Manchester attack, Channel 4 News interviewed a White Mancunian, Martin Hibbert, who had accompanied his daughter to the Grande concert. He recounts the anguish and stress of that night in highly affective and moving ways, including how he thought his daughter had died whilst he himself was dying on the floor. Hibbert was hit with twenty-two of the nuts and bolts from the bomb and was left paralysed from the waist down. Despite his horrendous injuries, Hibbert's race and gender mean that he exists only just below the trapdoor to *the basement*. 'The basement' is an often overlooked metaphor in Crenshaw's scholarship, one she developed to explain the ways that power and inequality become structured and sedimented within hierarchies of domination.[17] Applied to Hibbert then, if it were not for the 'singularity' of his impairment, he would reside in the 'upper room' above the basement where he could move more freely. But even within the basement, Hibbert's White masculinity allows him to stand upon and 'squash' many (racialized) others who are multiply and simultaneously disadvantaged. His head not only 'brush[es] up against the ceiling' but his 'privileged position – relative to those below' means that he is 'permitted to squeeze through the hatch' and return to the 'elevated' realms of society.

This White *capacity* to exist beyond the confines of Crenshaw's symbolic cellar is further reinforced through being given a prominent voice in broadcast and print media. Here his White male northern-ness, articulated through local argot (often read as a sign of 'honesty'), makes Hibbert legible to a White nation. In addition to *discursive* capital, Hibbert also benefits from a healthcare system that hails him as 'deserving' and offers emergency and ongoing medical care. These *material* resources *capacitate* a recovery programme in which he is given the social and economic support to move from his bed, to a gym, swimming pool and into a performance wheelchair, in order to compete in the Manchester 2018 10k race. Within the raciological circuitry of White nationhood an *affective* economy is also produced, animated by Grande's re-appearance at One Love Manchester, a concert attended by 50,000 people to support victims in the aftermath of the attack. The transmission of affective capital takes place in the shared stadium space between and through bodies. It is also signed in the textuality of the live broadcast and in the outpourings of sympathy, love, belonging, coming together and staying strong together. What becomes apparent in unpacking Hibbert's story vis-à-vis his affective, discursive and material resources is that 'some bodies may well be disabled but are also capacitated'.[18]

The theft of lives, livelihoods and leisure experienced by the Grenfell Tower residents is also a theft of attachments, citizenship and homes. Coded by the same themes of race, space and place that the victims of the Manchester bombing experienced, this is a different type of haunting. It is a different haunting because many of the victims were PoC and/or were from poor communities, who, in the first instance, are *debilitated* by the ideas of race and class. Whilst taking notice of the 'disavowal of the disability elsewhere',[19] citizens of the global elsewhere also reside here, but are rendered invisible and denied social justice. Disability is entangled with illness and old age, but is not often articulated as having the *exceptional* circumstances that qualify one to claim disabled status.

The majority of the victims of Grenfell were poor people of colour; many were also elderly with chronic illnesses. They lived with the psychosocial damages wrought by a racist society that makes it difficult for them to function. Unlike Hibbert, who has achieved disabled 'folk hero' status through his 'exceptional' tragedy, Black and Brown people continue to be read as 'folk devils'. Their dis-ease is often illegible to a post-racial society that as well as being ahistorical, fails to recognize how everyday racial microaggressions cause anxiety, isolation, fear, stress, high blood pressure, strokes and diabetes. A racialized society is therefore also a debilitating and disabling society for PoC. Yet, becoming disabled is an increasingly privileged category, in which the resources of the state are closely guarded and policed. Ethnic others are the most likely to fall through the cracks and, instead of receiving the economic, social and political benefits of being authenticated as a disabled citizen, experience debility. Puar describes debilitation as the 'slow wearing down of populations instead of the event of becoming disabled'.[20] Why were poor debilitated/disabled people of colour housed at the top of the tower? This form of containment traces its history to slavery and empire, of plantation politics and White colonial power that debilitates, disables and punishes people of colour. For some this analogy may go too far, but for those who are conscious of colonialism's continuing legacy, *its long claw*, there is a recognition that despite slavery ending in Britain 200 years ago, we are, as Christina Sharpe alerts us, still living in its wake. She argues 'in the wake, the past that is not always the past reappears, always, to rupture the present'.[21] Grenfell demonstrated to us that Black people, Black disabled people, Black, debilitated/disabled and poor people are placed in positions of precarity: being a person of colour, being debilitated/disabled and having limited financial resources runs against the neoliberal rhetoric of the free possessive individual. As bodies that transgress White ableist norms, they are unloved and uncared for. Doreen Lawrence, the activist and mother of the murdered teenager Stephen Lawrence, described the plight of the Grenfell residents as 'institutional indifference'.[22] However, it would be wrong to suggest that there is no support for the victims of Grenfell; the regular silent monthly marches are a testament to the quiet power of dignity and solidarity of the residents and their allies, and on the first anniversary of the fire, 5,000 people walked in silence to commemorate the seventy-two people who died. In the final part of this chapter I want to complicate further the ways that Black bodies, which are multiply read as debilitated, disabled, defective, damaged, deviant and dangerous, coalesce.

Bodies out of place[23]

I am currently undertaking PhD research that investigates leisure lives through the intersections of race, disability and gender. One of my participants, a Black, disabled man, describes some of his everyday experiences. Johnny (a pseudonym), who has a walking difficulty, tells me: 'it's different when you are disabled and Black or minority ethnic … I used to go on the bus and people sometimes don't give you a seat. I'm disabled, and I've got crutches … but somebody [White] walks on with a stick and they give him a seat!' He goes on to discuss driving, and the problems he experiences when trying to park his vehicle: 'you try and park in a disabled bay and the parking attendant will be at your window [saying], "You can't park here!" They assume that there is no possibility of a Black disabled person having a car [or] that we don't know the law or that we will just break the law anyway'. Johnny has an accredited impairment and is a Blue Badge holder with an entitlement to accessible parking. However, the racialized discourses that surround Black men mean that, at the very least, they are met with suspicion if not regarded as full-blown criminals. It is in the seemingly trivial interactions of the mundane that the problems of being a Black disabled man manifest, particularly in Brexit Britain where Black disabled masculinity is often rendered illegible to the White world. For Johnny this results in being 'viewed differently, viewed like you are not fully disabled'. The urban ethnographer Elijah Anderson insightfully picks up on this theme when he argues that Black people, whoever they are, 'move about civil society with a deficit of credibility in comparison with their White counterparts who are given a "pass" as decent and law abiding citizens'.[24] I continue exploring these intersectional opacities below.

In 2016 the Black Paralympic athlete and Disability Rights campaigner, Anne Wafula Strike, highlighted again how everyday places can also be disabling and humiliating places. Wafula Strike, who is a wheelchair user, was forced to urinate on herself because there was no working accessible toilet on the three-hour train journey she undertook between the city of Coventry and Stansted Airport. She writes viscerally of her dehumanization:

> I was completely robbed of my dignity by the train company ... Having access to a toilet, especially in a developed nation like the UK, is one of the most basic rights. I tried to conceal the smell of urine by spraying perfume over myself. When I finally got home after my nightmare journey, I scrubbed myself clean in the shower then flung myself on my bed and sobbed for hours.[25]

What is interesting in the reporting of this story is that although there are pictures of Wafula Strike, no mention is made of her also being a Black woman. She is embraced by the Disability Movement (whose membership, I assert, is drawn from an overwhelmingly White community) and aided by a liberal press, only on the basis that her race plays no part in the discussion. I have argued elsewhere of the brilliance of the Social Model in disaggregating impairment from disability, which is a socially constructed form of oppression.[26] However, its single-axis approach that takes no account of racist structures and cultures has the effect of marginalizing Black disabled people from disability politics and theorizing.

In a fundamental argument, one of the founding fathers of Critical Race Theory (CRT), Derrick Bell, cogently illuminated that it would only be possible for Black people to receive racial equality if there was a clear convergence with the interests of White people.[27] This *interest convergence* shows up in the Wafula Strike case. Here her race is silenced, in order for the more 'palatable' issues of access to be taken on board. It is an interest convergence with the disabled White community where race has no place and is sacrificed or dismissed in order to promote the issues of disabling barriers. Far from being strategic, it is a form of control, which says that your (Black) story is important only to the extent that it helps to strengthen the (White) argument of fair and equal access.

Wafula Strike's case is related and interconnected to another Black woman, the actress, singer and television presenter, Jamelia Niela Davis. Davis also took a train journey. Whilst seated in the first-class carriage with her daughter, she was challenged by a fellow passenger, an older White woman who aggressively questioned whether she had a first-class ticket. She, in turn, asked the White woman if she had a first-class ticket, and also if she would make such a demand of a White man. Her interlocutor made no answer to the second question. Although not disabled, in a racist society Davis is *debilitated* and marked out by the entwining of race and gender. Here the intersectional discourses of race, class, gender and age swirl around the Black female form, rendering her as a 'body out of place'. Mindful of the way Lorde was sometimes perceived by her 'sisters', I bring Wafula Strike's and Davis's experiences together here, to highlight their connectedness through their shared Blackness and womanhood. In another instance it could easily be Strike's race and its intersections with impairment, disability and gender that could be regarded as deviant and problematic (as was the case with Johnny). Both Davis and Wafula Strike, as prominent and successful Black women, are able to publicly speak about their different but related experiences. This is not often the case for other Black women who are contradictorily hyper-visible in White cultural spaces, but whose social voices remain hidden and irrelevant.

Wafula Strike in a later piece for the *Guardian* does identify herself as a Black woman but mentions it only in relationship to the ways that she is 'looked down' upon and 'marginalized' in Kenyan society for being a woman and disabled.[28] She highlights the lack of 'respect' and the way that impairment can often be attributed to sinister forms of 'witchcraft'. Of course, these modern hostile responses are troubling, and Strike obviously speaks from the structures of feeling that have shaped her life. Yet the imposition of colonial cultures including religious beliefs should not be forgotten, and nor should evidence that disabled practitioners of Obeah were once venerated and gender non-conformity embraced in Africa. I contend that, in contemporary times, the cruelty and contempt that is also housed in communities of colour impel Strike to identify more with her disabled identity than her Black one, because of the support she receives from the White disabled community, however contingent that may be.

The dichotomy of Stuart's emotional evocation is again brought back into view: 'am I Black or [a] disabled man?' He continues this affective articulation by arguing 'for almost as long as I can remember I have loathed myself. It was a loathing that was renewed every time I looked into the mirror',[29] which speaks to the distancing and disavowal he experiences in relation to non-disabled Black men. The 1960s dictum that *Black is beautiful* has failed to penetrate the social carapace that surrounds disabled Black bodies, who are stubbornly met with fear and anxiety. CRT has successfully disentangled the biology of race from its social construction. It has revealed its biological fallacies whilst attending to the everyday racial fantasizing that is at play. Yet disabled Black personhood is still somehow self-evidently a condition and process of disease. Erevelles's[30] piercing and compelling account of these elisions reveal that in the dominant imaginary, disability, whether physical, sensory or cognitive, and including mental health issues has a far more immutable stamp; regarded as recalcitrant, Black disabled people seem to carry a discernible pathology that is hard to deny. This is particularly true when manifested in the medical language of signs, symptoms, diagnostic categories and surgical interventions (see also Chapters 3 and 2 in this volume, by Katucha Bento and Annabel Wilson respectively).

Paradoxically, scientific rationality lends credibility to the individualizing of disability, even when the 'pseudo-scientific' ideas involved in the violent social production of Black bodies have been so strongly criticized and dismantled. Think here of the social and psychic damage manufactured by the eugenics movement, Jim Crow in America and the school-to-prison pipeline. The uneasy emotions and negative attitudes towards disabled people of colour from within our own communities can be understood through these brutal histories, but the need to challenge, change and transform these arrangements is an urgent requirement of CRT. If the feelings of Lorde, Stuart and countless other people of colour are to be heeded, then the intersectionality of race, disability and gender needs to be taken seriously. This allows the *spirit death* and hegemony of fear and loathing, deposited in the *outcast* Black disabled other to be relieved, bringing into focus a White supremacy of cultural, economic, historical and political forces that have shaped this becoming.

I highlight the importance of thinking about Blackness, race and racism in this chapter when discussing disability, because it continues to be elided or unevenly addressed. Intersectionality as a central component of CRT instructs us to grapple with the complexity of simultaneous oppressions whilst not 'losing sight' of race in the process.[31] Moreover, enabling physical environments is only a first step of access; it does not necessarily consider the way that racism, disablism, sexism and heteronormativity intersect, and are also culturally produced and structured. In this chapter numerous Black crip killjoys have helped to prise open society and culture, revealing the many inequalities and injustices that continue to persist, but culture is also a place to grow, find kinship and transform. Therefore, thinking simultaneously and multiply, I join Black/Brown disabled personhood with Black/Brown women, Muslims, queer, trans and non-binary others in political alliance. Here at the boundaries' edge where our identities converge and intersect, is a meeting place, where we can gather to disrupt, deconstruct and decolonize social spaces to create the accommodation that our myriad Black/Brown forms deserve. We are thirty years on from Crenshaw's distinguished 'Demarginalizing' paper, where, in her denouncement of intersectional politics, she excavates and exalts the voice of Anna Julia Cooper from a more remote history, and, in so doing, reminds us that we are all still tasked with doing the work that demonstrates 'when they enter we all enter'.[32]

Racializing femininity

Mary Igenoza

This chapter is about femininity. It is also about race. It is about the necessity to draw attention to the racialization of femininity within Western culture, and from there to evaluate the ways in which the images of femininity that can be seen everywhere in popular culture affect the lives of both White and Black women. It is important to state here that this chapter mainly focuses on the concept of femininity from within the modern culture of Western Europe and North America or societies whose foundations are based on Judeo-Christian traditions. The use of the term 'Western' is controversial because Western societies are cultures of pluralism and diversity made up of subcultures and countercultures and are places where there is ever-increasing cultural syncretism resulting from globalization and human migration. However, when I use the term 'Western' or 'in the West' I am simply referring to cultures of European origin. I am also referring to countries to which the term 'Western' can be applied, countries whose history has been strongly influenced by European immigration or settlement such as the Americas and Australasia.

From the outset, and drawing from the works of White Western feminists, I want to clearly explain what I mean by the concept of femininity and how this term will be used throughout this chapter. The female body is not an unchanging fixed biological truth; it is an historical, plural and a culturally mediated form.[1] In the West, the female body has been physically, socially and culturally constructed to represent the characteristics of femininity. Therefore, appropriately, Moi defined femininity as a set of cultural attributes assigned to the female sex.[2] De Beauvoir informed us that for the female body to be considered 'woman' that body must share in the mysterious and mythical 'reality' known as femininity.[3] De Beauvoir enabled us to understand that gendering should be understood as a form of 'becoming', for a female body does not automatically equate into being a woman. Womanhood is something that is learnt and developed, a state of 'being' that the female body is changed or transformed into. It is femininity that transforms the female body into a feminine one for it to be labelled 'woman'.

Ultimately, femininity is about gender; it is about transforming female bodies into socially constructed feminine roles. According to Bordo, femininity is always a representation of the aesthetic ideal of the time and this ideal within contemporary Western culture is thinness; the slenderness of the female body.[4] The aesthetic image of femininity is a woman with a slimline figure and for a woman to be considered feminine she must display a replication of this image. Hence, femininity becomes an obsessive pursuit for women; their bodies must be trained and shaped through the utilization of diet and exercise if they are to reflect femininity. It is this cultural manufacture of femininity and the aesthetic images of femininity that are all over popular culture that this chapter is concerned about.

'Seeing comes before words. The child looks and recognises before it can speak', and femininity is a concept that is first learnt and understood through imagery.[5] Photographic images of women, whether from film, television or advertisements, are a significant part of Western culture. They also help to mould and shape our ideas of femininity. Though the female body is central to the concept of femininity, femininity has nothing to do with the female body. The images of femininity we see everywhere in popular culture are cultural representations of what female bodies should look like, and our knowledge and understanding of femininity primarily comes from those images rather than from biology.

Imagery dictated my initial knowledge of femininity. I first noticed a woman was feminine/beautiful about the age of five or six and it was the image of Fay Wray (Figure 1), the leading actress in the 1933 film *King Kong*.

I remember being mesmerized by her. As a young girl living in Nigeria at the time, I am not sure if it was her feminine beauty that captured my attention or if it was the fact that she was so different from the Black women I saw around me. As a child, I was unable to articulate my feelings; as Berger says, seeing which comes before words can never be quite covered by them. Being a Black girl, I knew that my reflection bore no resemblance to what I observed femininity to be and for me, Fay Wray was the personification of femininity. The concept of race played a fundamental part in my first perception of femininity, though at the time, living in Nigeria, I had no understanding of what race was.

As a teenager, and now living in Britain, through interaction with my White counterparts and the images of femininity that were everywhere, I saw that thinness was important if a woman is to replicate the feminine ideal. This was something I had not realized during my early years in Nigeria and living in a place where the ideal body shape could be described as plump.[6] In Britain, and as a girl whose bodily frame could be described as slim and petite, I realized that being thin was not enough when it came to femininity. I was different. I became conscious of the fact, as Mirza claimed, that as a Black girl I was judged by my 'otherness';[7] the colour of my skin, the shape of my nose, the texture of my hair and the curve of my body. My physical body, which is inclusive of my skin tone and hair texture, meant that I was excluded from the realms of femininity and I began to see the significance of intersectionality in my life. Femininity is not and cannot only be about gender, as White Western feminists have informed us. My body can never 'become' a woman, as De Beauvoir states, simply because the word Black will always prefix the word woman. It was not thinness that became an obsessive pursuit for me as a woman; it was not the slenderness of the female ideal that had a detrimental effect on the way I perceived myself or my body. This may have been the case for my White counterparts, but it was not the same for me. I simultaneously held the position of Black and female, and my experiences could not be reduced to just one category. The intersection between race and gender in my everyday experiences meant that the oppression I experienced differed from that of my White counterparts.

Carrie Mae Weems's 1987 artwork *Mirror, Mirror* enabled me to understand that beauty, femininity and Whiteness were synonymous. The image is of a Black woman in a mirror, with a White woman looking back out at her. The caption under the image reads:

> Looking into the mirror, the Black woman asked, "Mirror Mirror on the wall, who's the fairest of them all?" The Mirror says, "Snow White, you Black bitch, and don't you forget it!!!'"

These telling words made me realize that it was not Snow White's beauty that made her 'the fairest of them all', but her Whiteness. In fact, it was the Whiteness of her skin that made her beautiful and a Black woman could never be perceived to be 'the fairest of them all'; as Dyer states, 'the fair sex' has a distinct skin colour suggestion.[8] Foutz's analysis of eighteenth-century scientific racism claimed that in the eighteenth century skin colour was interwoven with European sentiments of aesthetics.[9] Major writers of this time such as Denis Diderot (1713–84) and Pierre Louis Maupertuis (1698–1759) bluntly stated that they considered Black people 'ugly'. Georges Cuvier (1769–1832) wrote:

> The White race, with oval face, straight hair and nose, to which civilized peoples of Europe belong and which is the most beautiful of all, is also superior to others.

These sentiments were also reinforced through literature and Art. For example, in nineteenth-century paintings, Andromeda, the daughter of Cepheus and Cassiopeia, king and queen of the African kingdom of Aethiopia, was always portrayed as White.

In classical English literature Black represents death, fiends, fearful men, hell and the devil's blood.[10] White is holiness and purity and feminine beauty. There was not only a gender difference of what feminine beauty was; there was also a clear racial difference. Whiteness was linked to femininity and beauty and being Black was linked to evil and fearful men. The Whiteness of Andromeda's body showed that for a woman to be labelled beautiful, Whiteness was a necessary component; making femininity and Whiteness interlinked. Dyer uses the Western portrayals of Cleopatra as an example of this. He claims,

> the history of the representation of Cleopatra provides one of the clearest instances of the conviction that Whiteness is the pinnacle of human beauty. Cleopatra became a byword for feminine beauty in European culture, but in the process, she had to be represented as White.

White is seen as beautiful because it is the colour of virtue, it is goodness, cleanliness and purity. This means that femininity is not just a representation of women but is a representation of White women.

Crenshaw's concept of intersectionality has been used as an analytical tool for understanding and responding to the ways in which gender intersects with other identities and how these intersections contribute to unique experiences of oppression. Intersectionality was also a great tool which enabled me to broaden my analysis of femininity. Rather than making subjects such as Black women and White women my starting point, the Westernized concept of femininity became my starting point, and in so doing I saw that femininity is a multidimensional concept that cannot be analysed on the single-axis framework of gender, as White Western feminists have done. I began by stating that this chapter is about femininity but also about race. To state that this chapter is solely about femininity is to inadvertently say that it is about gender and perpetuate the overarching belief that the concept of femininity only pertains to 'being' or 'becoming' a woman. As will be demonstrated, to talk of femininity is also unintentionally to speak about race and throughout this chapter, I will draw attention to the fact that femininity is by no means only gender specific but is an intersectional concept in which race also plays its vital part.

This chapter is derived from a research study that placed race at the centre of its exploration of femininity. The concept of femininity was researched empirically through in-depth semi-structured interviewing. A total of forty-two women, twenty-two Black women and twenty White women, were interviewed for this project. The rest of this chapter is divided into five sections. The first section will give definitions of race and Whiteness and how these terms will be used throughout the rest of this chapter. It will then go on to present the research on which this chapter is based, and its methodology, particularly the use of grounded theory as an analytical tool in examining the data collected.

The second section, drawing on the data in this study, will show that race is an important part of both Black and White women's perceptions of femininity. In the minds of the respondents (White and Black), femininity was an intersectional concept in which gender (female) and race (White) played their significant parts. The third section will begin with what is already known, which is, as Bordo argued, that femininity teaches women that rigorous dieting and exercise is essential if one is to replicate femininity. However, drawing from the data, when I applied an intersectional lens and looked at the gender and race of the women who attempted to reflect the thinness femininity represented, I saw that it was mainly the White respondents of this study. I will then give the reasons why some of the Black participants were not interested in replicating the slenderness of the female ideal. This section will end by showing why the White women who took part in the study felt that Black women were not interested in femininity because they were not interested in the thinness femininity represents. The fourth section will focus solely on the voices of the Black women who chose to be a part of this study. It will begin by focusing on Black women's attempts to reflect femininity and the Whiteness it represents through the alteration of their afro hair. I will then go on to argue that femininity is part of the racism Black women suffer, what could be described as 'gendered racism' because it makes a distinction between them and what is normally depicted as an acceptable form of femininity.[11] I will conclude this chapter by stating that femininity is not only about womanhood, but that femininity is as much raced as it is gendered.

Defining race and Whiteness

The concept of race and Whiteness is central to the Westernized concept of femininity; therefore, it is essential that I make clear here what is meant by race and Whiteness and how these terms will be used. There are no races in the biological sense of distinct divisions of the human species. It is also widely accepted that 'race' as such does not exist. It is an historically, culturally and socially constructed term. Thus, it is a contested concept both academically and politically. The idea of race came into common usage from the mid-eighteenth century affirming the popular, scientific and political discourse of the time. The concept of race enabled humanity to be divided into distinct groupings whose members possessed common physical characteristics.

If there are no races in the biological sense, then like race, Whiteness, or to talk of being White remains a social construction. Consequently, like race, the definition of Whiteness is hard to identify.[12] Dyer in his analysis of Whiteness concluded that Whiteness is an invisible perspective, a dominant and normative space against which difference is measured. However, seeing Whiteness as invisible is contentious. For example, Morrison argues that in American literature, it is Blackness rather than Whiteness that is largely invisible.[13] Thus, Whiteness is only invisible to those categorizing themselves as 'White'. Ahmed argues that Whiteness may be invisible to those who are White. However, it is highly visible to those who are not perceived to be 'White', thus to truly understand 'Whiteness' it must begin from Black critique.[14] When we attempt to define Whiteness from a Black perspective we see that at its core it is a set of racial interests often obscured by seemingly race-neutral words.[15] Western feminists who have written on femininity and the female body often fail to see Whiteness, and consequently race, as one of the main characteristics of femininity because for them Whiteness is invisible. De Beauvoir claims femininity is about 'being' or 'becoming' a woman, when in actual fact femininity is essentially about 'being' or 'becoming' a White woman. Thus, even though White Western feminists use race-neutral words, their racelessness of femininity is in itself highly racial.

Even though 'race' does not exist, it is difficult to argue that a person's experience of race/Whiteness is based on 'fiction'. Race and Whiteness are mythical concepts that are deep-rooted in Western culture both historically and socially. Ahmed argues that one's 'racial identity' is not simply determined by the 'fact' of one's skin colour. Racialization, according to Ahmed, is a process which takes place in time and space and 'race' is an effect of this process rather than its origin or cause.[16] Thus, in the case of skin colour, racialization involves a process of investing skin colour with meaning such that 'Black' and 'White' come to function, not as descriptions of skin colour, but as racial identities. According to Barthes, the subject of race, perhaps more than any other subject in modern Western life, feeds on myth.[17] This mythical concept of race, Barthes states, affects our reasoning and politics; it also aids in forming part of the way we see ourselves and others as well as shaping part of our everyday realities. Therefore, race 'lives' because it is part and parcel of the means of living.[18]

Although there is so much historical and social investment in skin colour and what it means to be 'Black' or 'White', there is very little, and often contradictory information on the differences between skin coloration. Despite this, it is important that I try to give a more precise definition of what I mean by 'Black' and 'White' in terms of skin tone and racial group. Rawlings states that pigmentation is the obvious difference in skin characteristics between different racial groups and that this racial variation is dependent on the quantity of melanin.[19] Melanin is a natural skin pigment which protects the skin from UV damage, and it is this that is responsible for the differences in skin pigmentation. When I speak of White women, I am referring to White British/European or White American women, those who Rawlings would describe as having a pinkish skin tone. This is because those with light skin pigmentation have approximately half as much melanin as the most darkly pigmented skin types. When I speak of Black women, I am primarily referring to Black British, African/Caribbean and African-American women.

As already stated, a total of forty-two women (twenty White and twenty-two Black women) were interviewed for the project on which this chapter is based. The women who took part in this study all lived in the city of Manchester, England. To access data that was not only informative but also rich in knowledge when it comes to the concept of femininity, respondents were chosen from women who regularly visited establishments such as beauty salons, hairdressers and gyms. My intention was to find women who made a concerted effort to reflect femininity.

Qualitative semi-structured interviewing was the favoured method for data collection. The interviews were approximately between thirty minutes and two hours and thirty minutes. Interviews were undertaken at a place of the participant's choice, and for half of the Black respondents who took part in this study, this was at the hairdressers. Despite my attempts to conduct one-to-one interviews, when discussing a subject matter as emotive as race, Whiteness and femininity in an open-plan Black hairdresser, many Black women who were not being interviewed spoke about their experiences of race and racism and gender and femininity. This played a fundamental part of my data collection and enriched the findings of this research. I also conducted an interview with two friends in a cafe, one White, one Black, one after another. I interviewed the White woman first with the Black woman present and then the Black woman with her White friend present. This also enhanced the findings of this study, and I will elaborate on this later in this chapter when discussing the data.

The interviews were analysed through the main principles of grounded theory. Grounded theory methods consist of systematic inductive guidelines for gathering, synthesizing, analysing and conceptualizing qualitative data to construct theory, and the strength of grounded theory lies in its empirical foundation.[20] Grounded theory helped me to see the gaps within feminist theory and theories of race and racism when it comes to the effects Westernized femininity has or can have on both Black and White women's lives.

Poran, in her study on Black women and body image, argues that grounded theory is necessary when attempting to explore what has been missed by other studies especially in relation to the female body.[21] An open approach enabled me to locate what concerned Black participants by offering them the space to define issues of femininity for themselves. It also allowed me to establish White women's racial perceptions of femininity and how they related those perceptions to themselves and their own bodies. Through the use of grounded theory, I saw that it was the Black women who discussed their experiences of femininity in relation to their race and ethnicity and what it was like for them as women from Nigeria, Jamaica, Uganda. However, the White respondents through their race-neutral words saw themselves as being outside race and racialization.

'The fairest of them all' and 'the English rose'

Through Weems's artwork *Mirror, Mirror*, I attempted to relay how I as a Black woman felt in the face of femininity, and the Whiteness femininity represents. The idea of the 'fairest of them all' being the most beautiful gives women, both White and Black, the subliminal message that Whiteness signifies beauty. Through the words of participants who took part in this study, the fairest of them all, which indicates Whiteness as the most feminine/beautiful was still prominent in the imagination of my respondents. During my interview with Crystal, a thirty-five-year-old Black domestic worker who grew up in Uganda, I asked her what her first image of femininity was:

> Crystal: Well, for me I grew up reading fairy tales, and I guess … I'm sorry I can't tell you how old I was, but I guess my first image of femininity must have come from those fairy tales.
> MI: Can you describe that image; how did you see femininity?
> Crystal: Umm, well most of the fairy tale books I had, had pictures. Snow White was obviously White, Goldilocks had blonde hair, so she was White, and Rapunzel had really long hair, and the prince used her hair as a rope, so she was also White … I knew Rapunzel could not be Black because you cannot climb up afro hair (laughs). So even though I grew up in Africa, I guess my first image of femininity was White.

Through the popular writers of fairy tales such as Grimm and Hans Christian Anderson women learn the sinister connotations of Black, the favourable implications of White, and the lovability of blue-eyed princes and blonde princesses. There were many respondents (Black and White) who identified fairy tales or Disney princesses as their first perceptions of femininity. This is the mythology of the dark and fair. This myth is not only established but has become historically and geographically universal. In addition, the mythology of the dark and fair is extremely pervasive, and it has a considerable influence on Western culture. Black and White girls internalize the myth of Whiteness, particularly the myth of White beauty,[22] and they have attached value to the feminine ideal that has been portrayed to them through fairy tales. Tate argues that when we judge beauty or femininity, then we are making racialized judgements based on societal and global norms of beauty.[23]

I asked Phoenix, a twenty-seven-year-old Black teacher, who personified femininity for her, and she picked Keira Knightly, a White British actress who has appeared in many period dramas:

> Phoenix: It's because of, you know the English rose persona, you know …
> MI: Does the English rose persona mean White?
> Phoenix: Yeah, English rose, yeah it is, she does like period dramas … [race] is an issue to me because when I was growing up that was what I saw in the media … Everything was very Caucasian and umm, so, therefore, maybe as time has gone on I have developed to think that maybe Keira Knightley's image is the ideal.

The English rose persona is an image of Victorian femininity and angelic perfection. It is also the reason why June, a twenty-five-year-old White student, picked Keira Knightley when asked which image most fits her image of femininity:

> I think it's … umm, it's a bit of a tough one really, I would say Keira Knightley. I just like that sort of very English rose delicate kind of look …

As can be seen from the above examples, race/Whiteness, even when not mentioned, do play a significant role in the respondents', both Black and White, primary perceptions of femininity. Subsequently, femininity cannot and should not be defined in terms of the strict dichotomy of gender.

White women and the thinness of femininity

This section explains the ways in which the White women who took part in this study perceived femininity to be mainly about the slenderness of the feminine ideal. Some White respondents even argued that Black women were rarely influenced by the concept of femininity because, according to them, they had no desire to be thin.

Most of the White women interviewed argued that cultivating and maintaining a thin figure was important for them when it came to femininity. White respondents claimed that they endeavoured to reflect what they saw as feminine through utilizing the practices of diet and exercise. Sara, a twenty-four-year-old White woman, working in retail, said:

> It is important for me to stay slim because I feel better when I am slim … I feel more presentable, more beautiful. When I put on weight after Christmas or a holiday I cannot bring myself to buy another dress size, I just work really hard to lose the weight.

Many of the White interviewees were like Angela, the twenty-eight-year-old White nurse who told me how she constantly struggles with her weight:

> Well … I go through ups and downs with my body; I mean I know I'm slim, I'm not over-weight, but I could do with losing half a stone. I've always been like that but umm … I know I've got quite skinny legs, but I also know I've got a bit of a tummy … I had a little bit of an eating problem when I was eighteen. I was two stone lighter than I am now and I thought I was fat … I'm bigger now, but I could still do with losing half a stone …

Jeffreys argues tha there needs to be a 'taking away' from the female figure if it is to be a representation of femininity.[24] Drawing from the data, it was primarily the White respondents who talked, some for hours, about the struggles they had with their weight. Thus, what has been perceived as a normalized gendered way of performing femininity, which is replicating thinness, has always been a White racialized way of attempting to reflect femininity.

This continual constant monitoring of one's food intake is something that has not transpired nor is it entrenched within Black subculture, and both Black and White participants testified to this fact during the interview process. Florence, a twenty-nine-year-old Black health care officer, said when asked why she was not influenced by thin images in the media:

> They don't reflect who I am. When I see those images, and some people would say that they're feminine [but] I don't take any notice of them, all I see is skinny White people. It is not talking to me as a person; it is not about me as a Black woman …

Florence describes the image of femininity that she sees in the thin White female body as a racial image. As a Black woman, for Florence, Whiteness does not masquerade as universal; therefore, she recognizes Whiteness and thinness as being compatible, and she does not perceive herself as reflecting the images that are labelled 'feminine' in Western society. Many of the Black women who took part in this study claimed that though they noticed the thinness of femininity, it rarely spoke to them as women. Crystal, the Black thirty-five-year-old domestic worker, said:

> Our food is very important to us and dieting is not something that is part of our culture. To be thin has nothing to do with femininity and beauty. In Uganda to be thin is to be sick, dying of malaria or AIDS.

White participants thought that femininity was something only directed at them as White women even though they failed to speak about themselves in racial terms. When I asked Laura, a White nineteen-year-old trainee hairdresser, why she thought Black women were not influenced by extremely thin images in the media or why we rarely saw Black celebrities labelled as 'too thin', she replied by repeating a common Black stereotype, commenting that 'I don't think femininity affects them and, well, Black people have a culture of food, don't they? They love their chicken'.

Julie also claimed that the cultural labels that are placed on a large White female body compared to that placed a large Black female are completely different:

> I think people expect … they expect Black women to be voluptuous and they expect Black women to be more like that … Whereas when you see a fat White woman walking down the street, and you see fat hanging out of her, and I have noticed this before, if you are really, really, really pale it looks dreadful and blotchy, it just looks worse, yeah it really does … I think if you are Black you can be big, and it does look more beautiful. I think it is also an image we've got in the UK of a big fat White

woman which is scary, people just think they are just sitting there doing nothing all day eating pies and getting fat and I think that is part of it, that association of a lazy fat White person on the dole.

Julie informs us that there are more negative connotations associated with being fat and White than there are with being fat and Black. Society expects Black women to be fat; it is not a problem if Black women are fat because they have never been associated with beauty or femininity. On the other hand, White women have long been the 'most' beautiful women, and in occupying that sacred position, they must look after their bodies to maintain their femininity and beauty. It is they who must sculpt their bodies into what is culturally perceived to be beautiful. One of the most prevailing stereotypes of the Black woman is the image of the Mammy, the obese Black woman. It is one of the most pervasive images of Black women and it is an image that is ingrained in the minds of both White and Black people.[25] This is exactly the image Sandra, a White thirty-year-old probation officer, has when she thinks of Black women, explaining that 'when I think of Black women I think of them as big, they look cute and cuddly'.

Black women's realities of femininity and race

I would like to begin this section by clearly stating that women, both White and Black, are oppressed by the Westernized concept of femininity, and Bordo is correct in describing it as a form of gender oppression. However, no social group is homogenous. Knowing quite simply that a woman lives in a sexist society is insufficient information to describe the complexity of her daily social interactions when it comes to femininity. Diverse life experiences such as stereotyping, silencing, and marginalization do not lend themselves to simple, categorical analysis based solely upon gender. As Hill Collins states, the oppression of the aesthetic ideal, like any oppression, frames everyone's lives, and everyone's life is subject to a varying amount of penalty, and the prescriptive feminine ideal presents a normative yardstick for all femininities in which Black women are relegated to the bottom of the gender hierarchy.[26] Femininity enables White women to be described as women without having to preface it with the word 'White', unlike their Black counterparts. The intersection of femaleness and Whiteness in the image of femininity holds enormous power.

The worldview that has been created by White people enables White women to be completely oblivious to Black women's experiences in relation to race and the Whiteness of femininity. The White women interviewed in this study had no clear understanding of how marginalized Black women may feel because of representations of their skin and hair in Western culture. hooks claimed that White people never realized that there is such a thing as 'White privilege' until they developed non-White connections.[27] Yet, even when White people have close 'non-White connections' they may remain ignorant of Black women's racial experiences. A telling example of this was the interviews I conducted with two friends one after another in which both were present at the other's interview. Sara, a twenty-four-year-old White woman working in retail, was interviewed first, and then Leanne, a Black twenty-four-year-old fitness instructor. When I asked Leanne if she thought Black women were considered feminine she answered:

> Leanne: No, not in the media, no, not generally.
>
> MI: What about Beyoncé? Do you think she is considered feminine?
>
> Leanne: Yeah, but she is light-skinned so she can be both, so the lighter the better … but then again that's with me growing up where my cousins have been mixed race, and us lot was dark, and they used to say: 'We are better than you because we are mixed race, we are light skinned' …
>
> MI: How did that affect you?
>
> Leanne: It made me feel like crap, to be honest … I felt it would be better if I had long hair. I used to put a shirt on my head just to think my hair was dead long … isn't it weird, but as a child, I used to think long hair, long hair and maybe that's why I am like this now [respondent had a long Black weave] …

What was important during these interviews was that Sara, who is White, knew nothing about how marginalized Leanne, who is Black, felt in relation to femininity because of her skin and hair. Sara, who has been a close friend of Leanne since childhood, was perplexed by the fact that Leanne, when growing up, put a shirt on her head to replicate White women's hair. She asked questions such as, 'Why, what did you do?' and 'You put a shirt on your head pretending it was hair?' When it comes to femininity, Whiteness has created a different culture for Black women that White people do not see or are blind to.

Hair was a major topic for every one of the twenty-two Black women that were interviewed. The idea of putting a shirt or something on your head to replicate long hair was an experience shared by twenty of the Black women interviewed in this study. Florence, the twenty-nine-year-old Black health care officer said:

> This is so funny, but I remember putting a towel on my head pretending it was long hair. I vividly remember flicking it pretending I was like the girls at school as I walked around the house (laughs). It's embarrassing now when I think about it.

For the Black women of this study, hair was a vital part of their performance of femininity, and the privilege that comes with the long flowing hair for Black women is something that is learnt very early on. Many Black respondents painfully spoke about their first images of femininity and their childhood. These experiences centred around their hair. Phoenix, the Black twenty-seven-year-old teacher, said when talking about her first images of femininity:

> Phoenix: Umm, well I think I even remember watching *Super-Girl* as
>   a young girl and Super-Girl was a long blonde-haired woman and
>   I thought she was really pretty and beautiful but that was, I think,
>   I was about nine or around that time. But I would think even before
>   that, even cartoons if I can use animation. You saw the warriors and
>   the females with the long hair fighting …
> MI: Hair was the most prominent thing you noticed?
> Phoenix: Yes, definitely.

Like Phoenix, many Black respondents argued that hair was part of their first realization of femininity. Gloria, a Black twenty-year-old student nurse, told me that 'although I knew I was racially different, that my friends at school were White and I was Black, but for me, it was my hair that was the real issue'.

Leanne agonisingly told me how she knew she was not a representation of femininity because of her interaction with boys. Through those boys she realized that femininity was not a Black girl with afro hair:

> MI: When did you first notice that a woman was feminine?
> Leanne: How old?
> MI: Yeah.
> Leanne: At nine … Because when all the guys wouldn't want to date me
>   because my hair was not straight and umm (pause) and I guess I was
>   told that I was ugly … They would tell me that I was ugly because my
>   hair was not straight …

MI: Was it just your hair?

Leanne: My hair and I was too dark, and my nose, and you know I used to get called things like 'flat nose', things like that. But then I used to look at my friends … boys were more attracted to straight-haired girls … Naomi Campbell, you know that was the first Black woman I saw with straight, long, beautiful weaves and I thought, 'Wow, I want my hair like that and because it just looks amazing' … I can't imagine my hair being afro again. It is hard work; it does not suit me …

Femininity for Black women is largely about the imitation of Whiteness, simply because Whiteness is one of the primary characteristics of femininity. If a Black woman chooses not to reflect femininity she can still be judged in relation to it and the Whiteness it represents. Margaret, a Black thirty-year-old drama teacher, talked about being judged in relation to the image of femininity at her place of work:

Margaret: Yeah when you talk about femininity, it is White, and if you as a Black woman and don't try and look White then you are too different.

MI: Too different how?

Margaret: Different because you don't try and look White. People think that society has changed, and there is no racism but that's not the case, it's just that racism is not in your face as it used to be. Last year I was teaching in a mainly White school, and I had my hair in afro twists, and I was told that it was not an appropriate hairstyle because pupils may be intimidated by it …

Danielle, a Black thirty-one-year-old solicitor, spoke of the importance attempting to reflect femininity and the Whiteness it represents as she endeavours to secure a 'privileged' position in a place that could be described as 'White space':

Once I went on maternity [leave] just before I had my baby I decided to stop relaxing my hair. I just thought that it would be easier to go back to having an afro and I can just put my hair in braids or cornrows so that I didn't have to worry too much about my hair. But then I got an interview whilst on maternity leave with a really good law firm and I thought, 'Oh God I'm going to have to get a weave', but I just bought a wig, went to the interview with the wig on (laughs), and when it was over I got home and took the wig off, and I was back to being myself again.

Danielle highlights the importance of reflecting femininity and the Whiteness of femininity, especially for Black middle-class women. It is important to state here, drawing from the words of the participants of this study, that their lives as women had become fabricated representations of femininity. However, this is not to say that they had no power or agency at all or that the Black respondents had no control when it comes to replicating femininity. The Black women who took part in this study did not always want to reflect the Whiteness of femininity, but they had skilfully learnt how to navigate through society, and to use Danielle's wig as an example, they knew when to put on femininity and when to take it off at their own convenience.

Femininity is part of the racism Black women suffer, and what could be described as 'gendered racism' because it makes a distinction between them and what is normally depicted as an acceptable form of womanhood within Western culture. This distinction is made because a Black woman's body does not reflect the Whiteness femininity represents, taking her out of the category 'woman' into the combined category 'Black woman'. Femininity discriminates against Black women on the basis that their bodies are associated with a racial group that is not White, and this discrimination takes place on a day-to-day basis, as can be seen from the above examples. If I am to offer a way of thinking about racism in relation to the concept of femininity and beauty, I would have to say that we need to think of it as a form of everyday racism. Femininity is a historically constructed racial image that affects Black and White women's lives on an everyday level. Essed argued that everyday racism is about seemingly small injustices that one has come to expect and because they recur so often they are taken for granted, even though they are nagging, annoying and debilitating. Everyday racism is a subtle form of racism that is rooted in the pervasiveness of White culture, of which femininity plays a part. For many it is automatic, taken for granted, often covert and hard to pinpoint. I would like to give one example from one of the Black women who was not interviewed but was present at one of the interviews I conducted at a Black hairdressers, Hayley, a Black twenty-six-year-old:

> I was out with a couple of friends, and we were thinking of going into a bar, but it was still quite early, so we asked a guy smoking outside who was in the bar, and he said, two ladies and three Black women. As we walked away, I just thought, 'That means there are five ladies in the bar. What makes the three Black women not ladies?'

It is important to note that Black women have never been given the opportunity to be feminine.[28] Historically, they were never helped into carriages, carried over mud puddles, or given the best of anything, and they have never really been treated like ladies.

I would like to conclude this chapter by saying there is a need to remove the cloak of normality and universality that helps secure the Whiteness femininity represents, and which continues to protect White women's racial privilege of racially theorizing femininity without ever mentioning race. Femininity is about womanhood, but it is not only about 'being' or 'becoming' a woman. It is about transforming female bodies into feminine roles, but gender is not the only sociocultural concept that defines femininity. Femininity is a representation of thinness within modern Western culture, but being thin is not enough to label a female body feminine. When it comes to the subject of femininity, gender and race operate in tandem, and there must be an awareness of intersectionality; the interconnected nature of social categorizations such as gender and race but also class, sexuality, religion, disability and even age, which create overlapping and interdependent systems of discrimination or disadvantage. Intersectionality provides an avenue for researching complex inequalities when it comes to the concept of femininity. Femininity at its core is a racialized construction of gender that excludes Black women from what can be described as traditional and accepted ideals of womanhood. Gender, and femininity as an aspect of gender, are forcefully racialized concepts, and we see polarizations of insiderness and outsiderness organized around the axis of race.

'It's not even an attitude … but a way of being!': Negotiating Black British women's lived experiences

Dionne Taylor

Knowledge of Black British women's lived experiences is often restrictive, maligned and unrepresentative of the nuances and complexities of their lives. The lived experiences for Black women in Britain involve a complex process of negotiations. Black women are having to negotiate through conflictual and oftentimes conflated axes which are racialized, gendered, classed, nationalized and so on. Through an ongoing and often relentless navigation of responses to discourses of Black womanhood, representations of Black women are often limited to stereotypical and controlling images such as 'hypersexualised video vixens' or culturally inept 'welfare queens', 'baby mothers' and 'strong matriarchal emasculating super women', just to name a few.[1] Arguably, Collins's framing of controlling images is broadly ascribed to Black women in a US context. While this is helpful, what is needed is a specific focus on Black British women's lived experiences.

Paradoxically viewed either as 'victims' or 'enterprising actors',[2] for Black women in Britain, while there are nuances in their lived experiences, they are largely in alignment with systemic oppressions that operate through processes of negotiation. For Black British women, their lived experiences are discussed at a personal level in this chapter through the exploration of questions such as: what are the lived experiences of being Black, being educated, living and working in Britain? How do their engagements with educational, employment and health institutions affect them? Do they feel a sense of belonging or exclusion, based on their racialized, gendered, nationalized identities? What impact do other negative representations of Black womanhood have on their sense of selves? Addressing these questions will allow for a more intersectional examination of the dominant discourses negotiated by Black British women in their day-to-day lives, with the anticipation that some of the restrictive and unrepresentative narratives can be negated and resisted for more nuanced variations.

Two aims will be fulfilled in this chapter. The first is to outline the complexities of Black British women's experiences, which are located in racialized, sexualized, classed, nationalized, and other such axes of identity. Embedded within a theoretical framework of intersectionality and Critical Race Theory, which is both a Black feminist politic of survival and an analytic interested in how race, gender, class and sexuality interact in complex ways that shape subjects and institutions alike.[3] Disparities experienced by Black British women are relational and contingent to those of other women (White) and men (White and Black), therefore contributing to the systematic social inequalities.[4] Drawing on the narrative extracts of Black British women from interviews fulfils the second aim, which is the centring of their experiences in the public and private spheres; outside of the maligned and limited discourses which are stereotypical and restrictive, and are ultimately damaging to Black women's lives. The interview extracts are drawn from my PhD research on young Black British women's lived experiences of negotiating their identities in relation to popular culture and also postdoctoral research with Black university students, their self-perceptions of their academic experiences. The narrative extracts are pivotal to creating new knowledge on Black British women. It is important to note that there are vast experiences ranging from feelings of inclusion, marginalization, exclusion, pride, shame, visibility, invisibility and hypervisibility. Therefore, their lived experiences are complex and at times ambivalent and contradictory. The chapter concludes by emphasizing the importance of centring the lived experiences of Black British women, which will enable the negating, resisting and challenging of the stereotypical representations of Black womanhood, many of which persistently affect their everyday lives.

Structural and systemic inequalities of Black women in the UK

I would like to begin by calling into question how discourse works to inform, reconstruct and create knowledge of Black British women's lived experiences. How is it that for Black women in the UK our experiences, both as individuals and as a group, are often located and bear the brunt of structural and systemic inequalities; which are central to the interlocking systems of race, gender and class oppressions, but further compounded by the nationalized context we are living in and governed by? The impact of the inequalities and disparities faced by Black women has devastating and long-lasting consequences on our health, wellbeing, self-esteem; in short it affects our overall life experiences. Take, for instance, Britain's austerity measures between 2010 and 2019, which have hit Black women hardest.[5] Black women in the poorest households have lost on average 14% of their income (over £2,000 a year) as a direct impact of state benefit cuts and tax changes.[6] Racialized and gendered inequalities are embedded within political and economic policies which have, and will continue to have for generations to come, severe and detrimental consequences, thus unwittingly affecting Black British women's lived experiences.

There is a plethora of research evidence pointing to the fact that Black British women are statistically more likely to engage in low-paid jobs with lower levels of job security and employment protection rights.[7] Regardless of educational outcomes, minority groups were disproportionately more likely to be unemployed or underemployed.[8] Those in the labour market had to negotiate an 'ethnic penalty' which depresses wages and concentrates minority groups in low-paid, temporary and unstable work.[9]

Significant social divisions are in employment and educational opportunities afforded to Black women in the UK who often occupy a subordinate position in relation to employment opportunities and career progression. This has continued to be an ongoing and collective experience for Black women since labour market data statistically reported on the demographic profile of individuals' labour market contribution according to gender, ethnic/racial backgrounds. In this respect, structural factors pertaining to the young women's lived experiences are directly related to macro-level patterns of social organization or divisions. The structural domain in this instance addresses issues of power and inequality in the institutions and structures of society that govern the allocation of resources such as job/employment opportunities and positive educational attainment and progression.[10] The effects of the structural divisions have a detrimental impact on Black British women. There is a plethora of research evidence pointing to the fact that Black British women are statistically more likely to engage in low-paid jobs with lower levels of job security and employment protection rights.[11]

Even more devastating, what we know as a 'global pandemic' of 2020 brought to the public's attention the systematic and disproportionate impact of COVID-19 on Black people's lives in the UK and globally. It is reported that Black African and African Caribbean women are twice as likely to die of COVID-19.[12] The explanations, excuses and at times the outright denial of why and how this impacted Black women were inconsistently audible, while simultaneously being imperceptible. One explanation which pointed to the wider structural inequalities is that Black women are more likely work in key frontline roles and therefore to be at higher risk of exposure to the virus itself because of the jobs they perform are located in health and social care roles. Black women in the UK are faced with the duality of being structurally disadvantaged not only through their economic circumstances but also through the types of work they do.

Similarly, through late 2019 and 2020, we were alerted to reports in the national press which pointed to something that many Black people were already well aware of, but it is still nonetheless traumatic to hear of; that is, Black women in the UK are more likely to die from complications surrounding pregnancy and childbirth than White women. Reports into the maternal morbidity in the UK found Black women to be five times more likely to die in pregnancy, childbirth or in the postpartum period than White women.[13] The questions of why and how these figures are so distressingly high for Black women beg to be answered. Sowemimo writing for *The Independent* states, 'The 2019 statistics were so appalling that they could no longer be ignored; BBC *Woman's Hour* featured a special episode on the issue and a parliamentary petition was launched in March 2020, in the hope that there would be greater government support in tackling the root causes'.[14] The parliamentary petition 'Improved Maternal Mortality Rates and Health Care for Black Women in the UK' gained traction by receiving over 187,500 signatures. The government response came in June 2020, which was the funding towards a research project which examines factors associated with the higher risk of maternal death for Black and South Asian women. Questions of the efficacy of yet another report will need to be asked; why a report and no immediate action? What will it change? How many Black women's and children's lives will be saved and their overall experiences be improved as a result of this report and its recommendations? Will there be targets set to reduce the disparities and financial and legal ramifications, if these aren't met?

Medical professionals in the UK have long assumed the death rate can be explained by pre-existing conditions amongst Black women such as high blood pressure, or the higher prevalence of pregnancy complications such as pre-eclampsia, which explains why 'the likeliness of an adverse outcome for someone like myself – a Black, healthy, middle-class professional – increases, rather than decreases'.[15] Whereas, in most cases, adverse health outcomes would be aligned with poverty, lack of education and poor housing. If we look at the experiences of Black women in the US and elsewhere across the globe, there are some significant differences, as the issues around class become nuanced. Many of these pre-existing conditions are non-communicable diseases which are driven by social determinants of health such as poverty, education and housing. Therefore the issue within the UK context is located within structural inequalities.

I will not be your baby mother

The discourses around Black mothers and Black women more generally have been presented in unfavourable and maligned terms. In the UK, the media has routinely linked households with single Black mothers to increasing youth violence and London's knife crime epidemic; with little regard for the other structural factors at play.[16] Reclaiming and resisting the use of dominant ideas concerning Black women's subjectivities is vital to situating and examining Black British women's lived experiences.[17] It is essential to understanding the impact of how their racialized, sexualized, classed and nationalized identities 'affectively mediate' their everyday lives.

Examining processes which are oppressive and limiting to Black British women's lived experiences can be viewed through the lens of both intersectionality and Critical Race Theory (CRT) frameworks. It is important to explicate the relationship between CRT[18] and Intersectionality[19] which operate in alignment with each other to conceptualize race as 'recursive' and fundamental to discussions of societal structures, representations and identity formation.[20] Centralizing racialized experiences in tandem with sexualized, classed, gendered and nationalized discourses allows for more complex and nuanced ways of understanding, interpreting and building new knowledge on the everyday lives of Black British women. An intersectional analysis can and should ensure that knowledge on oppressed or marginalized groups helps to reveal the unequal power dynamics in operation. So too should its application unveil structural, hegemonic and interpersonal dimensions of power to expose how oppression is constructed and maintained through everyday social practices.[21]

There is an onslaught and damaging denial of normative gender relations afforded to Black women,[22] for instance in the stereotype of a 'baby mother', which in most cases is noted negatively as an unwed single Black woman, with one or more children: 'Immoral, neglectful, domineering', 'slack', the notion of being 'hypersexualised' women that are accused of 'overbreeding'.[23] This is apportioned to the 'beige' (asexual) image of motherhood that is the norm. The depiction of 'baby mothers' or 'baby mamas' is rarely showed positively, nor is she shown to get on well with her children's father. Rarely shown as self-sacrificing, hardworking and resilient, instead, she is well known to be emasculating, bitter and acrimonious. In this sense, the 'insidious nature of discourse is revealed'[24] of which Black women are often framed against unattainable racialized gender ideals.[25] This is an example of the co-constitutive, anti-Black and misogynistic racism directed at Black women, particularly in visual and digitalized cultural formats.[26]

For Critical Race Theory scholars, the functionality of the *welfare queen* trope is embedded within racialized discourses, which are powerful, purposeful and functional. Often noted to be single, with children, passively reliant and a recipient of state benefits, she is welfare dependent. *The welfare queen*, or *benefit scrounger* or *chav mums*[27] in the UK context are those women whose very existence is bound to an oppressive class structure which maligns them to an underclass deeming them irrelevant and invisible, yet simultaneously scapegoating them for the social ills within Black communities. Despite having education qualifications, and being more likely to go to university, Black British women from African and Caribbean households are disproportionately more likely to be living in poverty compared to White households. Black women are over-represented among single-parent households.[28] While many of the same households are more likely to receive state support, Black households were the most likely to receive Council Tax Reduction and Housing Benefit.[29] Support with covering basic living costs for themselves and their families is what the data shows is more prevalent for Black women living in Britain; thus, hardly a passive welfare/state benefit recipient, instead there is much more nuance at play. Another way of perpetuating the myth of the *welfare queen* is the way in which it can be used to reboot classed and racialized discourses that have historically positioned Black and working-class mothers outside of the hegemonic ideal of White, middle-class maternity.[30] Further creating constraints by boundaries of class, 'Black working class' or 'Black middle class', there is always a racialized disclaimer, that is, in alignment with historic and contemporary readings of Black bodies.

Being Black, British and female

Racism depends on its perceptibility to highlight difference making Blackness hyper-visible.[31] The result then is to devalue Black women, who are positioned as working class, uneducated and overly sexualized. The denial of femininity beyond sexualization/reproductive capabilities relegate Black British women to the lower echelons of womanhood in the hierarchy of femininities.[32] Sexuality is bounded to notions of heteronormativity; there are heavy penalties for Black women when attempting to resist or refute stereotypical representations of hypersexualized women such as the video vixen and cultural ineptness of the breeder women 'welfare queen' and 'baby mother' narrative. In short, resistance, and an unwillingness to accept stereotypes of Black womanhood demonstrate how racialized, gendered, classed and sexualized discourses continually impact on young Black

British women. This positioning is used as a tool of denial and maligning of Britishness; Blackness and Britishness operate as an 'oxymoron', as Britishness has historically been synonymous with Whiteness. Black women are thus excluded from this definition of Britishness.

To be affectively mediated by one's lived experiences for Black British women is to embody the representations of Black womanhood. This embodiment (i.e. living through and within) is demonstrable in their everyday lives, such as education, employment, health, where they live and the quality of life. In short, it affects how they are viewed, treated and subsequently respond to stereotypical representations. Being labelled and referred to as 'uneducated' and 'ghetto' is how one university student describes challenges of being stereotyped based on where she lives. This and other such instances of being negatively labelled for many Black British women is unrelenting. There is a need to navigate and negotiate feelings and emotional responses to the representations of Black womanhood which they endure through daily microaggressions, hostility and blatant racism. Microaggressions are often described as subtle, yet hostile common verbal, behavioural, and environmental indignities which are both gendered and racialized.[33]

Microaggressions are what Black women face in their everyday lives; they are experienced whether intentional or unintentional, unconscious or conscious, and communicate insults and putdowns that have harmful psychological impact on targeted individuals or groups.[34] Take for instance, Mya (twenty-six) a fully qualified quantity surveyor, who describes how she was often assumed to be the 'note taker' in meetings with external contractors. Mya goes on to explain how she 'left' the workplace, as it began to affect her mental health and well-being. Microaggressions are insidious, chronic, and traumatizing.[35] They affect Black women through pervasive and insidious undermining, harmful, contradictory and negative treatment.

Through strategically navigating and identifying the differentials in awareness of knowledge of discourse, Black British women's lived experiences are varied and differentiated but are nonetheless situated within a racialized, classed, sexualized and nationalized context. The result and impact of this can be oppressive and detrimental to their lived experiences. Black British women's identities have been forged through stereotypical representations of Black womanhood, such as being culturally and intellectually inept, sexually pervasive and deviant, and 'such myths need to be understood within the socioeconomic and political context of our position in Britain'.[36]

For Black British women, there is a range of strategies that one might employ when faced with microaggressions which affect every part of our lives. In the summer of 2018, the British newspaper the *Guardian* ran an article entitled 'How to Deal with Micro-Aggressions as a Black Woman',[35] which acknowledges that Black women are questioned in public settings like workplaces with queries such as 'How long does your hair take to do?' The article states it isn't a Black women's responsibility to 'decode' Black culture or identity for others. The experiences of Black women within this context, oppressive, maligning, and liminal, are bounded to a racist, sexist and classist setting. The setting, the geographical location of the UK, is where stereotypes, microaggressions and negative labels of Black British women are maintained. Black British women must continually negotiate their lived experiences – against a backdrop of hostility and exclusion, facing a duality of marginality and resistance.[36] Being a Black British woman is to have lived experiences which are varied, differentiated but are nonetheless complex and nuanced.

Black British women's experiences have been and will continue to have an impact on the axes of their social identities. Bryan, Dadzie and Scafe in their 1985 book *The Heart of the Race: Black Women's Lives in Britain*, the first published book about the experiences of Black womanhood in Britain by Black women, advocated for an awareness of their sociocultural, economic and historical experiences in the UK context. Being affectively mediated by their social, cultural, economic, historical and political experiences is symbiotic of the women's racialized, sexualized, classed and nationalized categorizations.

In 2018, two young women wrote *Slay in Your Lane: Black Girl's Bible*. Adegoke and Uviebinené interviewed Black British women on a range of issues: education, work, representation in popular culture, health and relationships and dating. Stemming from exasperation and frustration, yet unwaveringly optimistic, the text offers anecdotes and insights into Adegoke's and Uviebinené's and other Black women's personal journeys which address their identity formation both socially and personally and in cultural politics. Adegoke notes, 'Growing up, I felt keenly the dearth of visible Black British women in the stories our society consumed and it made me feel all sorts of things'.[37]

While Uviebinené explained the impact of the accumulation of microaggressions experienced at work, she states she was 'done with feeling conscious of my Blackness and femaleness and apologising for just existing'.[38] For both women, their lived experiences are located and embedded within their identities of being Black, female and living and growing up in Britain. Being hypervisible, yet simultaneously invisible, it is important to recognize that the subjugation and pathologization of Black womanhood is integral to the maintenance of present inequalities.[39] As such, Black British women are faced with a range of both oppressions and inequalities which affectively mediate their everyday lives. To examine the impact of these inequalities, which are both structural and systematic, it is imperative to draw on intersectionality as a theoretical framework. Intersectionality, in this sense, provides a vital framework for theorizing identities and oppression.[40]

Intersectional lens

Intersectionality was used by Crenshaw to unpack and decipher how specific racialized identities (Black and female) are bound by particular sexualized and gendered oppressions (violence against women) reinforced through law, politics and perception.[41] In a similar way, this paper utilizes a key thematic area of intersectionality and CRT as outlined above to interrogate the ways in which young Black British women navigate through the representations of Black femininities as they work to shape their identities. The importance of examining this is to understand how these inequalities persist and impact on the everyday lives of Black British women. Recognizing how discourses infiltrate knowledge and contribute to unequal power relations, thus reproducing inequalities, is, it will be argued, vital in bringing together Blackness, womanness and Britishness at the intersections. From this perspective, processes of negotiation, resistance coupled with conformity to representations of Black womanhood continually submerge lived experiences which are considered to be ambivalent and multifaceted.

Recognizing the complexities surrounding the social inequalities faced by Black British women, it is imperative to assess how the nationalized landscape with its history of empire, coloniality, imperialism and racism perpetuates and maintains its unequal power relations. Fundamentally, it can be contended that race, class and gender and national identities are not equally salient, but rather they are intertwined into a complex matrix of social relations which are linked to immigrant experiences and British 'multiculturalism'.[42] Hence, it requires a more expansive analysis which incorporates sexuality, nation, ethnicity, age and ability in parity with the broader categories of race, class and gender.[43] The unpacking but tying together of the themes of analyses which include nation, nationalism, nation state and national identity has aimed to align power relations of the nation with structural analysis of racism, capitalism, and patriarchy.[44]

Britain was built on and continues to strive and reap the benefits of the unrecognized labour of Black women. There are structural inequalities which are detrimental to Black British women, yet enable and privilege White, middle-class, heterosexual men and women. Reynolds notes the importance of this as 'Black women were judged purely on their reproductive labour capacities and they were positioned as breeders whose role involved reproducing the future labour force'.[45] Due to this disparity Black women's identities were constantly in the dichotomy of 'men/women', 'virgin/whore', 'work/home' and 'dominant/subordinate'.[46] Black women were not deemed worthy of their femininity, they were as capable at the 'men', they were the 'whores' who symbolized the antithesis of sexual purity which was afforded to White women. They were regulated to work, which was laborious, demeaning and physically painstaking. Adhering to the myth that Black women are able to do more than physical labour, thus they can do more than the average woman can; they are self-sacrificing, emotionless and less feminine.

Negating stereotypes in higher education

For some of the young women discussions diverged into stereotypical discourses such as 'Black girl attitude', the 'angry Black women' related to experiences they have had in education. A final-year student Shay (twenty-one) explains, 'I constantly stand against the idea Black women have attitudes or are "ghetto" and uneducated'. Shay, while studying and working part time is also aware of the stereotypes of Black women and girls in education. Therefore, in her communication and interactions with her tutors, she actively attempts to refute and subvert the notion of herself or her friends being the Black girl with 'an attitude' or coming across as 'uneducated' or not prepared for the final stages of her studies and subsequently the world of work, which she'll be moving on to.

Mirza explains this in terms of invisibility and visibility in higher educational settings, 'the construction of the invisibility/visibility split in terms of Black women's embodied experiences as Black bodies "out of place"'.[47] Yet so too can Black women be 'celebrated' in colourful promotional brochures, thus they can be objectified and commercialized. Given the lack of Black women, particularly in some professions, this can cause discomfort for students. A postgraduate student, Cassandra (twenty-eight) explained that 'in my chosen field there is a lack of women of colour (WOC) and in my experiences, I often feel discriminated against or treated differently'. Feeling out of place in the university and excluded for Cassandra has become the norm; this is a sacrifice she is willing to make in order to get to the desired career she wants.

Education was an important feature for many of the young women, as many mentioned wanting to better educate themselves to respond to representations. In this sense, education can operate as a buffer against racialized and gendered portrayals of their womanhood. For some this is used a strategic response to navigate the overtly sexualized images of Black women, which work to limit their identities. In this regard, many felt that they had to 'work twice as hard' to prove themselves outside of stereotypical images of Black womanhood. Many Black women feel that they must constantly prove themselves by working harder than their White counterparts work to combat negative stereotypes.[48] A final-year music student, Mary (twenty-two) explained, 'being a classical singer is already negating any stereotypes but I feel I do have to work harder to be considered, mostly due to my lack of experience in comparison to other singers'.

Mary's experiences can be considered from several perspectives. Firstly, she is in the area of classical music, which is not commonly associated with many Black artists and singers. Secondly, she aware of this and feels that she has to work to negate stereotypes of Black women and Black people more generally, simultaneously, feeling inexperienced in comparison to singers. The lack of experience which Mary speaks of could stem from a lack of networks, contacts, and ultimately garner opportunities to develop in classical music.

Tionne (sixteen), a college media student, feels that working hard to subvert dominant portrayals of Black womanhood would be useful to her when attempting to resist stereotypical representations. From this viewpoint, some Black women feel that their strength is necessitated by the challenges presented in a racist and sexist society.[47] Tionne explains how she negotiates this in her personal life 'by ignoring, not paying any attention and trying to better educate myself'. Education for Tionne is a way of negotiating her status in British society as a young Black British woman. The education which she speaks of isn't from a British school or college perspective, nor it is based within the Eurocentric/Anglicized curriculum. What Tionne is referring to is the personal education of reading and exploring knowledge of herself and outside what is formally taught in education. She will see knowledge and understanding of herself, Black people and others in history and the current context which impact her so she is able to challenge and refute discourses which seek to malign and distort who she is.

Similarly to Tionne, Mary and Cassandra are negotiating their identities through attempting to subvert and refute stereotypes of Black womanhood. They are all too aware of the negotiation from a personal and social categorization perspective which has created obstacles and disjunctures for them.

For economic survival taking on representations such as the strong matriarchal superwoman may be necessary for some women's survival. Black women need to navigate both material and discursive obstacles – about whose crisis counts, who can legitimately speak on their behalf, and who can mobilize for social justice.[48]

The chapter has provided a preview into the lived experiences of Black British women while presenting just a snippet of their lives. It demonstrates that being Black and women, being educated, living and working in Britain presents challenging and multifaceted experiences reaped in systemic racism, gender and class inequalities and stereotyping of Black womanhood. Although the picture isn't all bleak, as the lived experiences are and will not just be consigned to stereotypes, or maligned misrepresentations or tropes, there is much work to be done for Black women, Black men and our allies. There is the need to work together to reinform, reconstruct and create knowledge of Black British women's lived experiences. There will be many negotiations for Black women, such as, 'Do I immediately challenge these insidious microaggressions from the class teacher who consistently questions, "Where are you really from?" or do I leave this place of work which fails to treat and pay me equally?' The negotiation process is consequential, pervasive and can have severe life consequences. It is complex and conflictual and often conflates axes which are racialized, gendered, classed, nationalized and other aspects of a Black British women's identity.

This chapter is a call for action to challenge, refute and resist the skewed discourses within which Black British women are framed. For all of the Black women reading this, yes, we'll face many challenges and obstacles, but so too are we pioneers, enterprising, educators, inventors, resisters and so much more. There is pride, inclusion and much to celebrate for Black British women.

Part Three

Counter-narratives

Fierce intersections: Thinking through portraits of Black queer youth in Britain

Eddie Bruce-Jones and Ajamu X

I also have a different physical relationship with this type of print. I have to brush the paper with things. With digital, it's mediated somewhere else, by a big conglomerate somewhere. With analog photography, I am not separate form the process, I am a part of it, I am in the mix. With *Fierce*, the image is an artefact or object that involves reflection on the process and the medium of photography, to try to break down these binaries. A lot of the meaning in the photograph is what the viewer brings to the image. Stuart Hall said, people see what they want to see. So I try to create beautiful, meaningful images that people can connect to.

Ajamu[1]

Ajamu Ikwe-Tyehimba, known by his artist name 'Ajamu', is an acclaimed fine art photographic artist, archive curator and radical sex activist based in London. His work grapples with, among other things, the intersection of queerness and Blackness, by reading Blackness through a queer lens and queerness through a Black lens, and he has developed the reputation as an artist who is always ready to challenge society's perceptions of Black queerness through his art, and particularly, through his photography. Ajamu's work, his combination of activism and photography, and this exhibition in particular, have been featured on independent media sites, such as Afropunk[2] and OpenDemocracy.[3]

There are many notable queer Black UK artists doing extraordinary work, in Roderick Ferguson's terms, in the service of 'intersecting particularities' and in opposition to the universality of the (White) racialized heteronormative citizen. These include performance artist and poet Travis Alabanza, poets P. J. Samuels, Dean Atta, Lassana Shabazz, Jacob V. Joyce and Keith Jarrett, mixed-media visual artist Rabs Lanzicot, and dancer Zinzi Minott, to name but a few. Their voices are thought-leading and lend invaluably to a broader social critique of power, particularly around race, gender and sexuality.

Fierce: Portraits of Young Black Queers is a photographic exhibition of Ajamu's work, which opened on 1 February 2013 in Guild Hall, in the City of London. I thought a joint analysis of the *Fierce* exhibition would be a productive entry point from which to discuss intersectionality in the UK for several reasons. First, the portraits – large-scale, black and white platinum prints of queer British young people – coupled with the exhibition title *Fierce*, leave us to contemplate the layers of meaning and value of the exhibition as a work. Second, Ajamu's negotiation of the art world in the UK and elsewhere, given his own identity and the political identification he attributes to his work, tells a story of how Black queer subjects and artists are positioned within visual narratives of Britain. Third, Ajamu's work as a visual artist should be recognized for its beauty, consistent presence in the Black queer community of the UK, and in its constant un-covering and uplifting of under-represented people in the UK. Fourth, Ajamu's prominence as an artist and outspoken champion within the queer Black community over several decades in Britain gave me the immediate sense that the discussion would be multidimensional, in terms of longstanding artistic practice and political vision that has helped pave the way for newer queer Black artists to emerge.

Ajamu and I know one another from queer Black events and through mutual friends, and I have viewed a number of his exhibitions. Through discussing *Fierce*, we discuss joy, strength, desire, and pleasure. Ajamu reflects on the connotation of strength that underpins the term 'fierce' and, in the same context, I ask what his chosen descriptor 'queer' conveys in his work. 'Queer is not used as an identity but rather as a politic in this work', Ajamu says quickly as we excitedly dive right into the heart of the matter, after brief and warm *hellos*. 'A lot of the work on Black LGBTQ+ people is framed around a deficit model or paradigm in which it is hard to discuss celebrations and aspirations'.

I raise the question of whether and how the exhibition contributes to a wider archive of queer Blackness, whether it attests to and enables the public to witness the rounded reflection of some aspect of queer Black life. It is the foundational work of Crenshaw in developing a theoretical lens of intersectionality that demands an examination of the invisibilized intersections of experiences of identity and to 'defend a politics of social location rather than to vacate and destroy it'.[4] It is also central to the work of writers and academics who have used an intersectional perspective to take forward what Roderick Ferguson describes as 'queer of colour critique'[5] and what Fatima el-Tayeb gestures toward when 'queering ethnicity in post-national Europe'.[6]

We agree to have a longer, in-person discussion. 'We need to talk about pleasure of Black LGBTQ+ people outside of the context of sexual health',

Ajamu says. 'We mean second-generation Black British people as well. People *get* "Black" to some extent, or they *get* "LGBTQ+" to some extent, but "Black LGBTQ+" or "Black queer": hmmm. Much of the politics is based on a binary framework'. By this I understand Ajamu to mean that certainly mainstream politics but also even some Black and queer movement politics of struggle, respectively, can tend towards single-issue approaches.

After sitting with the transcription of our conversation for some time, I broke the conversation into four acts, lifting from the two-hour exchange a few core sections that resonate with the analytical drive of this volume.[7]

Act 1: The lens is the frame

Ajamu and I sit down in the living room of his flat in Brixton, clutching two mugs of tea, and excitedly begin to connect aspects of his artistic creative process, his politics of identity and his vision for how his work might start conversations that interrupt common conceptions of Blackness, queerness, youth and British identity. The first thing to mention is Ajamu's careful conceptual consideration of his subjects and the form in which they will be portrayed. This is obvious for an artist, but for someone without much of a photographer's eye or depth of appreciation for the history of the form, I gain a fuller understanding, as we leaf through the portrait prints, of how they are meant to engage with the world they have been ushered into.

The prints are large, kept in a large box, which Ajamu does not retrieve and open until mid-way through our conversation. Before opening the box, he describes the process of producing platinum prints. Ajamu mentions that he, as an artist, has a different relationship with the platinum print than with digital prints – a physical relationship, requiring the artist to literally brush the paper with a solution. He notes that the blending of analogue and digital technologies is a gesture toward showing the complexity and interconnectedness of the image and the production of the image, which is akin to disrupting the binary between the politics and identities of his subjects. He states:

> Platinum prints are softer. The softer tone gives you more of an intimacy. With that, the print looks more painterly. You then get a bit of a photograph-versus-painting dynamic. Historically, you had photography killing painting, and then digital killing analogue. So how do we hold it all together and keep it straight? It's the same as holding together the Black-versus-White, straight-versus-gay, the gender binary. We need to move beyond identity, and move to processes and mediums.

Platinum prints are the most archival of processes, and I am interested in the materiality, the physicality of the print.

In some ways, when Ajamu mentions moving beyond identity, he does not suggest abandoning identity, but moving beyond the binary, single-lens view of identity that we are socialized to understand. He uses two methods, analogue and digital, to create something different, which mirrors the complex intersection of identities at the intersection. Additionally, of course, there is an attentiveness to the production and deployment of identity for some outcome – a form of staging or, thought of differently, inhabiting identity through an act of politics.

During the conversation, he reminds me several times that he is 'taking these photographs with Bessie', and when I finally ask who Bessie is, he reveals that Bessie is the name of the old camera he uses. It is a slow-process camera, with a cloth that goes over the photographer's head to block out light. He tells me that while slow-process techniques slow things down and open up the photographic practice to chance and experimentation, digital photography speeds things up. This element of risk when using the older camera, for him, had been important in the early development of his work on pushing the boundaries of race and gender. This makes me think of the improvisational but purposeful and profound nuance of jazz. According to Ajamu, using this older method of photography slows things down and creates a certain intimacy, a type of foreplay, between the photographer and the sitter.

Bruce-Jones: Describe *Fierce* for me. What type of portraiture is *Fierce*?
Ajamu: You have the sitter looking straight out at the viewer. It's a
    face-to-face encounter. Richard Avedon is one of my favourite
    portrait photographers, this work was in homage to him. His subject
    was typically against a White backdrop. It removed them from their
    environment. White backdrop is usually used in advertising – in
    baby photographs, and food photographs. It's trying to be celebratory
    or trying to sell something; it's high key, very bright. That's the first
    feel I wanted it to have. These twenty-five queers could come from
    anywhere in the world. I've located them in the world but pulled
    them from their cultural backdrop. I wanted to get across that fierce
    Black queers exist around the world, and these twenty-five are not
    unlike others in the world. I'm using queer, here, as a shorthand, even
    though I'm opposed to using queer as an identity, and that's part of
    the complexity around it.

Over the last fifteen years or so, we've seen these radical shifts within the field of photography, especially with social media. Independent production and independent darkrooms have closed down; the most popular images in the world are being taken from a phone in your back pocket. I am now linked with people online who I never knew existed. I would argue that since there are not a lot of social spaces that we meet in physically. Lots of our LGBTQ+ POCs meet virtually, in a virtual space, on the web. That's part of the backdrop for the style of these portraits.

Bruce-Jones: And so the White backdrop is for pulling your portrait subjects out of their everyday contexts?

Ajamu: That's right. The portraits are of a second generation of African, Afro-Caribbean and Black British-born people, under thirty-five years of age. For those of us whose parents came to Britain in the 1960s, we'd be the first generation of Black British-born people in the UK. We were the first 'out' generation. We'll be the first aged generation of Black British-born LGBTQ+ people. But the portraits are of the second generation, and so while context matters, the project was an attempt to speak also to the new digital age, and to reflect the everywhere-ness of Black British LGBTQ+ people … Part of it is to insert young Black queers into a nineteenth-century tradition that we weren't part of in such a visible way, certainly not in portraiture. I also wanted to create images in that tradition of young Black folk which are not based on the noble savage. Take a look at this platinum print of Keith.

Bruce-Jones: Stunning. There is something warm about the image, although it is in black and white.

Ajamu: The tones are more muted, the blacks are black, shadows deep, whites more delicate. So for me, the tonality of the print is a metaphor for how I want to talk about race, gender, and sexuality – how to deal with the nuances within those concepts. So we ought to move away from the banners of talking about those identities and move into looking at something far more entangled …

Bruce-Jones: I notice you say LGBTQ+ sometimes, and sometimes you say 'queer'. How are you distinguishing those terms?

Ajamu: I'd say I'm a gay man with a queer politic. 'Queer' should never be about an identity, because for me, anything should be able to fit into that framework. In its first movement, queer was like punk – it was more mischievous, more radical, more deviant. But now it's been cleaned up. The more LGBTQ+ politics and culture aspire towards the mainstream, the more it becomes sanitized, made palatable, it's more – it becomes trapped within the confines of respectability politics. Being 'respectable' requires a certain type of labour. The frustration is that queer is being read within a binary framework, 'queer versus heteronormativity'. Being so limited and responding all the time to heteronormativity, queer is sometimes seen through the prism of mainstream LGBTQ+ rights. It could become quite frigid and side-line non-binary people and people with different politics and practices around sexuality, love and gender, forcing them out of the equation and out of the conversation … The politics that brings in the dirt, and grit and messy stuff, is bound up in our creative power. Within our queer spaces in the UK, we are caught up in the deficit model because queer is being used as an identity and not a politic. That's not to say that you can't identify as queer, but what does that mean in your everyday experience? 'Queer' needs to be about doing something. It's what you do, politically and creatively.

Ajamu reflects on the tensions that arise between photographic form and the digital age when he decides on the format of his portraiture for *Fierce*. He re-envisions what a cannon of portraiture could look like if it featured Black queer people, and brings it into the digital era by 'lifting' the sitters from their contexts. Paradoxically, it is the lack of perceptible context that provides a strong indicator of context. It reminds us of the virtual commons, the rise of the selfie, and the constant marketing and promotion of lifestyle and aesthetic through social media platforms. In some ways, the virtual world allows us to imagine a different world, though in other ways, it is a nod to the impossibility of replacing the real with the virtual. We must acknowledge that virtual media is produced, framed and expressed within the realm of our social realities, even as it conveys the desire to transcend them.

The simultaneous blending together and transcending of fast-paced, market-oriented digital photography of the twenty-first century and the portraiture of the nineteenth century figuratively parallels the dialogic relationality that keeps identity categories and critique, play and even rejection of those categories within the same orbit. Ajamu mentions that, for him, the use of platinum prints allows him to engage with nuances in the image, the detail and soft tones that can make a black and white image look warm and rich. The banners of identity that seem to be in a different space for Ajamu are not necessarily absent in the images he produces, but they do a specific type of work. The type of representation of the *Fierce* sitters connects them through the common photographic form and style, while leaving the vastness of possibility of their differences to be imagined. This space of imagination is important so as not reproduce hegemonic ideas about who Black, queer young British people are or should be. It instrumentalizes the form and the image in the service of a critique of the time and circumstances of nineteenth-century portraiture, and is a critique of history, at the same time as it lifts aesthetic aspects of beauty, warmth and Black queerness. Ultimately, it seeks to be subversive in a particular way that is not immediately related to a rights-based framing of identity, but it does its work on the level of representational intersectionality, by countering an aesthetic that would seek to erase or ignore the particularities of being Black and queer at the same time.[8]

Ajamu also evokes the question, in his portrait series, of a togetherness of Black queer people. Is there a Black queer community? What does it look like? I think of the photos produced by Afropunk, the social platform and media collective, which are about fashion and eye-catching creative expression. This is quite the opposite. It is celebratory, but in muted tones; it is trying to isolate something, some essence. This may be demonstrative of what he is pushing for, beyond certain types of difference, but not beyond identity. After all, the form is meant also to critique the type of representation possible for Black queer people. What happens when we are put onto an austere pallet?

Ajamu's work, over the years, has been dedicated to exploring the relationship between Blackness, queerness, embodiment, desire, love and real human emotion, never compromising Blackness or queerness in his artistic representation of the people he works with. For this particular project, he chose sitters not only on the basis of identity but on the basis of the action and engagement the sitters have with this intersection – their politics, broadly defined. Keith Jarrett, a poet and writer featured in *Fierce*, engages with the embodiment of Blackness and queerness in his poetry. He writes:

> God of blue glove
> God of scanner wand
> Who has searched me and known
> How well I have folded
> These unsmiling frontiers
> Can't you see how I have steadied
> All my inflections?[9]

Jarrett weaves the insights from what might be imagined as a Black or queer or Black queer person passing through a security checkpoint or, maybe, some other figurative or literal policing situation in their everyday life. With a juxtaposition of the rules of state regulation with those of religion, he integrates the bodily with the ephemeral (knowing), personifies the institutions of state bordering and surveillance, and demonstrates how the speaker 'folds' and 'steadies their inflections' around the demands of the contesting authority. These are themes that comprise the ebb and flow of Black queer engagement with the state, but also themes that crosscut Black and queer individually in different ways, including in family and religious life. The intersection, here, is the recognition that such demands take on a multitude of dimensions when one experiences them in a composite register – 'how I have steadied *all* my inflections'.[10]

For both artists, keeping the connection to experience and keeping the criticism of social power relations centrally in the frame is important. Ajamu and Keith Jarrett do this in different ways, but both are in tune with the convergence of representing both Blackness and queerness in the same print and stanza. With art, the framing is in the centre; it's a deliberate centring. With politics of social life or legal change, we may forget that there are also frames, and that rights-based logics are strategic deployments rather than postmodern aspirations. This is something that certain criticisms of intersectionality tend to overlook.

Act 2: The politics of location

I wondered why Ajamu had chosen the Guild Hall as a venue for *Fierce*. The Guild Hall currently serves as the seat of local government for the City of London, housing the City of London Corporation which governs the 'Square Mile', now associated with a significant portion of London's banking commerce. It was built in the early part of the fifteenth century, and was a significant site during the Reformation.[11] The building is of great national symbolic import, including historically during a period where England was busy forging the machinery and techniques of imperial rule.

I asked Ajamu about the challenges he faced getting the exhibition *Fierce* and other projects shown in the various spaces he has approached. He mentioned having found that some gallery and museum curators do not approach queer Black artists partly due to the conservatism of their curatorial practices and collections, but also partly through a debilitating fear of tokenizing artists at the intersection, which paradoxically results in failure to show their work at all. I hadn't considered how that fear would stifle engagement by curators to approach artists. Ajamu said that he needed to approach certain venues proactively to help alleviate some of this fear, but also to 'prove that there was an audience' at this intersection – that Black queerness or Black British queer youth were not conversations too specific to advance by way of his portraits. He mentioned that, at the Guild Hall, he was not aware that other Black queer artists had ever occupied that space, and that occupying this space was part of the appeal.

> Ajamu: Ah, yes, Guild Hall. Well, it is an amazing public space. The Pre-Raphaelites – I love those artists and painters. But there are notions in that space about colonialism and the very question of Britishness. At the opening of *Fierce*, in this space, we'd have young Black queers having an intergenerational conversation about how they imagine and relate to Britishness … The space had only attracted a particular demographic, and particular types of events. I wanted to bring Black LGBTQ+ people into the Guild Hall because of its history. This is its first Black exhibition and first queer exhibition, in the centre of the City of London, I think. *Fierce* is about celebrating a young generation of Black queers, and the opening was packed. Everyone, coming into a space they'd never been before, right in the heart of London.
>
> … Vocalist, David McAlmont closed out the opening evening with a wonderful performance of 'Diamonds are Forever', how Black and queer is that!
>
> The space that it was in was a place it could do a lot of work in. I love shiny new galleries, but there's a different conversation that you can have in a building that has been around for hundreds of years. I love Victorian spaces, anyhow. Think about the National Portrait Gallery and the many buildings that house art, slavery money is in the mix. But it's a stunning building and stunning space as well, and it's important to grapple with those tensions and deal with what the space upholds and what we can do with it.
>
> Bruce-Jones: Yes, and to acknowledge that history is actually the present – we see it all around us.
>
> Ajamu: Indeed. And how do we play with some of these temples and go, 'Okay, I'm going to chip away at this bit here by doing this type of work'? People come to see portraits, but aren't just seeing portraits. Surreptitiously, they're feeling and getting a certain politic, and those things inhabit the same space. That's what I like. One week you had all these Black queers in the space, and the next week, the Lord Mayor. (Laughs). For me, it does something.
>
> Bruce-Jones: Interesting. I suppose the stories about how people did or did not wish to engage in what has turned out to be quite an intimate and publicly visible project are important too, almost as important as the artistic renderings themselves. How did you envision you would archive the portraits and also the process of making *Fierce*?

Ajamu: In 2005, Topher Campbell and I launched The Queen's Jewels, which became Europe's first dedicated Black LGBTQ+ archive, and *Fierce* is ultimately a photographic archival project. It's archival in the sense that it's capturing a moment of another generation of Black LGBTQ+ people emerging. This is a group of people you will hear about now or in the next few years. So how do we tell stories that reflect our experiences? And these twenty-five people will have links and connections around the world, we can't forget. It's saying that this moment is happening now. And there are other movements happening the same time, and around our Black LGBTQ+ experiences, this is what we may need to look toward. Because in ten or twenty years' time, this will still be around. I'm saying this, because this is a history of the now, and of the future. We're creating history. It's not only about the past, it's about doing a history of the new. *Fierce* was about that. Now, most of these young people are coming up to thirty-plus ... Also, putting things in institutions tries to clean up the queer archive, cleans up the messiness. So how do we maintain a break from the linear framework? The work I did in my masters was about juxtaposing objects from the past in a way you don't expect. So part of my thinking will always be not only who is included, but what is excluded and how we account for that, and what stories and experiences of Black queers we also exclude, through LGBTQ+ respectability politics or the politics of Black respectability.

Bruce-Jones: So is the temporariness of the exhibition of *Fierce* in the Guildhall important for being able to, as inclusively as possible, include and archive Black queer people and their stories – in other words, not committing *Fierce* to an institution?

Ajamu: Sort of. How do we feel the archive? What is the effect of the archive? What do we want the archive to do to us? With *Fierce*, when they came into that space, the work did something to us, it did something to those Black queer people. It was about a moment, that we can remember, but the moment changes. So time, as in permanence, has to go. And then these big clunky things around identity have to go as well, actually. And we go back to something that is experiential. And how do we talk about that without the default to identity or race, gender, etc.? I'm not saying identity is not included in that, but there has to be a way to articulate these things in a more sensory experience. There's a danger when we only look at ourselves through a lens of identity or visibility or rationality, when there are some things we don't or can't talk about because we don't have a sense-logic to it. When we move through the world too wedded to time, and to the world's sense of order, we've actually put those other ways of being in the world on hold. Because we can't grasp it or hold it. *Fierce* and this project is trying to grapple with that.

As we discuss the ways *Fierce* engages with history and identity, I am struck by the effect that the form will have on us as viewers of the work, both now and some ways into the future, in disrupting our sense of time and place – using nineteenth-century photographic techniques to render Black queer young British people in the Guild Hall, which is a nation-building space. I had the sense that he was speaking to a future audience of Black LGBTQ+ British youth by creating a vision of this disruption in the present. In some ways, as he mentions, *Fierce* is dependent on the recognition of identity in order to achieve the subversive dissonance that causes this disruption. However, the aspiration of going beyond identity, at some stage in some unwritten future moment, still undergirds the artistic aim – to transcend the 'clunky' conceptual boundaries that threaten, like concrete ogres, to crush the delicate and subtle beauty of the people in the portraits. This is a constant tension, a political and social paradox of power, rights and recognition, borne just as much by art as it is by law.

We talk a bit more about identity and the staging in the Guild Hall. Ajamu's beautiful image, of 'chipping away at temples', resonates with the physical spaces, demystifying them and divesting them of the symbolic power and exclusivity that they represent. It also applies to the temple of identity – the narrative and expectations that go along with inhabiting roles that set the terms of our political and social engagement. Sometimes the constant self-protection and self-defence from the dangers of falling out of line with expectations around race, gender and sexuality occupy so much of our energy that they distract us from being able to realize all of our creative potential. But sometimes, occupying the particular space of speaking from an identity position, to secure a right or to make particular form of violence legible, for instance, is indeed a question of survival.[12] In a sense, the conundrum describes the longstanding question of reform versus transformation, where we hold on to the aspiration of our transcendence of social problems of power and difference even whilst we strategically deploy that difference in the form of identity to gain otherwise impossible traction.

Law, like art, constantly mediates and intervenes in social life with the different ways in which it emphasizes and mutes, embraces and disavows identity. Given the formal and informal, sanctioned and discouraged forms of recognition and deployment of identity in social life, the response of 'identity does not exist' would not be a sufficient response to the continued relevance of identity politics. It is clear that default stereotypical assumptions about groups stymie social progress, but perhaps art, like laws, demonstrates that the momentum of critical, forward change can be best recovered by grappling with the concepts and vocabulary that we have at our disposal, to leverage radical change possibilities against impending ones, radical change against banal, ongoing reform.

Ajamu has gone into schools to engage with young people on Black British LGBTQ+ experiences, and his work asks how narratives of experience from his generation fit with the experiences of young people. He noticed, during the various uprisings of young people in London over the decades, including the 2011 protests, that young people, particularly young Black people, were being criminalized, and that this featured heavily in discussions with Black LGBTQ+ youth. Additionally, as an out person who is prominent in the Black queer community, Ajamu came into contact with some Black LGBTQ+ people who were not out and did not want to be photographed. The virtual world, where anonymity can be preserved in some way with pseudonyms and cropped photographs, enables a different negotiation of privacy than a head-and-shoulders portrait. This was a particular feature of the *Fierce* project that related to the various circumstances facing the community.

To this end, Ajamu presents his portrait series as a 'history of the new', or of the now. He is speaking to present and future generations about the present conjuncture, in which young Black queer artists are taking forward a range of positions and interests without compromising the unique convergence of their Blackness and queerness, in a political and social sense. Underscoring that the circumstances and experiences of Black queer British people is also shaped by the political context and social imaginary of their respective generations is important for Ajamu in his work, as he accounts for these differences by calling them into productive tension, rather than blending them out – one of the most crucial components of any intersectional project.

Act 3: Fierceness as futurity

As Ajamu and I leaf through the box of large prints from *Fierce*, he stops when we come to the portrait of Julius Reuben. He lifts the portrait from the box, and holds it up. I imagine it displayed in the austere Guild Hall, which I visited several times while working as an attorney in the neighbouring building, and I smile. Reuben is staring directly into the camera, unsmiling but with an open face, arms crossed, wearing a structured scarf and hat styled like one worn by many an elder woman of the African diaspora, but made with a shiny metallic and futuristic-looking fabric.

When I ask Ajamu for his thoughts on the term 'fierce', he describes 'fierce' as a future-looking, aspirational concept. This strikes me, particularly because the associations I have with the term relate to making a radical impact on the present – I had not considered the future. At the same time, it certainly resonates with the portrait of Reuben.

> Ajamu: Fierce is that extra thing you're trying to get to … How do you explain that thing right outside your grasp, that thing that's always there? It is that set of things you can't explain in logical terms. The senses, the sensual. There are ways in which we experience identity that we don't always talk about. Fierce is also those warriors fighting White settler colonialism – my Fierce sitters are warriors, this is our genealogy.
>
> Bruce-Jones: Yes, that intangible ever-present, or ever-future something that we can nevertheless perceive. I get it. And I also get the reference to genealogy or inheritance, of struggle, and that the struggle is about racism and colonialism, as much as it is about sexual and gender liberation.
>
> Ajamu: Yeah. That's also what I mean by aspiration – putting the struggles together.
>
> Bruce-Jones: A particularly queer Black tradition of aspiration.
>
> Ajamu: Yeah. Well you know, there is no real template to being Black and LGBTQ+ in this country. Notions of play, imagination, fiction, myth-building, all have to come into it as well … The word 'fierce' has cultural currency beyond race and sexuality. Naming a project is a key part of the process. You know, naming is centre to one's identity. Even the word 'fierce', I'd need it to do what it needs to do. I didn't want to call it 'Black Gay Portraits'.
>
> Bruce-Jones: Like tapping into something that allows people to draw their own associations, in the hope that the associations draw out some form of broader social critique.
>
> Ajamu: Yes, yes. Like years ago when Rukus! did the thing about 'The Queen's Jewels', it's about bringing humour into the politic as well. The queen's jewels – it's negative. But jewels, is about private parts as well, and when people would google 'the queen's jewels', they'd come across us and the Buckingham Palace. So that's part of British humour. (Laughs). There's a double entendre. So fierce is something people can hold and work with. It doesn't mean Black and gay, but it's that thing, that thing you can't articulate. So that's it.

Also, the thing around 'fierce' – the Marlon Riggs, Snapology,[13] that was all my reference point in the nineties. It was about choosing something Black and gay, and drawing upon our multiple histories, pulling on the resources of our multiplicity from around the work. It's part of our history. So then *Fierce* draws upon that as well.

In Ajamu's work, one can readily recognize what Roderick Ferguson calls a 'queer of color critique'. According to Ferguson, 'a queer of color critique addresses minority cultural forms as both within and outside canonical genealogies, pointing to the ruptural possibilities of those forms means that culture is not simply exhausted by its complicity with regulation'.[14] Ajamu plays with tropes of portraits that make a statement as contemporary art, juxtaposing old formats with subjects that subvert the imprint of the canon, while always calling upon something just beyond the image. This 'something extra that you're trying to get to' that Ajamu defines as fierce mirrors the possibility of rupture, of going beyond the 'canonical genealogy' that Ferguson describes.

Ajamu draws inspiration, in part, from a transnational discussion on Black queer life, by way of Marlon Riggs's contribution to exploring the cultural significance of Black gay men's social experience in US cities in the eighties and nineties. Through the transnational aspect, he emphasizes the multiple sources, experiences and systems of meaning among Black queer people that, while different, can be connected and co-extended.

The relevance of Ajamu's connecting Black queer stories across national borders, but still noting the differences among them, and of juxtaposing the important openness, the fierceness of Black queer creativity and politics with Black and White portraiture, is at least in part to situate the political critique he is making with art in the explicit and implicit tension, and importantly also the corporeal aspects, of being both Black and queer, and capturing that in an image. This imaging (or imagining) work has nuanced local meaning, but it also undoubtedly has broad international resonances.

Act 4: Keeping desire at the intersection

A core aspect of Ajamu's engagement with Black queerness, one that he insists should not get swallowed up by the respectability politics of commercial sensibilities and mainstream social acceptability, is desire. As a proposition at the intersection of Blackness and queerness, his is particularly crucial because of the ways in which Black queer people have been made to encounter both racist and anti-queer logics of sex, desire, and body politics, which threatens to mute the richness of experience and fullness of political contribution of Black queer people.

> Ajamu: The last project I did, on Black male sex-workers, shows that there are still voices that are marginalized within our LGBTQ+ communities, and if you're going to have your narrative down pat about what heterosexuals are doing to you, we have to have our politic down pat about what we are doing within our own communities as well. And *Fierce* is part of that jigsaw puzzle. A lot of my work is not about finding answers, but about rethinking ways in which these dots can be joined up, if they can, because sometimes they can't, but that's okay too. It's about mining this space, as Ajamu, activist, actor, lover, son.
>
> I don't find a lot of the politics sexy. So if we are going to sidestep our sexiness and fierceness, and talk about only what's been done to us, we're missing a trick. For me, it's about people realizing when I kiss my partner, it's still political, when we fuck, it's still political, and people need to know that within our Benetton LGBTQ+ community, there are still things we don't talk about.
>
> We can talk about homophobia, but we need to still address transphobia, sissyphobia, and racism within our own communities as well.
>
> Bruce-Jones: It makes us reflect on our own roles in domination and exclusion, our own complicity.
>
> Ajamu: And submission too! If we are in a system of domination, if we submit, we're benefiting too. How do we try and work through that? All of it is entangled. The frustrating thing is that we cannot unravel it all, it's meshed already. So then to talk about someone else's power, we always also have to reflect on our own power too, and how we navigate that power. Even if that power seems quite limited according to others, we also have agency.
>
> And central to that point, my own lecturer says, 'If things were otherwise, what would the otherwise look like?' That's what we're gesturing toward. How would we learn how to inhabit that space that is enmeshed and not clear cut? Entangled is my word of the moment …
>
> Bruce-Jones: A significant critique of the same-sex marriage campaigns has been that a focus on marriage has emphasized a certain type of sexual politics that can be presented as respectable, and has lost track of the liberating concept of 'queer'.[15] How do you view that criticism?

Ajamu: I get that. One of the projects I have in the works is called
Blissful Chaos. This project is around looking at the first generation
of Black queer people in Britain, doing work around kink, BDSM
and pleasure. We have stopped talking about the body and dirt, and
intimacy and grit. It's been cleaned up. It's not actually okay.

Lots of conversations are around sexual health. But we need to get
back to talking about sex. We do things behind closed doors that are
private, but things that are shaped by public discourse we need to talk
about identity in this messy, sensuous kind of way …

When I do portraits, I come into the eyes with the focus, and
everything else is a bit less focused, also with my fierce sitters, I
wanted them to be looking straight at you. There's also focusing
in on what I as a photographer find attractive as well. Everyone I
photographed, there is always something about them that I find
sexually attractive, and I focus in on that. I like the fact that the
people in the work will be desired as well. And then there's something
soft and gentle that comes into it.

Fierce is like trying to do intersectionality without doing
intersectionality. It creates hierarchies around identities; that's
important work, but not as interesting. It may exclude other ways
in which we can be and are in the world already. There are primary,
recognizable identities, there are hierarchies of oppression. But what
about the unsaid things? If you talk about my race, religions, etc., also
talk about me being a kingster, a top or bottom, an SM master as well;
it leaves those ways of being out of the frame. However, it's important
work. It needs to do that other thing as well, because what it sounds
like is that queer has been cold and clinical or left out. It's not doing
the thing that it needs to do.

Bruce-Jones: What you're saying reminds me of Audre Lorde's essay,
'The Uses of the Erotic', where she describes the political power of
claiming and standing in one's own desires and connection, including
sexual connection, with others.[16]

Ajamu: Yes! I was thinking the same. We talk about sexuality without
talking about sex. It leaves out the body. It forgets pleasure and
forgets desire. Let's embrace the things that are not respectable for a
change. And that way, we complicate these other kinds of narratives
simultaneously. And for me, it doesn't sound sensuous. It should be
sensuous. It's important work, but there is a danger of always framing
our experiences about the social and cultural and excluding sexual
and political, the sensual-philosophical, all the stuff we don't talk
about publicly.

Essex Hemphill, in one of his pieces, he said he wanted people to know that he was a good fuck as well, to keep the body in the mix. If not, it's weighted towards one thing, and all of it was a part of his sexual politics. In the same way that we should not create hierarchies of oppression, we should not leave sexual politics out of our understanding of who we are, and we have multiple complex and nuanced experiences.

Bruce-Jones: Of course, we always have to be vigilant that desire is not flipped back on us in a way that allows us to be merely consumed.

Ajamu: Of course. But I ask myself: does my politics feed me, does it nourish me? Of course there is shit to fight, but we should not lose sight of the joy, pleasure, desire, and the things that make us who we are, actually. Sometimes the victim narrative is not always our narrative. Sometimes people pull us into the narrative, because that is the only way they can deal with us. As much as possible, I try and set my own agenda, so as not to be instrumentalized that way. I think as Black LGBTQ+ people, we should never be afraid of our fierceness. Maybe, it's because we're afraid of our fierceness, we be pulled into things that don't nourish us. 'Tone it down', 'you're too Black', 'you're too queer'. We should not be afraid of our own fierceness. Whether it's coming from our families, or the community, we should challenge that also. Wherever it comes from, the 'tone it down' is a big problem.

For me, the word 'intersectionality' sounds cold, it sounds clinical. Like I'm in this laboratory, and that's how my experience is being viewed. Of course, great things happen in a laboratory. But does the concept seduce me? Not as much as 'entanglement', but I suppose they do different work.

Ajamu demonstrates that there is intersectional work being done at every stage of his conceptualizing and execution of his art. The aesthetic negotiation of how this plays out, grappling with grit, desire, and aspiration, takes control of the use of identity politics, equipping it with the ability to do work that is aspirational, almost utopic, driven by a necessity to explore the full possibilities of our beings, without losing sight of the importance to give regard to the strictures of that convene on our positions and our bodies. This enables us to make certain positions visible where they were once invisible, and to subvert the narratives that would relegate the fullness and diversity of these positions to a register of illegibility. 'Lots of galleries can get their heads around Black *or* LGBTQ+, but Black *and* LGBTQ+ or Black *and* queer? What do we do with that?' Ajamu reflects. '*Fierce* was doing something that was not the default model that I had'.

Ajamu's juxtaposition of the concepts of intersectionality and entanglement prompted me to think of the symposium on the work of Sadiya Hartman that we both attended in 2017 in London's Serpentine Gallery, where she described entanglement as a practice. With that in mind, perhaps we can consider that entanglement is layered on top of and enmeshed with intersectionality, sort of like Black queer politics are layered on top of and enmeshed with standing in, or occupying one's own intersectional identity.[17]

> Ajamu: The messiness, the grit, is the entanglement, it's also a process. It's what you can't articulate, and we use what we can articulate to try and approximate, to get as close as we can to the mess. So having a creative process helps us grapple with and inhabit that entanglement. How do we ever inhabit that which is always already entangled? We do it all the time.

Mediating the praxis of intersectionality: Curatorial poaching on Tumblr

Kadian Pow

Intersectionality names the compound discrimination in United States law that Black women often experience due to race and gender being treated as separate categories of experience. The concept has existed for centuries in the lived reality and works of Black women, but Crenshaw's term gave the phenomenon an accessible identity. More than thirty years later, intersectionality is becoming common parlance in the realm of social justice. The modern movement for Black Lives is inextricably tied to the affordances of social media platforms like Twitter and Tumblr.[1] Our lives are increasingly mediated by digital spaces, affecting the ways we communicate and interpret the world around us and ourselves. What interests me is the praxis of intersectionality and the implications for its use within the mediated nexus of popular culture. This paper seeks to understand the productive ways in which intersectionality theory is being deployed in the popular consciousness on social media, the porous boundaries of which complicate attempts to contain intersectionality to a geographical area. I will analyse the intersectionality I engaged on Tumblr, and then theorize the term 'curatorial poaching' and its relationship to intersectionality. Finally, the paper will consider the contours and limitations of relying on social media to understand the framing of intersectionality.

Intersectionality has been a key pillar of Critical Race Theory (CRT), which examines the intersection of race, law and power in society. The applicability of intersectionality allows us to make visible the axes of discrimination – class, race, sexuality, to name a few – that are often obscured, or made invisible, in feminist and anti-racist discourse. Writing about his increasing focus on CRT praxis outside academia, law professor Robert A. Williams (1997) notes that CRT reaches more people with messages aimed at those outside academic and legal communities.[2] The praxis of intersectionality is the method by which the theory is practised or engaged. In twenty-first century mainstream, online media publications in the USA and UK, it is not uncommon to see 'intersectionality' published in the title of an article when addressing feminism, politics and culture.[3] Moreover, even when not reflected in the title, the journalists grapple with how intersectionality is present in racial dynamics of the television we consume or matters of environmental justice.[4] The examples above reflect just one of the ways in which intersectionality is now presented for popular consumption. But critical understanding does not always accompany increased visibility. Crenshaw has lamented that she is 'amazed at how [intersectionality] gets over- and under-used; sometimes I can't even recognize it in the literature any more'.[5] It is true that the term has become 'buzzy', and depending on the context in which it is used, virtue-signals one's politics, particularly in online social circles.

A buzzword is not a praxis, and intersectionality's function in the online space is not necessarily synonymous with the performative or uncritical. The Twitter hashtag #SolidarityIsForWhiteWomen was created in 2013 by Mikki Kendall, a Black woman writer and activist, to collate responses to systemic patterns from White women who use their power and privilege to dismiss race as a feminist issue, and whilst building their platforms on the targeting of women of colour as aggressive actors in the feminist movement. Kendall's response was on a digital platform because that is where the injury took place. Moreover, it allowed her to signal to other injured Black women, creating intersectionality discourse for themselves and others to learn from. Since then, the hashtag has gone on to become shorthand to critique a feminist agenda that centres Whiteness and obscures intersectional oppression in the lives of Black women, and other women of colour. This is but one example of the ways in which the architecture of social media enables reification of intersectionality. The #BlackLivesMatter hashtag, and the subsequent constellation of movements and organization created around The Movement for Black Lives further exemplify how the boundaries between digital and physical space become intertwined through the praxis of intersectionality.

Tumblr and participatory culture

Intersectionality's praxis in the digital space matters because of the way in which that space is shaping the production of popular culture, and, in turn, being shaped *by* popular culture. Stuart Hall notes that the popular is an arena of constant struggle, negotiation over meaning, and a place in which hegemonies are challenged.[6] Studies have shown that African Americans use social media platforms at an average rate 8% higher than their White counterparts.[7] Perhaps the most consistent, multi-axes framing and circulation of intersectionality's reach into modern culture and politics can be found on the social media platform Tumblr. Founded in 2007 by David Karp and now owned by Verizon Communications subsidiary, Oat Inc., Tumblr is a micro-blogging and social media platform with a network of nearly 450 million blogs. Though more insular, Tumblr is nearly as publicly accessible as Twitter. It allows users to create and post their own multimedia content, as well as follow, comment upon, and circulate content of other users. Searchable by key words and hashtags, the platform has gained a reputation for being a place for artists, kids, activists and Social Justice Warriors (SJWs).[8] Whilst mainstream media outlets and commercial brands are represented on Tumblr, most of the site's networked blogs belong to individuals who use the space to create, curate and circulate content to which they are passionately attached. The site's motto is 'Come for what you love. Stay for what you discover'.

What makes Tumblr a compelling social media space to study is that it is a micro-publishing platform, providing its users with a set of easy-to-use tools to create and consume highly visual, multimedia content upon which the platform depends. Or, as Tumblr puts it:

> We made it really, really simple for people to make a blog and put whatever they want on it. Stories, photos, GIFs, TV shows, links, quips, dumb jokes, smart jokes, Spotify tracks, mp3s, videos, fashion, art, deep stuff. Tumblr is 434 million different blogs, filled with literally whatever.[9]

Tumblr's tools effectively transform the producer and consumer into one identity known as the 'prosumer', a term coined by Alvin Toffler to describe the increasing amalgamation of those two identities in the post-industrial age, and the impact on the urban landscape.[10] With the means of production more accessible due to the proliferation of smartphones and internet access, the blurring of the two identities can seem opaque. Communications theorist John Fiske notes that this lack of distinction is essential in the functioning of the popular because consumption is itself a productive act. Fisk summarizes by saying that 'every act of consumption is an act of cultural production, for consumption is always the production of meaning'.[11] These mutually constitutive identities are enacted on social media, the architecture for which is dependent upon the prosumer identity.[12] These platforms have no intrinsic content of their own, save what their users produce and consume. Given that Tumblr prides itself on passionate creativity, and its reputation for attracting politically engaged users concerned about 'identity politics' and 'callout culture',[13] I now turn to examine ways in which the cultural producer identity discursively manifests in intersectionality discourse on the platform.

Methodology

I used a critical ethnography approach to gather and analyse qualitative data for this paper. To that end, the critical part of ethnography allows me, the researcher, to reflexively contextualize the situated knowledges I encounter and allow them to determine the path to my next piece of data. This grounded theory approach to ethnography works for a site like Tumblr, which often depends on intuitive behaviour in its production and circulation of content. Critical observation of how intersectionality is deployed was key, whilst the participation element was limited to reblogging (circulating content by posting to one's own blog) data to my own blog, omgphd.tumblr.com. None of the posts examined originate from me, and additional commentary was limited to tagging posts with '#intersectionality' to make them easier to recover for analysis.

To determine a partial understanding of how intersectionality is being framed on Tumblr, I typed 'intersectionality' into the site's own search function. I also entered '#Intersectionality' to bring up the most recent or most popular individual posts tagged with that term. Blog titles and URLs which contain the term 'intersectionality' indicate that the blog itself embraces intersectionality as a key content theme. Although hashtags can create lexical order out of overwhelming raw data, their use is not required on Tumblr and therefore present a limitation in data gathering. To that end, I explored the archives of blogs identifying themselves as 'intersectional' to find other data that may not have been tagged with the term. This untagged archival search may indicate the complex ways in which intersectionality is understood, framed and lexically deployed.

As of April 2018, there were eleven blogs using the term 'intersectional' or 'intersectionality' in the URL, blog title, or tagline (a summary of the blog's substance). A paltry return to be certain, it reflects the extremely literal search terms, and thus does not completely reflect the praxis. The tag page lists related search terms 'feminism', 'racism', 'ableism', 'race' and 'sexism', suggesting that those words frequently accompany searches for 'intersectionality'. This association indicates how people might employ and understand intersectionality. Below that are featured snapshots of over a dozen related blogs, in a horizontal scroll.[14] In the middle of the page are the results for posts tagged with #Intersectionality. The results can be filtered by 'most popular' or 'most recent', and filtered yet further by type (images, videos, text posts, etc.). Throughout this piece, I refer to the blog name and not the person behind the blog because, unlike Facebook, content is foregrounded to speak both for and about individual users, with a marked de-emphasis on biographical data typically found in a user profile.

In such a short paper, it would be nearly impossible to comprehensively assess intersectionality themes in a network of nearly 400 million blogs, which can produce upwards of fifty million blog posts in just half a day. I will analyse a selection of posts tagged #Intersectionality, or those retrieved from archives of blogs identifying themselves as intersectional. The key themes for discussion will be: what social media tells us about contemporary discourse on intersectionality; the sociology of curatorial poaching as a praxis of intersectionality, and, finally the limitations of engaging intersectionality discourse on the Tumblr platform.

'America was never great'

Intersectionalism.tumblr.com was one of the blogs in my search results. The blog's title is 'Dismantling the Master's House', which takes inspiration from the essay by Black lesbian poet and feminist Audre Lorde, 'The Master's Tools Will Never Dismantle the Master's House'.[15] This suggests a broad interest in dismantling oppression in non-hegemonic ways. There is no information to indicate the user's identity. Examining the blog's archives reveals a 2016 post about a young, Black woman named Krystal Lake, who wore a White baseball hat, emblazoned with the phrase 'America was never great'. The hat's message may be read as a rebuttal to then US Republican presidential nominee, Donald Trump, whose campaign continues to sell red baseball caps featuring 'Make America Great Again'.

The post interpretively curates media from Facebook, Twitter and Instagram, narrating the outrage expressed by people reacting to the candid photo of Lake, who seems unaware her photo was being taken whilst working at Home Depot, a DIY chain in the United States. The original photo was posted by the Fox News Channel's official Facebook page, captioned with 'LOOK: Home Depot Worker Wears "America Was Never Great" Hat'. Krystal Lake, twenty-two, was photographed by a customer at the Staten Island location and the picture quickly went viral. Fox News Channel poses a question to its followers about Krystal's hat: 'What do you think of The Home Depot employee's hat?' The question reads innocently enough, but given the conservative, patriotically racist bent of the Fox News outlet, the question serves as an invitation, for its audience, 94% of which are White,[16] to condemn Lake's attire and identity. The images depict people's vitriolic messages to Home Depot's social media teams about hiring someone who 'hates America'. These people also question why Krystal has not left the country; gone back to her 'shitty Third World country'; or been fired. The reactions culminate in tweets by Black people supporting Krystal and noting that the irony of the responses prove the statement on her hat correct. The constructed content highlights how Black people are not allowed to be critical of their own country, which enslaved their ancestors and continues to disenfranchise African Americans.

The post also contains manipulated media, designed to shape the discourse. Below Fox New Channel's Facebook post is a convincingly altered post from 'Home Depot Guest Relations' defending the statement on Lake's hat as being historically true to the experiences of African Americans. The false account invites Fox News fans to use it as a learning opportunity instead of fodder for a 'witch hunt'. A Tumblr user in the post's conversation thread notes the false account and posts screenshots of responses from The Home Depot's verified Facebook account, which do not defend Lake in the slightest. Instead, as most corporations do, they distance themselves from Lake's political gear and ensure customers that her hat 'isn't appropriate' or allowed. Only discerning readers would have noted the a-typical language and lack of verified status in the fake Home Depot Facebook response.

'Jamelia says embrace your roots!'

The 'popular' category for the intersectionality hashtag, on Tumblr's search page, led me to the next piece of data. Unlike the previous Tumblr, 'intersectionalism', 'biscuitsarenice' provides no pithy tagline, or description. This is far more indicative of the average Tumblr blog whose eclectic blogging behaviour can be determined by changing moods and world events. There is no descriptive information about 'biscuitsarenice' on his or her Tumblr page, though the blog description reads 'who was what girl?'. A look at her archive reveals other curatorial poaching efforts, taken from British documentaries and TV programmes tagged with #racism, #colourism, #civil rights.

User 'biscuitsarenice' distilled into several multimedia GIFs Jamelia's four-minute segment, entitled 'Jamelia Says You Should Embrace Your Roots!', aired on ITV's *This Morning* in 2016. Jamelia is a Black British singer turned advocate for natural afro hair. In the segment, Jamelia encourages Black women to embrace their afro-textured hair, giving a group of school-age girls encouragement and tutorials on how to style it (or 'tame it', as ITV describes). 'biscuitsarenice' layers a dozen GIFs with transcript from the video to create a story collage (or GIF set) that reframes an oppression specific to Black women into one of kinship and care. The result is a visual counter-narrative against European beauty standards, but not so critical as to make any morning viewers feel bad. Moreover, the images show Jamelia – a dark-skinned woman with shorter, kinky hair – caring for young dark skin girls with similar hair, as if they are her daughters. The visual juxtaposition between the British uniforms worn by the girls, and the smiling embrace of their kinky hair is powerful in its rarity in Eurocentric media spaces. 'biscuitsarenice' turned a rare event into something to be accessed by hundreds of millions of people, collapsing geographical barriers to access.[17]

'This is awful'

The third piece of data highlights the ways in which the lived epistemologies of Black oppression are digitally curated, poached and circulated to show the ongoing struggles with White supremacy. The blog, 'intersectionalityorbullshit', reblogged a photo collage originating from blog 'sixpenceee', where it was captioned with 'This is awful'. The photo set comprises a mixed-media tweet from Twitter user @Luge_Knight, in which he writes, 'The media when a Black man shoplifts bread to feed his daughter vs when a White man murders family and dissolves them in acid'. This is followed by two juxtaposed images of a sombre-faced Black man in orange prison uniform (left) next to a stock image of a relaxed White male with his smiling wife and child lying next to him. @Luge_Knight's tweet is used by sixpenceee to juxtapose @Luge_Knight's thin satire with a set of images depicting the reality. These images are tweets containing linked articles from verified news sources, illustrating the absurdity highlighted in @Luge_Knight's commentary.

The first image displays the mugshots of a Black man and woman and reads '2 people suspected of stealing ninety cans of baby formula from Walmart'. The tweet in the image reads 'St. Charles man killed daughters before telling wife to "live and suffer"'. The image displayed is a family photo showing a White man, one of his daughters and his wife, all three smiling joyously. There are two explicit points being made: the first is the insidious ways in which White supremacy is maintained in the association between Blackness and criminality, which is achieved using mugshots of the Black law-breakers and a happy family photo of the White murderer. The second is the power and complicity of media to shape narratives that maintain the racial status quo, so much so that @Luge_Knight was able to create a satirical script from the well-worn trope.

These acts of textual poaching from other platforms create additional discourse and enable perpetual circulation via Tumblr's digital archive. Once a post is reblogged by anyone other than the original poster, on Tumblr, the network's community guidelines stipulate that the content is part of the community discourse and can therefore not be deleted, even if the original poster deletes their blog. The examples I describe above are all posts that exemplify what I call curatorial poaching, and the ways in which it can be used to enhance the praxis of intersectionality discourse in popular culture. But it has its drawbacks as well, which will also be discussed in the next section.

Curatorial poaching as intersectionality praxis

The Krystal Lake example epitomizes Tumblr's propensity for curating a narrative theme using content from other social media platforms. Doing so speaks to the mutual constitution of media production and consumption described earlier. Consumption on one platform (Facebook, Twitter) leads to production and more consumption for another platform (Tumblr). The flows of consumption in the Tumblr-sphere add another layer of production each time a user re-blogs the post and comments. What builds up are layers of intersectional discourse about Krystal's act of resistance, and the historical context of the misogynoir-ist backlash. Black women are particularly prone to targetting for violence on social media, inspiring antagonism across race and gender identities. Online, abusive language is used against Black women nearly twice as much as that hurled at White women.[18] Twitter and other social media platforms remain slow to ameliorate the problem.

The Krystal Lake post also evidences a form of textual poaching common to the internet. Originally coined by de Certeau,[19] heavily influenced by Stuart Hall's[20] work on encoding/decoding active audience model, textual poaching was further developed by Jenkins in the context of challenging hegemony in fan studies. Jenkins writes, 'consumers are selective users of a vast media culture whose treasures, however corrupt, hold wealth that can be mined and refined for alternative uses'.[21] This is not dissimilar to the curatorial process of museums. When textual poaching meets the intentionality of advocacy, I call it curatorial poaching. While the term is not limited to The Movement for Black Lives, my analysis is within that context. Museums in Britain and America are littered with stolen treasure curated for public edification. A curator is a content specialist and care-taker of cultural heritage, who selects and interprets material, at institutions, for public edification. Curatorial poaching, then, selects and interprets cultural material that has been poached and bricolaged from multiple media platforms. Moments of culture are purposely selected, extending the boundaries of meaningfulness and creating multiple discourses around the content. Tumblr's tools also turn these curatorial poachers into digital archivists through its built-in archival system. Furthermore, users can create multiple meanings through the re-mixing and reframing of the limited material, just as a museum curator does. Curatorial poachers are more than care-takers. They are advocates against the injustice contained in the media they poach.

Jenkins' work mostly focuses on fan studies and its intersection with media. As fan activity increasingly bleeds into socially mediated popular culture, textual poaching has become a lingua franca of online media.[22] Though mostly used for entertainment purposes, its use can extend into activism, or what is derided as slacktivism, a term that is dubious of social media as a conduit for civic engagement.[23] Curatorial poaching is a twenty-first century manifestation of digital intersectionality praxis. It tells us how intersectionality is being understood and deployed in the social media space, taking intersectionality beyond academia and into public consciousness by embedding it in popular culture, particularly Black popular culture. I do not suggest that this praxis is always understood as such by the author of the content. These acts of curatorial poaching – however they are compelled – contribute to a layman's discourse on intersectionality.

In the example of 'sixpenceee's photo, the user succinctly juxtaposes the racial binary that exists in the media's language and representation of Black and White criminality. 'Sixpenceee's curatorial poaching is made of powerful imagery but does not expressly use the term or language of intersectionality. However, its circulation takes on a distinct meaning when reblogged by a blog like 'intersectionalityorbullshit', which categorically elevates it because of that blog's stated focus on intersectionality. The information is not new and placing 'intersectionality' in one's blog title does not make one an arbiter of the theory. But the intentionality of illuminating the 'everyday' ways in which multiple oppressions function is a key take-away.

Taken together, these acts of curation and poaching create a potent example of the multiple layers of racialized and gendered power struggle the term intersectionality was intended to combat. Moreover, this curatorial poaching in the digital space exemplifies what Manovich refers to as modularity.[24] Manovich thinks of the entire web as a modular structure, in that it is comprised of independent elements and web pages, each combination of which creates a new structure. Sorapure likens Manovich's concept to the structure of an essay, noting that while each sentence or paragraph may stand on its own, it is the clever combination of those elements that are used to explicate new contours of a single idea.[25] This is what curatorial poaching does as a praxis of intersectionality: explicate new contours and ways of expressing and comprehending historical injustices.

Does this advance understanding of intersectionality?

Like 'sixpenceee's examples, 'bisuitsarenice' does not use the term intersectionality but curates and circulates examples of intersectionality, particularly those interlocking forces of discrimination faced by Black women. Her example, taken from Jamelia's ITV piece on caring for Black afro hair, is an interventionist act that bears witness to the struggle and love of Black women and the hair that is a distinct marker of their identity. It is a marker historically used to marginalize Black women in nearly every aspect of their lives.[26] In 2016 there was a prominent protest by young Black girls in South Africa, wearing similar European uniforms as the girls in Jamelia's segment. They protested the ban against being allowed to wear afro-textured hair in school.[27] 'biscuitsarenice's curatorial poaching zooms in on select moments like these, interpretively isolating and de-territorializing content, making it globally accessible on Tumblr's platform. Sharing this content allows for greater empowerment as well as criticality. After all, oppression of Black women's hair is not territorial; it's global.[28]

Curatorial poaching can also be read as a justice-seeking exercise, or an attempt at reconciling the helplessness caused by marginalization. Curatorial poaching is an anti-hegemonic intervention and act of care-taking. It is textual poaching with a side of advocacy. As Jenkins notes of textual poachers, 'one ... can't change the world until one can imagine oneself as an active political agent'.[29] In a small way, 'biscuitsarenice' and others are active political agents spreading real world applications of intersectionality. By observing these instances of curatorial poaching, we come to understand how people process intersectionality and its meaning to their everyday lives. If a course-correcting intervention on the popular apprehension of the theory needs to be made, understanding how the theory is applied on social media platforms is critical.

Curatorial poaching demonstrates one of the productive ways in which the oppressed bear witness to their oppression, by using tools and algorithms meant to keep them engaged in these digital spaces for someone else's profit. Users put that functionality to use for something more meaningful. Tumblr's functionality is such that one cannot completely control what appears across one's dashboard. Therefore, people who would not normally be exposed to intersectionality are forced into pointed contact with it. This could cause them to grasp the threads of its function without necessarily comprehending the theory, eroding its potency in application.

Limitations of intersectionality praxis in social media

Use of curatorial poaching as a praxis of intersectionality may raise questions about intellectual property rights, but are largely outside the purview of this paper, given that textual poaching, upon which curatorial poaching is based, takes as its main conceit that 'poaching' can be anti-hegemonic intervention. However, in instances where people present the ideas of scholars as their own, those things can be disproved. The casual reader must care to investigate, and most do not. Another limitation here is in attribution and tagging. Not all posters practice tagging, so to rely on Tumblr's tools for quantitative research concerning the degree to which intersectionality populates Tumblr would be unreliable. Tumblr's technology does not intelligently scan visual media, and it cannot metatag data. This is only somewhat of a drawback as a research tool, not an educational one. Without a reliable curator to interpret the material, what may be labelled as 'intersectional' becomes more limited. Perhaps it is best that artificial intelligence, given its historically racist application[30] and potential for exploitation, cannot automatically index examples of intersectionality.

These approaches are not safe from deception, or state exploitation. In March 2018, Tumblr, during the height of the Cambridge Analytica scandal, revealed a list of eighty-four Tumblr accounts linked to state-sponsored campaigns.[31] Attempting to distinguish itself from the privacy policies of Facebook, Tumblr wrote the following on its website: 'Democracy requires transparency and an informed electorate, and we take our responsibilities seriously. We aggressively monitor Tumblr for signs of state-sponsored disinformation campaigns and take appropriate actions when we uncover anything'.[32] The list of eighty-four blogs reveals more than a dozen blogs with specific reference to the term 'Black' ('weproudtoBlack', 'starling-all-Black-all-day'), or terms coded as Black ('melanin-diary', 'hustleinatrap').

One of the reasons Russian 'troll farm' agents could be successful on social media is that mimicking the language of social justice, including intersectionality, is not too difficult. Social media, in many ways, is the Wild, Wild West, its boundaries and limitations are still being explored. For every good example of curatorial poaching, there may be a plethora of clumsy, reductive attempts that confuse or dilute intersectionality's meaning. As mentioned earlier, readers encountering this material may not necessarily grasp the theory but mimic its application. That is the danger, and one that political operatives exploited. In this instance, Tumblr users spread propaganda intended to specifically dissuade African Americans from voting for Hillary Clinton in the 2016 US presidential election.[33] The language of intersectionality has gained cache in 'woke' culture, a term from African American vernacular English (AAVE) that refers to social awareness and is firmly planted in the history of Black activism. Wokeness can be expressed in many ways, including through the praxis of intersectionality, as it challenges digital literacy. Fundamentally, being woke is an intersectional orientation to the world; how one navigates politics and community. But much like any cultural phenomena created and popularized by Black people, it gains currency as a trend. The lifecycle of all trends is that they reach a crescendo, wherein they become ripe for capitalist and political manipulation for an already overly-stimulated neoliberal culture.

Whilst Tumblr can be a space within which critical discourse and interpretive practices are supported in tandem with media consumption – especially by counter publics – it is still an arena without moderation, or appointed leaders. Because its tools place greater emphasis on the image over the written word, the praxis of intersectionality can be limitedly engaged to visual media. A popular set of images reblogged tens of thousands of times may have more to do with the content's emotional and aesthetic appeal than with what it expresses about intersectionality. The visual system isn't objective. It is already referential, and we bring to it a system of references that include entrenched ways of seeing.

Writing about the politics of Black Twitter's media consumption, Chatman observed that the geography of this consumption provides opportunities for 'resistance, pleasure, cultural politics, and identity construction'.[34] Curatorial poaching as a praxis of intersectionality becomes digital labour, hobby, and political agency. Platforms like Tumblr allow marginalized people to access political clout by way of the constant visibility and mobility of content. Though the content posted is often motivated by a desire for justice, it cannot be divorced from the psychological impact the largely neoliberal environment of social media is having on the drive for social status, especially the desire to post content that will guarantee impact.[35] The architecture of social media relies on the consumer being the producer, and as such, identity construction, and the search for belonging and power, are enmeshed in a complicated relationship with racial justice. Tumblr is an example of a digital space wherein the contours of intersectionality discourse are being shaped by the collapse of the line between production and consumption of culture. As we are thinking of how intersectionality should be reframed, it is imperative that this framing include the affordances and problematics of digital spaces in which intersectionality is being discussed and practised as both lived and performative reality.

Illuminating experiences among inner-city Black British single mothers and their sons

Miranda Armstrong

This chapter attempts to show some of the ways intersectional analyses make visible experiences usually rendered *in*visible. It centralizes the past experiences of women who raised sons to adulthood as single mothers and those of young men who were raised by single-parent women, all of whom are Black Londoners. According to the race equality think tank the Runnymede Trust, 59% of Black British Caribbean and 44% of Black British African children are being raised by single parents, who are predominantly mothers.[1] The proportion of single-parent households in Black populations has been used as a partial explanation for the over-representation of Black boys and men among students excluded from school, the unemployed and underemployed, the prison population and those within mental health institutions. This is due to the assumption that in single-parent households young men do not receive sufficient socialization, discipline or care.

Reductive narratives about Black single mothers and their children first emerged in the mid-twentieth century, amid anthropological studies of Black Caribbean families by Edith Clarke[2] in Jamaica and Sheila Patterson[3] in South London. The influential and controversial 1965 US report, *The Negro Family: The Case for National Action* by politician Daniel Patrick Moynihan positioned single-mother families within a 'tangle of pathology'.[4] Moynihan claimed these households reproduced poverty and deprivation and linked their prevalence to crime and juvenile delinquency. This association between single-parent households and pathology has been maintained by a range of surprisingly different voices.

In a speech on the 2011 unrest in Britain's inner cities, after the police killing of mixed-heritage man Mark Duggan, prime minister at the time David Cameron reinforced stereotypes of single mothers' sons, opining:

> I don't doubt that many of the rioters out last week have no father at home … Perhaps they come from one of the neighbourhoods where it's

standard for children to have a mum and not a dad … where it's normal for young men to grow up without a male role model, looking to the streets for their father figures, filled up with rage and anger.[5]

David Lammy, one of the few Black members of parliament, made similar comments following the unrest, which began in his constituency, in his 2011 book *Out of Ashes*. He wrote 'the angry young men in the riots had been lost to a nihilistic subculture long ago … because they had no one to steer them through their journey to manhood'.[6] Commenting on a perceived rise in knife crime in 2012, he also suggested that perpetrators typically came from single-mother homes, saying 'usually the child that has committed the offence comes from a background where the father has been absent'.[7] Single-mother households have even been implicated in their own tragedies. Following the murder of fourteen-year-old Jaden Moodie in East London, provocative journalist Rod Liddle responded with a column titled, 'Half of Black Children Do Not Live with Their Father. And We Wonder Why They're Dying'.[8] It is time for these reductive causal 'explanations' to be challenged.

This chapter draws on data from ongoing research on parenting and young manhood within Black British, urban single-mother families. Qualitative biographical interviews were conducted with thirty-five single mothers of sons and adult sons. The mothers' ages ranged from late thirties to early sixties, and most of the women were second-generation British. The adult sons were aged between twenty and forty-four years, although the majority were under age thirty, and were second- and third-generation British. The differences in generation provided important insight into how circumstances have shifted for people of African and Caribbean origin over time. Only a small portion of mothers and sons interviewed were biologically related, and so the study provided insight into a range of individual and family lives.

The term 'single mothers' is used to refer to all of the women here, but it does have a specific meaning, referring to women who raise their children with some level of involvement from the other parent. The majority of the women I spoke to fit this description, but a small amount of the sample could actually be described as 'lone mothers', those who raised their children without any involvement of the father. I use 'single mother' as it is the commonly used term, and I want to engage the image it conjures.

The brief discussion that follows is divided into two sections. In the first I discuss the gap between stereotypes of Black single mothers and Black men raised by them and their lived realities, which have been misunderstood and misrepresented. In the second, I try to show how people's experiences of motherhood and youth are shaped by the interaction of race/gender/class, family structure and geographic location.

Misrecognized

The single mothers and adult sons I interviewed did not match dominant portrayals. In the cases of mothers, the dominant benefit dependency trope was wildly inaccurate. They were all working mothers – as are the majority of single mothers. The majority of them had professional careers, as teachers, social workers and nurses, and some were self-employed business owners. Many of the women's careers were developed after gaining higher education degrees and/or postgraduate qualifications as student parents. The women spoke of using higher education to improve their prospects and attain financial security for their families.

Women described the economic survival of their families, as well as personal fulfilment, as their main motivations for attaining a profession. But respectability politics also seemed influential to their reasoning. The story of Natalie, one of the study's participants, is a striking example of this. The youngest mother to contribute to the research, she had become a mother just before beginning her A-levels and continued with her education while raising her son to eventually become a secondary school teacher. 'I was so fearful that if I took the time out from education, I wouldn't go back. You saw lots of people who had dreams of doing stuff. Had a baby and then didn't do anything else', she says. 'I didn't want that to be my story. And so I thought it better just to keep going. It was almost better to struggle and get it done, than take that risk of not trying … In the back of my mind, I was actually a failure, but there was that desire to prove people wrong'.

The image of the feckless single mother is classed, raced and gendered, its omnipotent spectre seemingly fuelling women to do differently. Most of the women similarly referred to such stereotypes in their accounts, differentiating themselves from it. Considering 'race' in tandem with single mothering does change the picture. The high economic activity of women of Caribbean and African origin, including mothers, has been documented in previous research.[9] It has been suggested that Black women are less likely to depend on state provision for income[10] and research by sociologist Tracey Reynolds found that being a good economic provider was intrinsic to Black Caribbean-heritage mothers' understandings of being a 'good mother'.[11] This is not about creating a good/bad single-mother dichotomy, but highlighting that the range of women's responses to single motherhood has not yet been fully explored.

The economic activity of Black single-parent women has been used against them. In 1982 Errol Lawrence put forward an analysis that remains relevant:

> The fact that many Afro-Caribbean mothers have to go out to work in order for their families to survive, easily gets translated into the

argument that they are neglecting their children ... the resultant 'maternal deprivation' then 'explains' the 'violence' of their children.[12]

Former chief inspector of Ofsted, which inspects schools in England, Sir Michael Wilshaw, made a similar point more recently in a discussion of gun and knife crime on *Good Morning Britain*:

> When I was teaching fifty years ago, when we had a problem with a youngster, Mum and Dad used to turn up ... you don't see that now ... dads are neglecting their children and providing terrible role models to their young men who then go astray ... You never see Dad. Mums are fully stretched and having to go out to work to support their family and worry about what's happening at home.[13]

Comments such as Sir Wilshaw's reflect assumptions that single mothers raise their children individually. Moral panic about single mothering is centred on the imagined circumstances of women trying to do it all alone. But another important factor overlooked is that single mothers do not typically raise their children alone. It could be said that the terms 'single' and 'lone' parent are in fact misleading, as they overlook the wider 'village' who play significant roles in the lives of single mothers and their sons. Mothers and sons spoke of the key supportive figures in their lives, including children's grandparents, aunties and uncles, family friends, and in many cases, fathers.

Single-parent Black women achieve economic self-sufficiency while, as women, bearing the heavy responsibility of their children's care. They try to perform a delicate balancing act between the two. Despite this their households and parenting are still found to be lacking, and blamed. They are misrecognized as key players within social dysfunction, rather than as social actors with significant resilience and agency.

The misrecognition of young men raised by single mothers is influenced by mutually reinforcing (mis)understandings of 'race', youth and masculinity. This is compounded by false assumptions about single-parent women's abilities to raise their own children. This is not a dismissal of the difficulties that occur, in all families, but to raise questions about the default problematization of single-parent women raising their boys to adulthood.

The emotional intelligence, maturity and thoughtfulness of the young men I met during the study suggested such anxieties were unnecessary. They were diligent university students, ambitious graduates, budding entrepreneurs and talented men pursuing creative vocations. They were negotiating their way in the world. Such images of young Black manhood are rarely seen at societal level, giving the impression they do not exist. Instead, stories and statistical patterns that perpetuate pathologies of race, youth and masculinity dominate, reinforcing patterns of misrecognition. Belief about the single-mother family structure have interacted with feared pathologies of Blackness and masculinity to construct the sons of single mothers as a problem. Despite changing understandings of masculinity, a belief persists that the instincts of young men are destructive and can only be tempered by a male authority figure. It is notions such as these upon which male role model discourse is based. But most of the sons valued their mothers, many crediting her for their survival in challenging conditions. The following quote from Lenny exemplifies this: 'the [2011] riots were right outside my window. I've seen police drive past, I've seen police chase people. I'm friends with gang members, so all of that is around me', he said. 'But I don't take part in it because of my mum. I can stand proud and say, "Yeah. I'm a strong Black man", thanks to my mum'.

It feels important to note that the non-residence of fathers did not always equate to father absence, because Black fatherhood has been discussed as a simple absence/presence binary.[14] For the sons of single mothers in my study, the lived reality of a separated father was much more varied and complex than dominant understandings suggest, a finding supported by previous research. A spectrum of experiences was described, from fathers deeply involved in their sons' lives (separated but present), to those who spent time with their sons rhythmically and regularly, to fathers whose visits were more intermittent, and finally to figures that sons did not know. The 'absent father' narrative does not reflect the variety of relationships between separated fathers and their children.

The discourse around 'fatherlessness' fuels the misrecognition of young men raised by women. It has repeatedly been claimed that young men grow up with unmet needs as a result of so-called 'father hunger', as suggested by Cameron above. Descriptions have become alarmist and slipped into hyperbole. For example, Tony Sewell wrote,

> these boys are like Hamlet, thinking too much about their absent fathers. This ghost has not been exorcised … There is an answer which lies not in more youth clubs or police on the beat but psychological intervention, where young boys can confront the demon within.[15]

Based on the accounts provided, this was not the experience of the young men I interviewed. Of all the experiences with separated fathers described, the one that seemed to be experienced as the most painful was that of fathers who maintained a relationship with their sons but were inconsistent and unreliable. Individuals described this as a private pain they processed over time. Samson spent some time eloquently describing the difficult emotions about his father he had wrestled with through boyhood and early manhood. 'When you get older, you realize [parents] are just people', he said. 'They are people with insecurities, people who have got shame, people who have got hurt and don't know how to deal it ... I mean I would be lying if I said this wasn't a frustration, but it's not like I want a dad at all costs'. Rather than misrecognizing particular family types and their members as deviant, perhaps closer attention should be paid to people's experiences of the social conditions.

Hidden realities

Despite longstanding anxieties about Black single-mother households and the young men raised within them, in truth our society knows little about their lived experiences. My study takes seriously the ways racialization, class, gender, family structure and geographic location work together to shape experience, which highlights the role of the social conditions. Issues such as policing, local crime and neighbourhoods became significant.

The London neighbourhoods in which the families resided are important, as they provide the backdrop of their everyday lives. Family structure and geography interact here, due to issues of affordability. The mother's income determines the quality of housing and neighbourhood space her family can access. The decision of where families root themselves is a pivotal one – it determines the educational institutions sons have access to, the social ties made, issues of safety, and whether or not children are exposed to criminality.

Most two-parent families generally face challenges navigating London's uneven housing and schooling markets. For Black parents there may be another dimension considered, that of local influences. A ground-breaking study on Black British middle-class families by Nicola Rollock and colleagues found that couples actively and strategically select residential areas in which to live in order to shield their children from unwanted influences of 'road' culture.[16] Single-parent women are less likely to have the ability to be as strategic, as they are funding their families with one income. Often their choices were subject to constraint.

Many of the single mothers I spoke to had lived in social housing at some point while raising their children as it offered the most stable and secure accommodation for their families. Council estates were viewed by a lot of mothers interviewed as a potentially contaminating space for their children. Accordingly, some of the mothers spoke of not allowing them outside to play, due to fears of what they might encounter. There was a sense of a proximity of danger and risk. Mothers' fears were not entirely unfounded. One of the sons I interviewed spoke of getting connected 'to the wrong crowd' on the estate he grew up on and getting into 'mischievous things' for a period. Another son recalled seeing a cordoned off area on his estate following a murder. Another spoke of former neighbours who had been imprisoned. But the environment did not determine the boys' fates. The young men successfully navigated these conditions, learning to straddle different worlds.

Paying attention to the interaction between race, class, gender, and location reveals the complexities and contradictions within families' lived experiences. Mary Pattillo illustrated such a pattern in her study of a Chicagoan African-American neighbourhood, which reflects certain aspects of some Black British experiences.[17] Pattillo's work highlights the significance of the geographic contexts in which Black children are often raised. The neighbourhood had relatively more poverty and crime, meaning young people were exposed to the temptations of crime because of proximity. Consequently, Pattillo observed, 'youth walk a fine line between preparing for success and youthful delinquent experimentation'.

In such environments, young men's futures are arguably precarious. Pivotal choices are made, and single mothers must carefully guide their sons to avoid pitfalls. Like this study, research by Cheron Byfield, documented in the book *Black Boys Can Make It*, shows that growing up in a difficult neighbourhood and being raised by a single mother are not barriers to earning admission at world-renowned universities.[18] This is not to suggest that conditions could not be improved for single-parent women and their children. Psychologist Suzanne Randolph suggests that there is a lack of political will to ameliorate the challenging contexts in which Black single mothers might raise their children, 'due largely to sexism and elitism'.[19]

For some people I spoke to, one aspect of their family lives involved dealing with the harassment of sons by police. Dominant stereotypes of Black male youth have legitimized this police practice. Approximately a quarter of sons whose experiences were shared with the study had had at least one such police encounter. One mother, Marie, expressed her frustration at her son 'constantly' being subject to police stop searches over the years,

> One thing we can't actually stop from happening, is this stop and search and criminalizing them … As soon as they start growing up and reaching secondary school age, they're the enemy, they're looked on like they are criminals … You can have the best behaved child that doesn't do any wrong, it doesn't matter.

One young man I spoke to, Donovan, described an incident in which he was physically assaulted and racially abused by officers at age sixteen, for which legal action was being taken. He also described being stopped and searched on the way home from school, an experience not uncommon among others. Young men were asked to explain their presence in certain neighbourhoods by police officers: 'What are you doing in this area?'

'Between the ages of thirteen to fifteen', Marie, a mother of two adult sons told me, 'they were stopped a minimum of three times a week without fail'. Vanessa, a mother to one son, said that during his teenage years her son was stopped and searched 'literally every day' despite no wrongdoing. In these circumstances mothers advocated on their sons' behalf, contacting local stations to complain. These accounts provide support for previous research showing that police practice has been discriminatory.[20] Interestingly, significantly fewer people in the second phase of this study, which included a younger sample, had experienced police harassment, which may suggest a change in approach. However, there have been recent calls to increase stop and search amid recent levels of street violence in London.

Single mothers and their sons navigate these challenges together. As well as a distinct but unseen experience of youth, the lived experience of racialization also produced a distinct experience of mothering for women raising Black sons. Mothers' awareness about racial inequality as well as negative narratives about Black male children through statistics and press reports created an additional pressure in their parenting task. The majority of the mothers I spoke to were concerned their sons might experience prejudice. They felt the need to educate their children about prejudice and inequalities. One mother said she felt the need to make 'soldiers' of her two sons 'in a loving way' so they might be less vulnerable in the social conditions. Mothers described raising their sons' socio-political awareness in various ways, including family discussions, attendance at educational cultural events and Black supplementary schools, the use of socially conscious music, movies and quotes from historic figures.

This chapter has attempted to demonstrate how race/gender/class, family structure and geographic location produce a distinct yet usually unseen experience of mothering and young male adulthood. Black single mothers and young men raised by them have been misrecognized and depicted in distorted and reductive ways. This is perhaps because their realities have been misunderstood. The demonization of Black single-parent families is arguably the product of mutually reinforcing prejudices: the stigma around single mothering for transgressing the patriarchal, heterosexual two-parent norm; the underlying sexism in the assumed inability of women to raise well-adjusted men; and xenophobic fears about Blackness and a mythical, homogeneous 'Black culture'.

Anxieties about the relatively high numbers of Black single-mother households have eclipsed research attention to people's actual lived experiences within these households. Links between this family structure and certain problems have not been substantiated by evidence. And yet anxiety, judgement and mother-blame surround Black single-mother households, acting as a repository for fears of and frustrations about Black British populations. I have tried to demonstrate how intersectional analyses provide a nuanced illustration of family lives normally unseen. It is only with such insight that our society can move beyond judgement and pathologizing to begin to consider how more equal experiences of youth and mothering can be produced.

'Stop killing the man dem': Prospects for intersectional Black politics

Kehinde Andrews

At the Reframing Intersectionality workshop in 2016, which turned into this book, Kimberlé Crenshaw showed a moving video of the Black women who had been killed by the state in the United States. Just a few of the names of the women killed include: Rekia Boyd, Kayla Moore, Megan Hockaday, Alexia Christian, Kyan Livingston and Mia Hall. More upsetting than the facts and the video were the stories of how the movement had been shunned by some at Black Lives Matters protests. There was genuine anger that saying the names of the women was causing a distraction from whichever man the protest was about. The image of Black people shouting down other Black people for raising an issue of Black women killed by the police was jarring and I spent the next couple of days trying to comprehend it.

Even at its most patriarchal the Black politics I have reference to would rally round the idea that we need to, as Malcolm X put it, 'protect our women'.[1] In Britain, riots were sparked in Brixton in 1985 after the police shot and wounded Cherry Groce. In the same year in Tottenham the death of Cynthia Jarret also lit the fuse of days of rebellions. At his keynote address at the inaugural Black Lives Matter Conference held in Nottingham in 2015, veteran campaigner Stafford Scott expressed his pride that they had been able to chase off the skinheads intent on attacking Black women. I've never come across a version of Black masculinity that would not mobilize the idea of protection from the violence of White people or the state. But something that Crenshaw said has stuck with me since: 'Black men are feared, Black women are despised'.

In trying to come to terms with the disturbing picture that was being painted my argument in this chapter is that we need to rethink how Blackness and gender intersect. There is a simplistic view that it is the Black man who is feared and gun downed by the state. The idea neatly fits into the hypermasculine narrative of the Black superman, who can only ever be viewed with suspicion. We are killed because we are a threat, a savage beast needing to be tamed.

'Stop killing the man dem' was daubed on t-shirts and chanted at rallies against police brutality across Britain. The refrain was at once a sign of both the limitations and potential of intersectionality in Black political activism. Just as in America, the issue of state violence has become centred around the male body, ignoring that Black women have always been, and continue to be, subject to the same forms of abuse. The call to 'stop killing the man dem' is an assertion of this right to be Black and male, and to be allowed to be the active agents in the community. In many ways it is a defence of Black manhood but as we will explore in this chapter the slogan was born of the wider Black Lives Matter movement, and campaigns for justice against state violence which have predominantly been led by Black women. The women in these movements have created truly intersectional politics, seeing the impact of a disproportionately gendered act through its intersection with Blackness. Too often Black politics has been guilty of intersectional failures, as we will explore in this chapter, but it is in these Black female-led movements that we have a roadmap for intersectional politics.

Fragility of Black manhood

In order to understand the roots of the rejection by some of Say Her Name we need to start with how and why Black manhood plays such a prominent role in Black political thought. The attack on Black men and boys that people like Dr Umar Johnson rail against presents the Black male as an almost unique victim.[2] There is a supposed effort to tame us, to 'feminise' Black men and boys. There is nothing new about these ideas; Malcolm chastised the nonviolence of civil rights activists for their tactics. He opined that the very idea of a sit in 'castrates you, brings you down. An old woman can sit. An old man can sit. A chump can sit, a coward can sit, anything can sit'.[3] In order to overcome racism men needed to regain their manhood and fight back against the oppressor. There is an implicit hypermasculinity in these messages, that the real Black man is the one who fears nothing and will take their respect by force.

Hypermasculinity as resistance has a long history in Black struggle. On the plantation the 'bad nigger' was a folk hero, an uncontrollable Black man who refused to be cowed by the oppressor.[4] After slavery ended the mythology of the bad nigger continued in the figure of the hustler, bad man or rude bwoy. Due to the marginalization of Black people in the West, a protective response has been to reject the mainstream and to create an alternative sphere of living. Being on the hustle provides economic but also social support and is a form of resistance. Hip hop is full of stories of how 'drugs kept the hood from starving'[5] alluding to the fact that when you cannot get a job the illegal economy is a rational source of income. Radical organizations like the Black Panther Party also saw the mandem as the revolutionary class, the 'Bad nigger off the block' who had nothing to lose and did not take prisoners.[6] But the embrace of what Cleaver called 'Lumpen ideology' was one that undermined the Party.[7]

The problem with embracing the bad nigger is that though it was a form of resistance 'road life' is not revolutionary. The hypermasculinity that lies at the heart of the hustler is a negative construction of Whiteness. We were enslaved because they viewed us as beasts of burden, more animals than people: stronger, more virile, more masculine. There is no liberation in embracing this lie, and it was the hypermasculinity of the men in the movement that destabilized it. The egos; the violence against women; Eldridge Cleaver's embrace of the gun as an extension of his manhood; Newton's collapse into the criminal underground.[8]

The defence of Black manhood has similarly problematic issues today as it leads to a position that marginalizes Black women. In the campaign to stop the so-called feminization of Black boys we collude in the terrible gender project of the mainstream. There is nothing wrong with so-called 'feminine' traits. Training Black boys to be hypermasculine supermen will not protect them from the system, and certainly not build beneficial relationships with Black women. This idea also leads to a set of ideas that marginalize LQBTQ communities, which cannot be accommodated in the outlook of the bad nigger. Rather than focusing on the real problems that our children face, we obsess over the imagined 'gay agenda' that is supposedly trying to brainwash our young men and castrate them.

Ironically, at the root of Black hypermasculinity is a deep-seated insecurity. When your resistance is predicated on your toughness, virility, manhood, then you are in a constant struggle to prove yourself. There is a constant need to preen and pose, to demonstrate you are bad. You literally have nothing but your reputation, so every little slight becomes a threat to your very being, meaning that the smallest of disputes can become matters of life and death. I'll never forget the experience of being on a bus in the historical Black community of Roxbury, Boston and someone accidentally stood on my foot. The look of terror on the man's face as he turned round to profusely apologize was something I never really understood at first. But as the relief spread across his face when I shrugged it off, I realized that he was fearful of my reaction. He was terrified of how a young Black man with a hoodie in the hood would respond to his violation of my kicks.

It is this insecurity that explains the reaction of some people to the Say Her Name campaign. Defending the mandem is (for some) an extension of protecting Black manhood. If Black women are killed too then we need a different explanation for the police killings. To muddy the water takes the focus off the conspiracy to emasculate Black men. Even worse, it is Black women intruding on the narrative, feminizing the issue. In fact, Black feminism is a dirty word in far too many Black political circles, viewed as something conjured up by White people to break the unity of Blackness and further undermine the issues of The Black Man™. This explains the vehemence with which some (and I hope this is a small minority) openly reject the presence of Say Her Name. Black hypermasculinity places a wedge between Black men and women in all instances, and this is just the latest example. Though it may seem like there is a relatively simple solution, to just abandon the allure of the bad nigger, it is far more complicated than that.

Attack on Black men

When Stafford Scott, veteran police brutality campaigner, keynoted the first Black Lives Matter (BLM) conference in the UK in 2015, he caused a stir. Scott is the definition of the mandem. He's been representing the bad niggers off the estate his entire life. BLM was set up because of the experiences largely centred around the mandem, but from a location very distant to the experiences on the road. At the conference there was rightly a lot of talk of LGBTTQ issues and critique of the gender binary. But Scott opened with an implicit dismissal of much of these debates, with the simple statement, 'I am a man'. He explained that the mandem had no choice but to embrace the masculine in order to survive and also protect the community. In his lifetime he had been active in fighting off the skinheads who would come in and attack people. The real fear of having their heads kicked in by the bad nigger is one of the reasons why racist attacks against Black people have been lower than for other groups. It is not an empty identity, but a genuine defence mechanism. The mandem are also produced by real material conditions of racism.

One of the key differences in which Blackness intersects with gender is in that there is oftentimes a lack of benefits accrued to being both Black and male. The enslavement of African people was predicated on using us as beasts of burden in order to toil on the plantations of the Americas. Hypermasculine Black beasts were therefore prized possessions and around two-thirds of those enslaved in plantation societies like Haiti were men, along with 80% of those enslaved on British ships.[9] We were inhuman, whipped, castrated and victims of sexual violence. After so-called emancipation the fear of the Black beast meant that Black men were more likely to be imprisoned, lynched and killed by the police. There are an estimated 1.5 million missing African American men, either dead or in jail.[10] In the UK, the marginalization of Black men from most forms of economic life means that Black Caribbean men are far more likely to be unemployed and in jail than their White counterparts. The attack on Black men is not some imaginary conspiracy but a genuine reality that is being felt keenly across the globe.

Black men simply do not always get the benefit of our maleness because of our Blackness. I am privileged enough to work in an elite profession and I come across so few Black men, I could count them on one hand. Of the six Black Studies staff at BCU there are two men and four women, and all of our PhD students have been women. There has been much noise made about the lack of Black professors in Britain, with there being only 140 out of 21,455, or 0.6%.[11] It has also been highlighted that Black women are far less likely to be professors. From the Higher Education Statistics in 2014/15 it was found that there were only thirty Black female professors in the entire country. This is an appalling statistic, but if we dig a little deeper into the intersection of gender and Blackness, we find a complex picture.

Women in general are far less likely to be professors than men due to sexism, representing only 25% of professors. The thirty Black female professors are a prime example of the double oppression of being both Black and female. Women are far less likely to be professors, and Black people are far less likely, and this hurts Black women the most resulting in just thirty professors in the entire country. A major explanation for this gap is the lack of female professors in the science subjects. Given the horizontal segregation in the subjects we see far more male professors in these subjects (though it is no less problematic). So there is nothing particularly surprising about the overall disparity between Black men and women in the professoriate. What does stand out is that the disparity between Black men and women was entirely explained by the situation of Black African academics, where there were sixty male, in comparison to ten female professors. For Black Caribbean and Black Other there were an equal number of Black male and female professors (30 and 5 respectively). Given the overall picture of gender and the professoriate there was clearly a significant under-representation of non-African Black men. This raises really interesting questions about the nature of the intersection with Blackness and gender across ethnicity and also class.

Caribbeans in the UK are descended from the enslaved and have tended to migrate into the country with less familial wealth due to the nature of migration. We will discuss how racial patriarchy causes different intersections in these conditions. But the disparity in professors has been discussed exclusively through the lens of double oppression, that there is something distinct happening here to Black women. Rollock, in an excellent report exploring the barriers that the handful of Black female professors have had to face, included racism, being undermined and undervalued.[12] These experiences are vital to understand for those navigating White institutions. But as one of the few Black (and Caribbean) professors I could identity with the majority of the experiences and issue raised in the study. A narrow frame that only sees the small number of Black female professors as an example of a double oppression misses some of the point.

One of the most bizarre manifestations of this kind of approach was Professor Iyiola Solanke compiling a list of black (meaning non-White) female professors, which was subsequently hosted by the Runnymede Trust.[13] The project eventually spawned a website called *Black Female Professors Forum*, which in its more expansive definition lists 350 non-White female professors.[14] The aim is apparently to 'generate positive narratives to underpin successful pathways and trajectories for Black women in education', though the initiative seems to do the exact opposite. Changing the definition of Black in a way that multiplies the number of black female professors tenfold seems like a terrible strategy to argue for change. Not to mention that the project utterly misreads the data that it responded to. Of course the low numbers of Black women professors is appalling, but this is not an example where Black men are being privileged because of our gender. This is an issue of racism, a Black issue, with gendered dimensions that necessitates us to come together.

Gender also intersects with Blackness in complicated ways for Black women. Whiteness is built on the exclusion of women from the public sphere, with perhaps millions of words being written about the role of the marginalized role of the housewife.[15] But this public/private split has never been the case for Black women. Women were enslaved and put to work both in the house and field, and have had to work ever since. Whilst there certainly are Black housewives in many families the idea is a completely alien one to many. In fact, in the post-war period the British government actually encouraged the immigration of Black women in order to prevent White women from remaining in the workplace.

Speaking of the public sphere, we are even seeing Black women outperforming men in political representation. There are currently thirteen Black female members of parliament, and only seven Black men. At the local level, I looked at the representation of councillors in Birmingham, which is the biggest local authority in Europe, and therefore gives us an idea of the wider picture. We would also expect more representation of Black people given the demographics of the city. Out of 101 councillors, in 2018, there were five Black women and no Black men. At the European level there is somehow not a single Black representative at all. It is too simplistic to transpose White gender relations when looking at Black people. The intersections are far more complicated, with the result being that Black men being equally under attack because of our gender, although this plays out in different ways.

Racial patriarchy

My point is not to argue that Black men have it worse than Black women because of less access to the professional jobs and politics, but to demonstrate that gender does not intersect in the same way for Black people as it does for White folk. There are specific cases where the patriarchal relations of the mainstream are recreated in Black communities, which are important to consider.

African America provides some good examples of the spaces where the Black community life was reconstructed in the image of White patriarchy. Under the doctrine of 'separate but equal' enclaves of Black communities based on White class and gender lines could emerge. Black teachers, doctors, nurses and other professions flourished under racial apartheid. There was even a hugely successful Black Wall Street in Tulsa, Oklahoma, showing that we could replicate capitalism. A warning was sent out not to be too good at this replication when it was burned down by White residents, supported by the state in 1921. Perhaps the best example of the mirroring of White values would be in the university sector.

In Britain, we are often jealous of the historically Black universities and colleges (HBCUs) because of the Black spaces we perceive them to be. But we must recognize that the values enshrined in many HBCUs are not for Black liberation, but an attempt to replicate the White universities. It is no coincidence that one of the most prestigious HBCUs, Howard, is remarkably similar in name to Harvard. Under the philosophy of separate but equal the aim is to replicate, not replace, so it is no surprise that we see all of the problems of the White university magnified in the HBCUs. Elitism, patriarchy, colourism have historically been features of these institutions.[16] Their inherent conservatism was a major concern for those who launched the Black Studies movement, which aimed to transform what a university education meant.[17] It is this conservatism that led to the leaders of the HBCUs being used as propaganda for Donald Trump during their visit to the White House in 2016. In these kinds of separate but unequal spaces White gender roles are reinforced in order to prove the legitimacy of the spaces. If patriarchy is a feature of White society, then they have to ratchet it up in order to show their credentials. This is one of the defining features of respectability politics.

The Black church is also an excellent example of where we can see White gender roles play out. Men are generally the church leaders, with women making up most of the congregation and doing the administrative work. Again, the Black church is generally a replication of the White one. Malcolm X scorned the racial politics of the Black church, saying that 'if God's White, Jesus is White, Mary's White and all the angels are White then that's White nationalism'.[18] He could just have easily said that if the pastor's a man, the deacon's a man but all the admin workers are women, then that's replicating patriarchy. Given the central role of the church in civil rights mobilizations it is no surprise that these gender relations spilled over into the activism, in the form of a particularly virulent respectability politics. The rejection of support for Claudette Colvin, who sat in the White section of the bus in Montgomery, Alabama, is a case in point. Colvin was not seen as an appropriate vehicle for the bus boycott because she was pregnant, teenage and single. Rosa Parks offered the kind of respectable figure (highly idealized in how she remains represented) that they felt they could build the movement around.[19]

We can also see how some of the gains from the Civil Rights Movement played out in typically patriarchal ways. For instance, in the male-dominated auto industry male workers on the production line were able to achieve pay rises based on race claims. White women in admin roles were also able to secure pay claims on the basis of gender protections. But Black women who were subject to lower pay and working conditions were unable to make pay claims because the race suits had been won by Black men and the gender litigation by White women.

We can also see the replication of patriarchal gender relations in the former colonies. One of the ways that Western empires were managed was by relying on a native administrational class. Western-educated elites were installed to run the colonial outposts and upon independence this group were charged with running the newly founded nation states. It should come as no surprise to see that both the racist and patriarchal relations of Whiteness were replicated within these structures. In the Caribbean the word 'pigmentocracy' is often used to capture the racial nature of hierarchy in the state.[20] I'll never forget a visit to Jamaica where I covered most of the island and saw just how dark skinned the vast majority of the population are. It was truly disorienting to look up at a television screen one day and see a parliament full of White or very light-skinned politicians. White patriarchal gender relations are also replicated in these contexts. It is no coincidence that it is Black African men who make up the largest group of Black professors in the UK. They are likely to be part of that post-colonial elite, trained for leadership and increasingly settling in the West.

We must recognize, however, that whilst these examples of replicating patriarchy exist they do so at a particular intersection of class. Professionals under separate but equal; academics in HBCUs; Black churches; colonial administrators and African academics all have a certain level of privilege. The aping of the White mainstream is reserved for those with the luxury to have either access to it, or a parallel system that feeds off the racist society at large. Once Black men have gained access to the privileges of the system then they are defended by the protections of patriarchy in the same way a White man would be. Elijah Anderson talks about how being accepted into a White space is possible once you have proven that you do not represent the 'iconic ghetto'.[21] One you have proven you can dance you are granted provisional status and for Black men this will mean being offered some of the protections of patriarchy. A classic example of this would be the defence of Clarence Thomas, and the vilification of Anita Hill, in confirmation hearings for his seat on the Supreme Court.[22] But Clarence Thomas, a well-to-do, high-profile right-winger does not represent the average African-American male. For those locked out of the privileges of society, patriarchy is actually used as a tool to attack Black people, both men and women included.

The notion that the problem of Black communities is down to the lack of Black fathers has long political history. In the US the Moynihan Report in 1965 laid the framework that explains racism on Black family dysfunction and lack of male role models, that negatively impacts on Black boys, who would grow into deviant Black men. We have seen this exact argument made in Britain, including from so-called Black commentators like Tony Sewell, who somehow came to the conclusion that 'more than racism, I now firmly believe that the main problem holding back Black boys academically is their over-feminised upbringing'.[23] Absentee fathers leave the mother raising the boys, who coddle them and feminize them leading to disastrous consequences. It seems like Black women are despised, not only by Whiteness but by large sections of the Black community. In response we see countless programmes to mentor Black boys in order to give them the male attention that will fix all the ills in the community.

After the death of Trayvon, murdered because he was a Black male who seemed out of place in a gated community in Florida, Obama demonstrated the violence of racial patriarchy. After lamenting that Trayvon was murdered and exclaiming solidarity by admitting that 'if I had a son, he would look like Trayvon', Obama eventually put his presidential power behind a project to address the problems that the killing had shed light on. No, he did not lend his voice, or power, to finding justice for Trayvon. He did not seek any legislative redress to Florida's 'stand your ground' laws, which played a major part in his killer's acquittal. He most certainly did nothing to address the structural issues of racism. In fact, his response actually poured gasoline onto the very stereotypes that lay at the heart of the assumptions that led to Trayvon's death. George Zimmerman followed Trayvon because he assumed he was from Anderson's 'iconic ghetto'. A thug, no doubt raised by a single mother, who was roaming the streets looking to do crime. Obama's response to this murder was to set up My Brother's Keeper, a mentoring programme for Black boys without a father, largely funded by the private sector. This would be bad enough, but Trayvon was visiting his father at the time he was killed. When Ralph Ellison said he was an invisible man, this is exactly what he meant. Trayvon was completely lost in this response; he was replaced by the iStock image of a young Black hood nigga, the same cardboard cut-out that Zimmerman shot to death. Obama was not just embracing Moynihan, he was actually more regressive than the fifty-year-old report.[24] Moynihan at least acknowledged some of the structural issues that prevented Black men from heading their families and recommended financial support for them to gain employment. My Brother's Keeper removed any structural analysis and presented the problem as deviant children, with their unfit Black mothers, which could be solved through modelling their behaviour on more appropriate male mentors. Watching Obama announce his policy in the company of the right-wing figures including the devilish Bill O'Reilly, who was responsible for a disproportionate share of the demonization of Trayvon, was the ultimate reminder that he was simply a Black man in a White House.

What we therefore witness from the state is increased attention on Black men and boys, but it is in no way positive or helpful, and reinforces the wider assault on all Black people. By framing the problem as a deficit within the community and then providing palliative care to the imaginary illness, the state is free to continue the marginalization of both Black men and women.

Intersectional politics

'Stop killing the mandem' was first printed on t-shirts by Sara Bristol-Abbott, who subsequently joined our Black Studies degree at Birmingham City University. At the time she did not realize that she was following in a long and distinguished tradition. Black women have historically mobilized on issues that predominantly effect Black men for the simple reason that racism is intersectional; whatever happens to Black men, happens to Black women and vice versa. When Black young men are killed we often see the mothers leading the campaigns for justice, whether it be Mamie Till, Lesley McSpadden or Doreen Lawrence. A system of mass incarceration that takes so many Black men can only have negative consequences for Black women.

Three queer Black women, Alicia Garza, Patrisse Khan-Cullors and Opal Tometi, birthed Black Lives Matter in response to the death of Trayvon Martin, because seeing your brother, son, cousin, or friend gunned down by the police is a trauma that reverberates across gender lines. Campaigns against state violence display some of the earliest intersectional mobilizations. Black women were not coming to the defence of Black men in these instances, they were mobilizing for the community.

Ida B. Wells declared that anti-lynching campaigns should be a feminist issue, chastising White feminists for not being involved.[25] Of the at least 4,000 African Americans lynched post-emancipation into the sixties, the majority were men, but for Wells this did not make it a male issue. Black communities are intersectional, so thousands of Black men being lynched has to be an issue for Black women. Wells also drew attention to the Black women who were lynched during the period. To take an issue which disproportionately impacts on men does not mean we have to focus solely on the masculine. Inspired by the Say Her Name campaign, Bristol-Abbott added a 'Stop killing the gal-dem' t-shirt to draw attention to Black women murdered by the police.

These movements should remind us of the interconnectedness of our struggles. It is too easy to condemn past movements for not focusing on women's issues. I've heard some version of the refrain that 'no Black organisation ever centred the needs of Black women' that has become almost a knee-jerk response. Such sentiment is as ahistorical as it is absurd. It is true that we have tended to view HIStory as a series of great men progressing the world forward as a sickness that plagues Black thought. Malcolm X, Martin Luther King, W. E. B. Dubois, Marcus Garvey, Frederick Douglass, Nat Turner, Kwame Nkrumah, Sam Sharpe and in Britain even an attempt to put the late Darcus Howe[26] into the hall of fame. In the same way that we need to say the name of the women killed by the police, we need to do the same for those who have been essential to the Black freedom struggle. To name a few: Assata Shakur, Yaa Assantewaa, Mbuya Nehanda, Fannie Lou Hamer, Queen Nanny, Cecile Fatiman, Amy Jaques and Amy Ashwood Garvey, Olive Morris. There is some excellent recent scholarship painting Black women into Black politics in the US and similar is needed across the diaspora.[27] No Black social movement was ever possible without the contribution of Black women and they were not struggling to only save Black men.

As we have already seen, issues like lynching and police violence are not male issues. Similarly, all the problems of the Civil Rights Movement (access to voting rights, desegregation and affirmative action) were not for men, they were struggles made for Black people, by Black people. The same is true for the Garvey movement, the Panthers and national struggles across Africa and the diaspora. None of these could have existed without Black women and the purpose was never to solely free Black men. We should criticize movements for their form (patriarchy), but it would be wrong, and a disservice to the women involved, to assume that missions excluded Black women.

The intersectional failure demonstrated in Stop Killing the Mandem and the framing of Black Lives Matter is the disproportionate focus that movement campaigns have had on the public sphere. Patriarchy is framed around this public/private sphere split and unfortunately we have fallen into that ravine in our activism. The oppression of Black men is largely in the public sphere, in the streets, in the prisons and courts. It is highly visible and therefore rallies public attention. Black Lives Matter co-founder Patrisse Khan-Cullors recounts how it was the police harassment of her brothers that politicized her growing, so obvious was the racist treatment.[28] On the other hand Black women tend to experience racial oppression in the private sphere. Domestic abuse, sexual violence, evictions and poverty are all aspects that both disproportionately impact on Black women and are also less visible. It is more difficult to film and put these on social media because they are felt most keenly behind closed doors. When feminists declared that the 'personal is political' it was to turn the focus precisely on the oppression in the public sphere that so disproportionately impacts on Black women.[29] We need to do much better at making so-called private-sphere issues part of our political imagination. But the way to do this is the same process that we need to do with those in the public sphere and stop thinking about these as women's issues.

Let's take the disproportionate experience of poverty and evictions as an example. One of the drivers behind these experiences for Black women is the far higher chance of being a single parent. There is no value judgement on single parenthood here, but raising a child on one income creates real financial pressures and around 90% of single-parent families are headed by women. The extent of fatherlessness and its impact is often overplayed by the right, but one impact that is undeniable is on the increased poverty rate of Black women. But there is no way to understand this phenomenon without connecting to the number of Black men being jailed, killed or unemployed. It is no wonder that the rate of single-parent headed families is far higher in Black communities in both America and Britain. We need to mobilize around this issue as a community because it affects all of us.

Even the issue of sexual violence is not a straightforward female issue. Women, and Black women in particular, are undoubtedly more likely to be victims of sexual violence and domestic abuse. Unfortunately, in today's society this is more likely to come from Black men than a threat external to the community. We could easily see this as a woman's issue but to make the personal political surely means to stop seeing acts such as sexual violence as both individual crimes and suffering of victims. In the same way that Black men, disproportionately abused by the police, are deeply connected into the lives of the community, so are the Black women, disproportionately subject to sexual violence and domestic. They are our mothers, sisters, partners, children, and we should be deeply concerned about the patterns of abuse. Anecdotally, it is equally shocking how many Black women have experienced domestic violence and that this is an issue we rarely talk about. It's only when you are close to someone the stories come out. These experiences are generally kept locked in the personal, the private sphere. If we are serious about intersectional politics we need to be putting campaigns to end this violence at the heart of our movements.

Racial patriarchy complicates this process. As discussed above hypermasculinity has been embraced by many in our communities to varying extents. Black manhood is defined so strongly in the image of hypermasculinity, the ability to be attractive, confident with the ladies and good in bed is often present whether or not we acknowledge it.[30] R. Kelly and his abuse of Black children should turn all of our stomachs. But too many of us drank the hypermasculine Kool-Aid, and cannot separate a li'l bump and grind from sexual violence. Central to hypermasculinity is the dehumanization of Black women who are the subject of the so-called real man's attention. Again, this is not a women's issue, it is one that we all need to work through and contend with.

Another problem with accepting the challenge that an intersectional frame necessitates is that because the disproportionate oppression of Black women happens in the private sphere it tends to be at the hands of Black men. We are good at calling out the actions of White people but generally terrible at turning the focus back on ourselves. White police harassing Black men is an easy source of anger. Far less attention is paid to the thousands of killings each year of Black men by other Black men. I can already hear the howls of disapproval of bringing up the idea of Black-on-Black crime. No one calls out White-on-White crime etc. But this is part of the problem. The murder rate for African Americans is absurdly high. Even in the UK where criminals have so few guns that the police are not usually armed you are significantly more likely to be killed if you are Black. The murder rates in places like Jamaica and South Africa are so high they may as well be warzones. To pretend that there is not something deeply problematic here is spectacularly wrongheaded. Police brutality is one of the deadliest forms of racism and of course should be resisted. But the disposability of Black life, at the hands of Black people, is also as a result of our racism and in large part racial patriarchy. The bad nigger goes a long way towards explaining both the disposability of Black life in general and of the disproportionate sexual and domestic violence experienced by Black women; and so do the racial patriarchal stereotypes of Black women as 'strong', able to bear more, even physical pain.[31] To produce an intersectional politics here means to understand how intertwined these issues are for all of us.

Black women mobilizing against the police, and earlier lynching, are a perfect example of intersectional politics: viewing an issue that disproportionally impacts on Black men at the point of delivery but understanding that this was a gendered issue that affected the whole community. Stop Killing the Mandem was a call that came out of this long history of struggle. Whilst the framing seems likely to obscure the killings of Black women, this was certainly not the intention of the organizers. Rather they were organizing around a gendered issue that impacted on the entire community. It is necessary to shift the frame so that it neither excludes the Black female victims of state violence, nor sees the issues solely through the eyes of Black men. The rejection of Say Her Name in some quarters of the BLM struggle is a reminder of the necessity to view the world through the perspectives of Black women. It is only at this intersection that we can see the full nature of racial patriarchy and the nature of the struggle that is necessary. In order to overcome our intersectional failures we must understand that we need unity in struggle, but not a unity based on erasing Black women. We need to understand our Blackness at the intersection of gender in order to make sure that we mobilize against all of the issues we face, whether they be in the public or private sphere. Ignoring the gendered nature of our oppression will ensure that we can never be free.

14

Blackness *is* the intersection

Kimberlé Crenshaw, Kehinde Andrews and Annabel Wilson

We were fortunate enough at both of the workshops to have good weather. Britain is so notorious for rain that there is no safe time in the calendar to pick out dates where it will be dry. After the final workshop, when almost everyone had left, we were sitting outside in the sun discussing how to shape the book. Editorial meetings are always easier when you can relax outside. Nicole Andrews was joining us for tea (a legacy of English colonialism) and was discussing the centrality of Blackness to all of the discussions and work presented at the workshops. She offered a simple but powerful amendment to one of the most well-used metaphors to explain intersectionality. In one of the founding papers of the concept Crenshaw articulates what happens when cars are travelling through an intersection of roads. Discrimination, like traffic through an intersection, may flow in one direction, and

> it may flow in another. If an accident happens in an intersection, it can be caused by cars traveling from any number of directions and, sometimes, from all of them.[1]

It is often cited because it captures how we cannot simply separate out the different axes of oppression that act simultaneously. Being in Britain, Nicole replaced the intersection with one of the most common features of roads in the country, the roundabout. For those unfamiliar with the term, a roundabout is the intersection where roads meet, but to make the traffic run more smoothly there is a circle in the middle that cars must navigate around to get to the exit they need. Britain generally does not do grid systems of road, so needs a way to bring together the various winding roads. As she was talking through the metaphor she narrated how Blackness was the roundabout, the terminal that everything else ran through, the connection of all the papers to each other. Whilst different axes of discrimination all acted at the same time, the inescapable truth was that they worked through Blackness. Or to put it another way, Blackness is *the* intersection to the chapters we have presented, shaping the way that oppression is enacted and overcome.

Understanding Blackness as the intersection is important because it roots the work in this volume to the two foundational theoretical contributions of intersectionality. As we have been at pains to stress throughout, Critical Race Theory (CRT) is an integral part of the intellectual framework that developed intersectionality. The main tenet of CRT is that racism is a permanent feature of society, an unmovable part of the social systems of oppression. This is not to downplay other forms of oppression but to centralize a race analysis. Racism is the external force that produces discrimination. Blackness should never be conflated with Western constructs of race but it does emerge in response to racism. We claim and organize around our Blackness in large part to challenge the oppression of race. Acknowledging Blackness as the intersection therefore places racism at the centre of the analysis. One of the problems with the way that intersectionality has been used is to remove racism from the analysis. This is possible because race is seen as a variable that can be taken away if there are no people of colour involved. But the lesson of CRT is that racism is always at work, even if there are only White people present. To centre Blackness as the roundabout is to remind everyone that you can never remove racism from the equation. Colour-blindness and intersectionality simply do not go together.

Throughout this volume we have also heavily embraced a Black feminist standpoint. Although not all of the papers were written by, or from the perspective of, Black women, the majority were and all engage with Black feminist scholarship. As we explained in the beginning, intersectionality is contingent on the context in which it emerged. In this case that context is Blackness. It is the glue that holds all of the pieces together, and so is more than an axis to be considered alongside others, but the roundabout through which everything must pass.

Of course, intersectionality can and should be applied to wider contexts than those from which it originally emerged. Blackness is the intersection for this collection of work and a wider intellectual movement but that does not hold that it always must be. The specific context matters and we are certainly not arguing that intersectionality can *only* be applied with Blackness at the core. For instance, it would be the definition of appropriation for a group of White scholars to organize a volume centring the work on their relationship to Blackness. Whiteness as the intersection would be the appropriate starting point for the hypothetical group of White scholars. We are arguing that Blackness is at the heart of the ways that we have mobilized intersectionality because our relationship to White supremacy is at the core of how we exist and resist. Furthermore, we hope that these kinds of uses of intersectionality will be picked up, unapologetically framing intersectionality through Blackness. We also hope that the insights gained from centring Blackness will be useful in other contexts. After all this is where the concept emerged and it has gone on to be one of the most influential ideas in shaping how we engage with the social world. To dismiss the wider applications of intersectionality through Blackness would actually be to do away with the concept itself. Black intellectual thought has always had ramifications that go beyond the initial contexts in which it arises. Attempts to apply concepts whilst removing the lessons of Blackness are the continued racist project of Whitewashing intellectual ideas and histories.

Blackness

Having made a case for Blackness as the roundabout, we should be clear that there is no monolithic, solid and unchanging definition of the concept. In fact, engaging through the process of the workshops and putting the volume together has impacted on how we think of the concept. Blackness is not an endpoint, and political ideas that see being Black as the solution are subject to the worst intersectional failures. If you believe there is a pre-colonial African identity to which we can return to solve our problems you are likely reifying a set of patriarchal gender norms that limit the roles for Black women. The same is true if you imagine that there is a modern Black identity, with clean living and a strong two-parent family form, which can erase racial oppression. Unfortunately, even some of the most progressive Black movements for social change have embedded within them a focus on men and their issues at the exclusion of women. Claiming Blackness is not enough, there are too many forms of Black nationalism that marginalize women. A perfect example of this would be the defence of Clarence Thomas from sections of the Black community when he stood for the Supreme Court, solely because of the colour of his skin. The fact he had sexually harassed Anita Hill, a Black woman, somehow did not disqualify him from community support. Thomas turning out to be the most conservative, anti-Black justice on the court is perhaps the outcome that those Black people championing him deserved.

Blackness is not the end, but the starting point. It is our Blackness that brings us together but we need to work collectively to define how we move forward from that point. To engage another metaphor, Blackness is the table, but we all bring our own dishes to make the meal. If we take this volume as an example, all but one of the contributors is Black and everyone brought an array of different dishes across the spectrum. We have different nationalities, genders, sexualities, ages, class positions etc., all contributing to the intellectual feast on display. The key to understanding Blackness is to strip it down to the connection between us as Africans and the diaspora, that which marks us as Black. But Blackness is also a choice that we make to embrace this connection as meaningful, and what makes it so is our commitment to improving the conditions that Black people face. It is not a natural, biological, or even cultural embrace but a political one. Once we frame Blackness in this way then to be anti-Black in any manifestation (sexist, homophobic, anti-trans, disablist) becomes disqualifying. Once we start to demarcate lines of acceptable or authentic Blackness we have destroyed the utility of the concept. More simply put, if we understand Blackness in this way then people like Clarence Thomas are never invited to the table.

Using the metaphor of the table is also useful because it points to Blackness as a co-produced space. The shape of the meal will be determined by what people bring to the table; there is a never finished process of becoming, rather than a set menu with a pre-defined course of action. Testament to the power of Blackness is that it brought such a varied collection of people and ideas to the table and we were able to co-produce what we have presented. Essential to this is to abandon some of the preconceived notions built into what we may have learnt Blackness is. Maleness is a dish we bring to the table, as is being heterosexual or able bodied. We cannot treat any of these as superior or more foundational. Obviously, given the history and present of how terms and politics are mobilized, this is not a simple proposition. We have to unlearn before we can go forward, which is precisely why we need to interrogate and trouble our notions of Blackness, using tools like intersectionality. It is relatively easy to clothe ourselves in the language of intersectionality whilst avoiding its practice.

Blackness is meant to be a tool to unify us in our response to racial oppression. If we can create truly intersectional visions of Blackness then they can help to reshape the social world. In this collection we have shown the embeddedness of racism in the social system; the manifestation of exclusions this creates; and pointed to counter-narratives that can challenge the status quo. All of this has been done through Blackness, bringing together a diverse range of people and ideas in order to provide a framework for engaging in scholarship. We aim for others to pick up the mantle of this work, to create unapologetically Black scholarship that is truly intersectional in its foundation and scope.

Workshopping

An essential tool in producing the kind of intersectional scholarship that we need is to build spaces where we can truly co-create knowledge. Without the workshops this book would not exist in the way that is does. We could have put together an edited collection but the editorial process could not be replicated. All the papers were subject to collective scrutiny and discussion in a supportive atmosphere. Over the five days there was a genuine exchange of intellectual ideas. This involved grounding sessions from Kimberlé Crenshaw and Devon Carbado in CRT and intersectionality; paper presentations from participants; group discussions as well as peer scrutiny. One of the most useful workshop tools was having participants read another contributor's chapter and then present the paper to the group. It really does highlight how strongly the key ideas in a piece of work come across if someone else can present them. These ways of working meant that the process was truly dialogic and collective. We were able to edit through discussion rather than by only sending corrections through email. The process was also a way to attempt to equalize out the power relations. Everyone's papers were subject to the same scrutiny, no matter their rank in the academic hierarchy.

Being away was also important because it meant we also spent time together socially. This is also vital in terms of breaking down hierarchical relationships. Once you've seen your professor die a theatrical fake death in a game of 'Wink Murder' (or 'Killer' as they call it Stateside), you are bound to have a less formal relationship. The building of community is an utterly vital part of producing this kind of this work. Too often we take for granted the notion of a Black community in which we will all magically get along because of the link to each other. Nothing could be further from the truth. Community needs to be built and this can only be done by communing together. At the start of the workshops most people were strangers, but by the end we had all got to know each other. That does not mean we all agreed, or even all got on. Community is not about sameness but about accommodating the various differences into a collective project. It should hopefully be clear that what we have presented in this volume includes areas of contestation as well as consensus. There is no one unified way to see the world, especially not through an intersectional prism of Blackness.

Building these kinds of scholarly communities is something we are committed to in the future and would encourage people to develop. The main barrier is of course cost. Taking groups of twenty people out into the country for a few days is expensive. We managed to mitigate this cost slightly with funding from the Arts and Humanities Research Council (AHRC) as part of a broader Black Studies research network for the second workshop, and had some institutional support from Birmingham City University for the first and UCLA for both. The lesson here is to leverage the resources that you have at your disposal in order to carve out these kinds of spaces. It is also useful to build partnerships across institutions to widen the pool of resources available. We are at a unique time in Britain in that there is now a critical mass of Black scholars in academia, and whilst we are starkly under-represented in both number and positions we must do all we can to hold the universities to account. Another approach we need to take is to build communities outside of the universities that can sustain our collectives. As part of the AHRC bid that part-funded the second workshop there was an aim to establish a Black Studies Association. That kind of work is essential as, if successful, it will mean that we will have resources to support these kinds of collective endeavours.

As much as we have made of the importance of being away, it is also possible to replicate many of the features of the workshop that were so important. Collective working, peer appraisal and social activities can all be done on a smaller scale that does not require the same expense. These are tools we can bring into our everyday working as we look to build localized collectives of knowledge production. What is vitally important is that everyone is invited to the space and is empowered to speak. If Blackness is the table, it cannot serve its function if people do not bring the multitude of dishes that constitute our experiences and struggles.

Future work

Our aim with the volume has been to present an intersectional analysis that is rooted in CRT and Black feminist standpoints. By doing so we hope to have shown the power and importance of these two intellectual frameworks in developing the concept and applications of intersectionality. The idea is by no means to limit intersectionality to Black experiences and struggles, and we envisage that the insights in the book will be useful to how intersectionality applies across a variety of contexts. This could be through both ways of working but also theoretical insights. Important in this regard is the CRT frame that argues race is always present and to exclude it from the analysis is anti-intersectional even when there are no people of colour around.

We also hope to inspire more work on intersectionality through Blackness as an essential tool for building and renewing networks of knowledge produced by Black scholarship. To see Blackness as the intersection is to understand the concept as foundationally intersectional. In the same way it is a mistake to remove race from our considerations of intersectionality, it is equally wrong to see Blackness as a single-axis struggle that does not engage at the intersection with other facets of identity.

Blackness at the Intersection outlines three areas that we feel are particularly rich for scholarship to explore in the future. Institutions are the mechanism through which oppression is delivered, applying the policy framework from the state. Whether it be the Home Office, NHS or universities, these institutions are the perfect sites for research. Highlighting the intersectional failures can illuminate the processes and narratives that promote discriminatory practices. By doing so we better understand the nature of how these systems and wider society operate.

We have also explored how voices are marginalized within these same institutions. Research of this kind is vital because it tells us the toll we take on as oppressed people as we move through some of the spaces we are told it is essential we are part of if we want progress. It also allows us to see the strategies for navigating through these spaces intact and to analyse the best strategies to disrupt rather than conform. Understanding how people are silenced also gives us a better understanding of the ways in which narratives of the powerful are maintained. If we hope to produce counter-narratives we have to understand the nature of what we are dealing with on both the wider and individual scales.

Producing counter-narratives that can unsettle the status quo is essential if we want transformative social change. We need to challenge the old by imagining the new, both in terms of how institutions work but also how we conceive of our own political engagement. An intersectional frame is not something we apply as an afterthought but one we must engage with from the outset. Reconfiguring societal narratives is essential and we would strongly encourage work that seeks to present alternative visions and understandings.

In many ways, one of the most important contributions of *Blackness at the Intersection* has been to present a counter-narrative of Blackness itself. Moving away from the single-axis, male-centric version of the concept, we hope this book has articulated a form of political belonging that can provide the intersectional glue necessary for us to mobilize a true collective for social justice.

Notes

Chapter 1

1   Wolfers, J., Leonhardt, D. and Quealy, K. (2015). 1.5 Million Missing Black Men. *New York Times*, 20 April.
2   Crenshaw, K. (1989). Demarginalizing the Intersection of Race and Sex: A Black Feminist Critique of Antidiscrimination Doctrine, Feminist Theory and Antiracist Policies. *University of Chicago Legal Forum* 1(8), 139–167.
3   Crenshaw, K. (2011). Postscript. Framing Intersectionality: Debates on a Multi-faceted Concept, in *Gender Studies* (pp. 221–233). Farnham, VT: Ashgate.
4   Eze, E. (1997). The Color of Reason: The Idea of 'Race' in Kant's Anthropology. In Eze, E. (ed.), *Postcolonial African Philosophy. A Critical Reader* (pp. 103–140). Oxford: Blackwell, 116
5   Andrews, K. (2021). *Empire 2.0: How the West Is Built on Racism*. London: Allen Lane.
6   Crenshaw, K. (2002). Background Paper For the Expert Meeting on the Gender-Related Aspects of Race Discrimination. *Rev. Estud. Fem* 10(1): 171–188.
7   Chief Justice Warren Majority Opinion.
8   Orfield, G. (2009). *Reviving the Goal of an Integrated Society: A 21st Century Challenge*. Los Angeles, CA: The Civil Rights Project/Proyecto Derechos Civiles.
9   Bell, D. (1992). *Faces at the Bottom of the Well*. New York: Basic Books, 198.
10 Crenshaw, K., Harris, L., HoSang, D. and Lipsitz, G. (eds) (2019). *Seeing Race Again: Countering Colorblindness Across the Disciplines*. Los Angeles: University of California Press.
11 Maylor, U. (2009). What Is the Meaning of 'Black'? Researching 'Black' Respondents. *Ethnic and Racial Studies* 32(2): 369–387.
12 Department for Education (2019). GCSE results ('Attainment 8'). *Ethnicity Facts and Figures*. Available at https://www.ethnicity-facts-figures.service. gov.uk/education-skills-and-training/11-to-16-years-old/gcse-results-attainment-8-for-children-aged-14-to-16-key-stage-4/latest#by-ethnicity
13 Andrews, K. (2016). The Problem of Political Blackness: Lessons from the Black Supplementary School Movement. *Ethnic and Racial Studies* 39(11): 2060–2078.
14 John, G. (2005). This Conflict Has Been 30 Years in the Making. *The Guardian*, 26 October.

15 Modood, T. (1994). Political Blackness and British Asians. *Sociology* 28(4): 859–876.
16 Malcolm X. (1964). The Ballot or the Bullet. Speech at Cory Methodist Church in Cleveland, Ohio, 3 April.
17 Named after the *SS Windrush* that bought over 400 migrants from the Caribbean in 1948.
18 Andrews, K. (2013). *Resisting Racism: Race, Inequality and the Black Supplementary School Movement*. London: Institute of Education Press.
19 Gillborn, D. (2005). Education Policy as an Act of White Supremacy: Whiteness, Critical Race Theory and Education Reform. *Journal of Education Policy* 20(4): 485–505; Warmington, P. (2019). Critical Race Theory in England: Impact and Opposition. *Identities: Global Studies in Culture and Power* 27(1): 20–37. doi: 10.1080/1070289X.2019.1587907
20 Rollock, N. (2019). *Staying Power: The Career Experiences and Strategies Of UK Black Female Professors*. London: University and College Union.

Chapter 2

1 Whilst this chapter was written by Annabel Wilson ('I' refers to Annabel's voice), the story presented is her mother's, and results from countless phone calls and conversations between Annabel and her mother, Paulette. This is why they are listed as co-authors.
2 Hill-Collins, P. (2009). *Black Feminist Thought*. Oxon: Routledge.
3 Hitchcott, N. (1997). African 'Herstory': The Feminist Reader and the African Autobiographical Voice. *Research in African Literatures* 28(2): 16–33.
4 Miller, C. and Swift, K. (1991). *Words & Women: New Language in New Times*. New York: Harper Collins Publishers.
5 A method used to focus upon a micro-level or individual experience whilst illustrating how such experiences derive from macro-level social processes that operate over an extended period.
6 hooks, b. (2000). *Where We Stand: Class Matters*. New York: Routledge.
7 Being detained in psychiatric hospital under a *section* of the UK's mental health act.
8 *Mental Health Act 1983, Chapter 20*. (1983). Legislation.gov.uk. Available at: http://www.legislation.gov.uk/ukpga/1983/20/pdfs/ukpga_19830020_en.pdf [Accessed 24 May 2016].
9 Barnes, R. and Royal College of Psychiatrists. (2015). *Information about ECT (Electro-convulsive therapy)*. Available at: http://www.rcpsych.ac.uk/healthadvice/treatmentswellbeing/ect.aspx [Accessed 24 May 2016].
10 Read, J. and Bentall, R. (2010). The Effectiveness of Electroconvulsive Therapy: A Literature Review. *Epidemiologia E Psichiatria Sociale* 19(4): 333–347.

11 Davis, N. and Duncan, P. (2017). Electroconvulsive Therapy on the Rise Again in England. *The Guardian*. Available at: https://www.theguardian.com/society/2017/apr/17/electroconvulsive-therapy-on-rise-england-ect-nhs [Accessed 7 September 2019].

12 Maultsby, M. C. (1982). A Historical View of Blacks' Distrust of Psychiatry. In Turner, S. M. and Jones, R. T. (eds), *Behavior Modification in Black Populations* (pp. 39–55). Boston, MA: Springer.

13 hooks, b. (1989). *Talking Back: Thinking Feminist, Thinking Black*. Cambridge: South End Press, 7.

14 Lorde, A. (1984). *Sister Outsider: Essays and Speeches*. New York: Crossing Press.

15 Ibid., 8–9.

16 Ali, S. (2011). *Mixed Race, Post-Race*. Oxford: Berg.

17 There are three forms of cultural capital. The first is embodied. It affects how one moves, appears and thinks. The second exists in one's possessions (e.g. books, art, toys, gadgets etc.). The final form is institutionalized, such as educational qualifications, which dependent on their type lead to different possibilities that affect one's social status and opportunities (Bourdieu, 2002).

18 Mental Health Foundation. (2016). *Fundamental Facts About Mental Health 2016*. London: Mental Health Foundation.

19 Care Quality Commission. (2018). *Mental Health Act: The Rise in the Use of the MHA to Detain People in England*. Newcastle upon Tyne. Available at: https://www.cqc.org.uk/sites/default/files/20180123_mhadetentions_report.pdf [Accessed 7 September 2019].

20 Care Quality Commission. (2010). *Count Me in 2009: Results of the 2009 National Census of Inpatients and Patients on Supervised Community Treatment in Mental Health and Learning Disability Services in England and Wales*. London: Care Quality Commission.

21 NHS Digital (2019). *Detentions under the Mental Health Act*. Race Disparity Unit. Available at: https://www.ethnicity-facts-figures.service.gov.uk/health/access-to-treatment/detentions-under-the-mental-health-act/latest [Accessed 7 September 2019].

22 Marmot, M. (2010). *Fair Society, Healthy Lives: A Strategic Review of Inequalities in England*. London: University College London. Available at: http://www.instituteofhealthequity.org/projects/fair-society-healthy-lives-the-marmot-review [Accessed 24 May 2016].

23 Hooks, *Aint I a Woman*, 52–3.

24 Crenshaw, K. (1989). Demarginalizing the Intersection of Race and Sex: A Black Feminist Critique of Antidiscrimination Doctrine, Feminist Theory and Antiracist Policies. *University of Chicago Legal Forum* 1(8): 139–167.

25 Tasca, C., Rapetti, M., Carta, M. G. and Fadda, B. (2012). Women and Hysteria in the History of Mental Health. *Clinical Practice and Epidemiology in Mental Health 8*: 110–119.

26 Jackson, V. (2003). In Our Own Voice: African-American Stories of Oppression, Survival and Recovery. *Off Our Backs* 33(7/8): 19–21.

27 Ibid.

28 Swartz, S. (1995). The Black Insane in the Cape, 1891–1920. *Journal of Southern African Studies* 21(3): 399–415.

29 Du Bois, W. E. B. (1920). Race Intelligence. *The Crisis* 20(3): 329.

30 Annamma, S. A., Connor, D. and Ferri, B. (2013). Dis/ability Critical Race Studies (Discrit): Theorizing at the Intersections of Race and Dis/Ability. *Race Ethnicity and Education* 16(1): 1–31.

31 Bruce, L. (2012). 'The People Inside My Head, Too': Madness, Black Womanhood, and the Radical Performance of Lauryn Hill. *African American Review* 45(3): 371–389, 371.

32 Brontë, C. (1999). *Jane Eyre*. Peterborough: Broadview Press.

33 Rhys, J. (1997). *Wide Sargasso Sea*. London: Penguin Group.

34 Bruce (2012), 372.

35 Ibid.

36 Keating, F., Robertson, D. and Kotecha, N. (2003). *Ethnic Diversity and Mental Health in London: Recent Developments*. The Kings Fund. Available at: http://www.kingsfund.org.uk/sites/files/kf/field/field_publication_file/ethnic-diversity-mental-health-london-recent-developments-frank-keating-david-robertson-nutan-kotecha-kings-fund-1-august-2003.pdf [Accessed 24 May 2016].

37 Harris-Perry, M. V. (2011). *Sister Citizen: Shame, Stereotypes, and Black Women in America*. New Haven: Yale University Press.

38 Hall, S. (1997). *Race: The Floating Signifier*. Sut Jhally. Available at: http://www.mediaed.org/cgi-bin/commerce.cgi?preadd=action&key=407 [Accessed 24 May 2016].

39 Fordham, S. (1993). 'Those Loud Black Girls': (Black) Women, Silence, and Gender 'Passing' in the Academy. *Anthropology & Education Quarterly* 24(1): 3–32.

40 Jordan, B. (1997). Authoritive Knowledge and Its Construction. In Davis-Floyd, R. E and Sargent, C., *Childbirth and Authoritative Knowledge: Cross-Cultural Perspectives* (pp. 55–79). London: University of California Press.

41 Harrison, P. (2016). Stephen Fry's Quite Interesting Moments. *The Telegraph*, 19 February. Available at: http://www.telegraph.co.uk/tv/2016/02/16/stephen-frys-quite-interesting-moments/ [Accessed 24 May 2016].

42 Time to Change. (2012). *Challenging Mental Health Related Stigma and Discrimination Experienced by Black and Minority Ethnic Communities*. Available at: https://www.time-to-change.org.uk/sites/default/files/Black-minority-ethnic-communities-position-statement.pdf [Accessed 24 May 2016]; Mental Health Foundation. (2016). Fundamental Facts About Mental Health 2016. Mental Health Foundation: London.

43 Keating et al. (2003).

Chapter 3

This chapter is part of my doctorate research entitled: 'Weaving an affective economy onto (post)colonial narratives of diaspora: Black Brazilian Women in the United Kingdom', funded by the Coordination for the Improvement of Higher Education Personnel (CAPES, Brazil). I acknowledge the rigorous and caring thesis supervision of Professor Shirley Anne Tate and the opportunity to learn and grow from her mentorship.

1 When referring to Black diaspora, in one hand I am talking about the result of involuntary, forced dispersal of Africans from the homeland to work for the colonial project, which remains racializing and Othering black people to the point of consistent dispossession, marginalization and subordination of this group in Western societies. On the other hand, I am situating the Racialized body through a nationalized category, connected with the condition of "immigrant".

2 Quijano, A. (1991). Colonialidad y Modernidad/Racionalidad. *Perú Indígena* 29: 11–21.

3 Fish, S. E. (1989). *Doing What Comes Naturally: Change, Rhetoric and the Practice of Theory in Literary and Legal Studies*. Oxford: Clarendon.

4 Arrizon, A. (2000). Mythical Performativity: Relocating Aztlan in Chicana Feminist Cultural Productions. *Theatre Journal* 52(1): 23–49.

5 McCall, L. (2005). The Complexity of Intersectionality. *Signs* 30(3): 1771–1800.

6 Such as Lykke, N. (2010). *Feminist Studies: A Guide to Intersectional Theory, Methodology and Writing*. Abingdon: Routledge.

7 Carbado, D., Crenshaw, K., Mays, V. and Tomlinson, B. (2013). Intersectionality: Mapping the Movements of a Theory. *Du Bois Review* 10(2): 303–312.

8 Ibid., 6.

9 Ribeiro, D. (2016). Feminismo Negro para um novo marco civilizatório. *Revista Internacional de Direitos Humanos* 13(24): 99–104; Ribeiro, D. (2017). *O que é lugar de fala?* São Paulo: Letramento.

10 Collins, P. H. (1990). *Black Feminist Thought: Knowledge, Conscousness, and the Politics of Empowerment*. London: Routledge, 19.

11 Ribero, *O que é lugar de fala?*

12 Fanon, F. (1952). *Black Skin, White Masks*. London: Pluto.

13 Ibid., 82.

14 I am using here the notion of 'crystallized ideas of Blackness' to question White-Wo/Man-Western-Euro-centric normative of stereotyping the black body and echo Shirley Anne Tate (2005) in the way she engages critically with Critical Race Studies by interrogating Paul Gilroy's expression 'changing same' to suggest the uniqueness of identifications of otherness that is simultaneously a radical sameness inscribed in Black women's discourses on their Black womanhood.

15 Gutiérrez Rodríguez, E. (2008). Lost in Translation: Transcultural Translation and Decolonization of Knowledge. *Transversal Texts*. Available at: http://eipcp.net/transversal/0608/gutierrez-rodriguez/en [Accessed 10 January 2019], 4.

16 Muñoz, J. E. (1999). *Disidentifications: Queers of Color and the Performance of Politics*. Minneapolis: University of Minnesota Press, 677.

17 González, L. (1988). Nanny: Pilar da Amefricanidade. *Revista Humanidades* 17(UNB).

18 Phoenix, A. and Pattynama, P. (2006). Intersectionality. *European Journal of Women's Studies* 13(3): 187–192, 187.

19 Gutiérrez Rodríguez, E. (2010). *Migration, Domestic Work and Affect: A Decolonial Approach on Value and the Feminization of Labor*. London: Routledge, 4.

20 Ibid., 5.

21 Kilomba, G. (2008). *Plantation Memories: Episodes of Everyday Racism*. Münster: Unrast, 16.

22 Tate, S. A. (2005). *Black Skins, Black Masks: Hybridity, Dialogism, Performativity*. Aldershot: Ashgate.

23 Ceci is a tupi-guarani name that means 'my mother' or 'the mother of crying'. It is known as a powerful name related to the mother Earth.

24 Gabriela: this name is inspired by Jorge Amado's book *Gabriela, Cravo e Canela*, a character who at the same time that is stereotyped by the hypersexualized seductive national imaginary of the 'mulata' – which generates a few problems, has a charismatic and strong personality that captivates everyone surrounding her. She ruptures with the patriarchy finding her liberation through her own strength.

25 González, *Nanny: Pilar da Amefricanidade*.

26 González, L. (1988). *Por um Feminismo Afrolatinoamericano*. Rio de Janeiro: Revista Isis; González, L. (1983). *Griot e Guerreiro*. In Nascimento, A. D. (ed.), *Sankofa: Resgate da Cultura Afro-Brasileira*. Rio de Janeiro: Achiamé.

27 Crenshaw, K. (1991). Mapping the Margins: Intersectionality, Identity Politics, and Violence against Women of Color. *Stanford Law Review* 43(6): 1241–1299.

28 Hunter, S. (2015). *Power, Politics and the Emotions: Impossible Governance?* Abingdon: Routledge, 48.

29 Leeds, U. o. and Services, L. A. W. s. R. (2015). *Latin Americans Migrating from Europe to the UK: Barriers to Accessing Public Services and Welfare*. Leeds.

30 Pacheco, A. C. L. (2013). *Mulher negra: Afetivide e Solidão*. Salvador: EDUFBA.

31 I refrained from exposing the details of this abuse to accommodate the emphasis Gabriela expressed during our conversation about the intersectional oppression sufferend in a British institution while giving birth, which is the point of this narrative. However, it was difficult to translate the tenderness and resilience in Gabriela's tone to talk about her

mother in a description of violence that flows with ethics of caring, respect and love as praxis of healing (Collins, 1990; hooks, 2000).

32 Nair, M., Kurinczuk, J. J. and Knight, M. (2014). Ethnic Variations in Severe Maternal Morbidity in the UK: A Case Control Study. *PloS One* 9(4): e95086.

33 Elattar, A., Selamat, E. M., Robson, A. A. and Loughney, A. D. (2008). Factors Influencing Maternal Length of Stay after Giving Birth in a UK Hospital and the Impact of Those Factors on Bed Occupancy. *Journal of Obstetrics and Gynaecology* 28(1): 73–76.

34 Mothers and Babies: Reducing Risk through Audits and Confidential Enquiries across the UK (MBRRACE-UK) (2018). Saving Lives, Improving Mothers' Care: Lessons Learned to Inform Maternity Care from the UK and Ireland Confidential Enquiries into Maternal Deaths and Morbidity 2014–16. Healthcare Quality Improvement Partnership and National Perinatal Epidemiology Unit, University of Oxford. Available at: https://www.npeu.ox.ac.uk/downloads/files/mbrrace-uk/reports/MBRRACE-UK%20Maternal%20Report%202018%20-%20Web%20Version.pdf [Accessed 10 January 2019].

35 Consterdine, E. (2018). Hostile Environment: The UK Government's Draconian Immigration Policy Explained. *The Conversation*, 04. Available at: http://theconversation.com/hostile-environment-the-uk-governments-draconian-immigration-policy-explained-95460 [Accessed 10 January 2019].

36 Sigona, N., Gamlen, A., Liberatore, G. and Kringelbach, N. H. (eds) (2015). *Diasporas Reimagined: Spaces, Practices and Belonging*. Oxford: University of Oxford.

37 Gutiérrez Rodríguez, *Lost in Translation*.

38 Ibid.

39 Spillers, H. J. (1996). 'All the Things You Could Be by Now If Sigmund Freud's Wife Was Your Mother': Psychoanalysis and Race. *Critical Inquiry* 22(4): 710–734, 712.

40 Hunter, Shona (2005). Negotiating Professional and Social Voices in Research Principles and Practice. *Journal of Social Work Practice* 19(2): 149–162.

41 Lewis, Gail (2017). Questions of Presence. *Feminist Review* 117(1): 1–19, 13.

42 Nascimeto, T. (2018). Fala Preta. In *DVD Vera Verônika – Show ao Vivo, Vera Verônika Oficial*. Available at: https://www.youtube.com/watch?v=YLBIspkJVbI&feature=youtu.be&t=4596 [Accessed 10 January 2019].

Chapter 4

1 Arshad, R. (1990). The Scottish Black Women's Group. In S. Henderson and A. Mackay (eds). *Grit and Diamonds: Women in Scotland Making History,*

1980–1990. Edinburgh: Stramullion Ltd and The Cauldron Collective, pp. 118–120.

2 Meer, N. (2015). Looking up in Scotland? Multinationalism, Multiculturalism and Political Elites. *Ethnic and Racial Studies* 38(9): 1477–1496.

3 Crenshaw, K. (1989). Demarginalizing the Intersection of Race and Sex: A Black Feminist Critique of Antidiscrimination Doctrine, Feminist Theory and Antiracist Politics. *University of Chicago Legal Forum* (1): 139–167.

4 James, S. M. and Busia, A. P. A. (1993). *Theorizing Black Feminisms: The Visionary Pragmatism of Black Women*. London: Routledge.

5 Bailey, M. and Trudy (2018). On Misogynoir: Citation, Erasure, and Plagiarism. *Feminist Media Studies* 18(4): 762–768.

6 Sobande, F. (2017). Watching Me Watching You: Black Women in Britain on YouTube. *European Journal of Cultural Studies* 20(6): 655–671; Sobande, F. (2018). Managing Media as Parental Race-Work: (Re)Mediating Children's Black Identities. In S. N. N. Cross, C. Ruvalcaba, A. Venkatesh and R. W. Belk (eds), *Consumer Culture Theory: Research in Consumer Behaviour Volume 19*. Bingley: Emerald, pp. 37–56.

7 University of Glasgow (2018). University of Glasgow Publishes Report Into Historical Slavery. Available at: https://www.gla.ac.uk/news/headline_607154_en.html

8 Palmer, L. A. (2016). Introduction. In K. Andrews and L. A. Palmer (eds), *Blackness in Britain*. London: Routledge, pp. 9–23.

9 Andrews, K. (2016). The Problem of Political Blackness: Lessons from the Black Supplementary School Movement. *Ethnic and Racial Studies* 39(11): 2060–2078.

10 hill, l. r. and Sobande, F. (2018). In Our Own Words: Organizing and Experiencing Exhibitions as Black Women and Women of Colour. In R. Finkel, B. Sharp and M. Sweeney (eds),. *Accessibility, Inclusion and Diversity in Critical Event* Studies. Oxon: Routledge, pp. 107–121.

11 Bryan, B., Dadzie, S. and Scafe, S. (1985). *Heart of the Race: Black Women's Lives in Britain*. London: Virago.

12 hooks, b. (1990). *Yearning: Race, Gender, and Cultural Politics*. Toronto: Between-the-Lines.

13 Hirsch, A. (2018). *Brit(ish): On Race, Identity and Belonging*. London: Jonathan Cape.

14 Scottish Government (2018). *Summary: Ethnic Groups Demographic*. Edinburgh: Scottish Government. Available at: http://www.gov.scot/Topics/People/Equality/Equalities/DataGrid/Ethnicity/EthPopMig

15 The Afro-Caribbean Women's Association (1990). Our Day of Awakening. In S. Henderson and A. Mackay (eds), *Grit and Diamonds: Women in Scotland Making History, 1980–1990*. Edinburgh: Stramullion Ltd and The Cauldron Collective, pp.121–122.

16 Dabiri, E. (2013). Who Stole All the Black Women from Britain? *Media Diversified*, 5 November. Available at: https://mediadiversified. org/2013/11/05/who-stole-all-the-Black-women-from-britain

17 hill, l. r. (2017). News Blackout – Why Aren't Black British Women Treated Fairly in the Media? *National Union of Journalists Scotland*, 30 March. Available at: https://nujscotland.org.uk/2016/10/11/women-of-colour-the-media-and-misrepresentation

18 Johnson, A. (2017). Getting Comfortable to Feel at Home: Clothing Practices of Black Muslim Women in Britain. *Gender, Place & Culture* 24(2): 274–287.

19 Sulter, M. (1985). *As a Blackwoman*. London: Akira Press.

20 Kay, J. (2010). *Red Dust Road*. London: Picador.

21 National Union of Journalists Scotland (2016). Women of Colour, the Media and (Mis)Representation. Available at: https://nujscotland.org. uk/2016/10/11/women-of-colour-the-media-and-misrepresentation/

22 Emejulu, A. and Sobande, F. (2019). *To Exist Is to Resist: Black Feminism in Europe*. London: Pluto Press.

Chapter 5

1 Wright, C., Weekes, D., McLaughlin, A. and Webb, D. (1998). Masculinised Discourses within Education and the Construction of Black Male Identities amongst African Caribbean Youth. *British Journal of Sociology of Education* 19(1): 75–87; Crozier, G. (2005). 'There's A War against Our Children': Black Educational Underachievement Revisited. *British Journal of Sociology of Education* 26(5): 585–598.

2 Archer, L. and Francis, B. (2007). *Understanding Minority Ethnic Achievement: Race, Gender, Class and 'Success'*. London: Routledge Falmer; Modood, T. (2012). Capitals, Ethnicity and Higher Education. In Basit, T. and Tomlinson, S. (eds), *Social Inclusion and Higher Education* (pp. 17–40). Bristol: The Policy Press.

3 Havergal, C. (2015). *Russell Group Access: Poorest Fall Further Behind*, https://www.timeshighereducation.com/news/russell-group-access-poorest-fall-further-behind

4 de Vries, R. (2014). Earning by Degrees: Differences in the Career Outcomes of UK Graduates. London: UK. Online. https://dera. ioe.ac.uk/30244/1/Earnings-by-Degrees-REPORT-1.pdf [Accessed 11 November 2018].

5 Solórzano, D. G., Ceja, M. and Yosso, T. J. (2000). Critical Race Theory, Racial Microaggressions, and Campus Racial Climate: The Experiences of African American College Students. *The Journal of Negro Education* 69(1/2): 60–73, 60.

6   Burgin, S. (2017). UK Higher Education Has 'Shrugged Its Shoulders' at
    Race and Gender Discrimination. *Times Higher Education*. Online. https://
    www.timeshighereducation.com/blog/uk-higher-education-has-shrugged-
    its-shoulders-race-and-gender-discrimination; Gabriel, D. and Tate, S. A.
    (2017). *Inside the Ivory Tower: Narratives of Women of Colour Surviving and
    Thriving in British Academia*. London: Trentham Books; Reay, D., Davies,
    J., David, M. and Ball, S. J. (2001). Choices of Degree or Degrees of Choice?
    Class, 'Race' and the Higher Education Choice Process. *Sociology* 35(4):
    855–874.

7   Elevation Networks Trust. (2012). *Race to the Top: The Experience of Black
    Students in Higher Education*. The Bow Group: London; Race for Equality.
    (2010) Report on Experiences of Black Students in Further and Higher
    Education. Online. https://www.nus.org.uk/PageFiles/12238/NUS_Race_
    for_Equality_web.pdf

8   Lamont, M., Silva, G. M., Welburn, J., Guetzkow, J., Mizrachi, N.,
    Herzog, H. and Reis, E. (2016). *Getting Respect: Responding to Stigma and
    Discrimination in the United States, Brazil, and Israel*. Princeton: Princeton
    University Press.

9   Goffman, E. (1962/2009). *Stigma: Notes on the Management of a Spoiled
    Identity*. New York: Simon and Schuster.

10 Ingram, N. (2014). *Being a Man and Getting Away with It? Working-Class
    Hegemonic Masculinity and Educational Success*. Unpublished Manuscript,
    Univ. of Bath, 29.

11 Bourdieu, P. (1984). *Distinction: A Social Critique of the Judgement of Taste*.
    London: Routledge, 466.

12 Bourdieu, P. (1990). *The Logic of Practice* (trans. R. Nice). Stanford:
    Stanford University Press, 11.

13 Gillborn, D. (2005). Education Policy as an Act of White Supremacy:
    Whiteness, Critical Race Theory and Education Reform. *Journal of
    Education Policy* 20(4): 485–505.

14 Phoenix, A. and Frosh, S. (2001). Positioned by 'Hegemonic' Masculinities:
    A Study of London Boys' Narratives of Identity. *Australian Psychologist* 36:
    27–35; Youdell, D. (2004). Identity Traps or How Black Students Fail: The
    Interactions between the Biographical, Sub-Cultural and Learner Identities.
    In Ladson-Billings, G. and Gillborn, D. (eds), *Multicultural Education*
    (pp. 84–102). London: Routledge Falmer.

15 Martino, W. (1999). 'Cool Boys', 'Party Animals', 'Squids' and 'Poofters':
    Interrogating the Dynamics and Politics of Adolescent Masculinities in
    Schools. *British Journal of the Sociology of Education* 20(2): 239–264.

16 Puwar, N. (2004). *Space Invaders*. Oxford: Berg Publishers.

17 Payne, Y. A. and Suddler, C. (2014). Cope, Conform, or Resist? Functions
    of a Black American Identity at a Predominantly White University. *Equity
    & Excellence in Education* 47(3): 385–403.

18 Wilkins, A. (2012). 'Not Out To Start A Revolution': Race, Gender, and Emotional Restraint Among Black University Men. *Journal of Contemporary Ethnography* 41(1): 34–65.
19 Goldberg, D. T. (2010). Call and Response. *Patterns of Prejudice* 40(1): 89–106, 90.
20 Puwar, N. (2004). Fish in and out of Water: A Theoretical Framework for Race and the Space for Academia. In Law, I., Phillips, D. and Turney, L. (eds), *Institutional Racism in Higher Education*. London: Trentham Books, Ltd.
21 Bell, D. (1992). The Rules of Racial Standing. In Bell, D. (ed.), *Faces at the Bottom of the Well* (pp. 109–126). New York: Basic Books.
22 Rollock, N. (2012). Unspoken Rules of Engagement: Navigating Racial Microaggressions in the Academic Terrain. *International Journal of Qualitative Studies in Education* 25(5): 517–532.
23 Gilroy, P. (1995). To Be Real: The Dissident Forms of Black Expressive Culture. In Ugwu, C. (ed.), *Let's Get It On: The Politics of Black Performance* (pp. 12–33). Seattle, WA: Bay Press.
24 Kaiser, C. R. and Miller, C. T. (2001) Stop Complaining! The Social Costs of Making Attributions to Discrimination. *Journal of Personality and Social Psychology* 27(2): 254–263.
25 Morrison, T. (1975). The Public Dialogue on the American Dream Theme, part 2. Black Studies Center public dialogue. Online. Available at: https://www.mackenzian.com/wp-content/uploads/2014/07/Transcript_PortlandState_TMorrison.pdf
26 Peterson, J. J. (2007). *The Effect of Social Identity, Social Power, Professor Gender and Race on Informal Student-Faculty Interactions*. PhD Thesis. Minneapolis: University of Minnesota, Online. Available at: http://Gradworks.Umi.Com/32/80/3280723.Html [Accessed 12 March 2018].
27 DuBois, W. E. B. (1903). *The Souls of Black Folk*. Oxford: Oxford University Press.
28 hooks, b. (1994). *Teaching to Transgress: Education as the Practice of Freedom*. New York: Routledge, 39.

Chapter 6

1 University College London (2018). *Legacies of British Slave-ownership* (Legacies). 'Context'.
2 Crenshaw, K. (1994). Mapping the Margins: Intersectionality, Identity Politics, and Violence against Women of Color. *Stanford Law Review* 43(6): 1241–1299.
3 Ahmed, S. (2017). *Living a Feminist Life* [Kindle Edition]. Durham, NC: Duke University Press, loc 216.
4 Ahmed, *Living*, loc 244.

5 Ibid., loc 328.
6 Cho, S., Crenshaw, K. W. and McCall, L. (2013). Toward a Field of Intersectionality Studies: Theory, Applications, and Praxis. *Signs: Journal of Women in Culture and Society* 38(4): 785–810, 787.
7 Cooper, B. C. (2015). Love No Limit: Towards a Black Feminist Future (in Theory). *The Black Scholar* 45(4): 7–21, 8.
8 Crenshaw, *Mapping*, 1249.
9 Williams, P. J. (1995). *The Rooster's Egg*. Cambridge, MA: Harvard University Press, 231.
10 Ibid., 231.
11 'Ann Eliza French', Legacies of British Slave-ownership database, http://wwwdepts-live.ucl.ac.uk/lbs/person/view/19966 [Accessed 18 April 2018].
12 University College London, 'Context'.
13 Ahmed, *Living*, loc 87.
14 Hall, S. (2001). Constituting an Archive. *Third Text* 15(54): 89–92.
15 Ibid.
16 University College London (2018). Legacies of British Slave-ownership (Legacies). Available at: http://www.ucl.ac.uk/lbs/ [Accessed 19 April 2018].
17 Flinn, A. and Stevens, M. (2009). 'It Is Noh Mistri, Wi Mekin History'. Telling Our Own Story: Independent and Community Archives in the UK, Challenging and Subverting the Mainstream. *Community Archives: The Shaping of Memory*, pp. 3–27, 4.
18 Fuentes, M. J. (2010). Power and Historical Figuring: Rachael Pringle Polgreen's Troubled Archive. *Gender and History* 22(3): 564–584, 566.
19 Fuentes, Power, 568.

Chapter 7

1 Du Bois, W. E. B. (1903). *Souls of a Black Folk*. New York: Dover Publications.
2 Hall, S. (1993). Culture, Community, Nation. *Cultural Studies* 7(3): 349–363.
3 Crenshaw, K. (1989). Demarginalizing the Intersection of Race and Sex: A Black Feminist Critique of Antidiscrimination Doctrine, Feminist Theory, and Antiracist Politics. *University of Chicago Legal Forum* 140: 139–16.
4 Hill Collins, P. and Bilge, S. (2016). *Intersectionality*. Cambridge: Polity Press.
5 Lorde, A. (1997). *The Cancer Journals*. San Francisco: Aunt Lute.
6 Kuppan, V. (2017). Spasticus Auticus: Thinking about Disability, Culture and Leisure Beyond the 'Walkie Talkies'. In Spracklen, K., Lashua, B., Sharpe, E. and Swain, S. (eds), *The Palgrave Macmillan Handbook of Leisure Theory* (pp. 595–616). London: Palgrave Macmillan.

7   Vernon, A. (1997). The Dilemmas of Researching from the Inside. In Barnes, C. and Mercer, G. (eds), *Doing Disability Research*. Leeds: The Disability Press.

8   Ahmed, S. (2010). *The Promise of Happiness*. Durham: Duke University Press.

9   Ahmed, S. (2017). *Living a Feminist Life*. Durham: Duke University Press, 13.

10 Stuart, O. (2005). Fear and Loathing in Front of a Mirror. In Alexander, C. and Knowles, C. (eds), *Making Race Matter: Bodies, Space and Identity* (pp. 172–181). Basingstoke: Palgrave Macmillan.

11 Tate, S. (2015). Mi Vex: Silencing, Anger and Insitutional Pain. Speaking the Activism of Black Feminism, 26 March, Trafford Rape Crisis Centre, Manchester.

12 Kuppan, V. (2018). Crippin' Blackness: Narratives of Disabled People of Colour From Slavery to Trump. In Johnson, A., Joseph-Salisbury, R. and Kamunge, B. (eds), *The Fire Now: Ant-Racist Scholarship in Times of Explicit Racial Violence*. London: Zed Books.

13 Puar, J. K. (2017). *The Right to Maim: Debility, Capacity, Disability*. Durham: Duke University Press.

14 Ibid., x.

15 Ibid., xvii.

16 BBC. Manchester Arena Attack: Bomb 'Injured More than 800'. *BBC* 2018; https://www.bbc.co.uk/news/uk-england-manchester-44129386 [Accessed 20 June 2018].

17 Crenshaw, Demarginalizing, 151.

18 Puar, *The Right to Maim*, xv.

19 Ibid., 89.

20 Ibid., xiv.

21 Sharpe, C. (2016). *In the Wake: On Blackness and Being*. Durham: Duke University Press, 9.

22 Sherwood, H. (2018). Doreen Lawrence: Grenfell Tenants Faced 'Institutional Indifference'. *The Guardian*, https://www.theguardian.com/society/2018/jun/02/doreen-lawrence-grenfell-tenants-faced-institutional-indifference [Accessed 2 June 2018].

23 Puwar, N. (2004) *Space Invaders: Race, Gender and Bodies Out of Place*. Oxford: Berg.

24 Anderson, E. (2018). Black Americans are Asserting Their Rights in 'White Spaces'. That's When Whites Call 911. *Vox Media*; https://www.vox.com/the-big-idea/2018/8/10/17672412/911-police-Black-White-racism-sociology [Accessed 10 August 2018].

25 Taylor, T. (2017). Paralympian Forced to Wet Herself on Train without Accessible Toilet. *The Guardian*; https://www.theguardian.com/society/2017/jan/02/paralympian-anne-wafula-strike-wet-herself-train-no-accessible-toilet [Accessed 20 August 2018].

26 Kuppan, Spasticus Auticus.

27   Bell, D. (1980). Brown vs Board of Education and the Interest Convergence Dilemma. *Harvard Law Review* 98: 518–513.

28   Wafula, Strike A. (2018). Disabled Women See #MeToo and Think: What About Us? *The Guardian*; https://www.theguardian.com/commentisfree/2018/mar/08/disabled-people-metoo-womens-movement-inclusion-diversity [Accessed 1 June 2018].

29   Stuart, Fear and Loathing, 172.

30   Erevelles, N. (2011). *Disability and Difference in Global Contexts: Enabling a Transformative Body Politic*. New York: Palgrave Macmillan.

31   Hylton, K. (2018). *Contesting 'Race' and Sport: Shaming the Colour Line*. Abingdon: Routledge.

32   Hylton, *Contesting 'Race' and Sport*, 167.

Chapter 8

1   Bordo, S. (1992). Postmodern Subjects, Postmodern Bodies. *Feminist Studies* 18(1): 159–175.

2   Moi, T. (1989). Feminist, Female, Feminine. In Belsey, C. and Moore, J. (eds), *The Feminist Reader: Essays in Gender and the Politics of Literary Criticism*. London: Macmillan Education.

3   De Beauvoir, S. [1949] (1997). *The Second Sex*. London: Vintage Classics.

4   Bordo, S. [1993] (2003). *Unbearable Weight: Feminism, Western Culture and the Body* (10th anniversary edition). Berkeley, CA: University of California Press.

5   Berger, J. (1972). *Ways of Seeing*. London: British Broadcasting Corporation and Penguin Books.

6   Igenoza, M. (2011). *Femininity as Portrayed Within Western Society*. Thesis, University of Sheffield.

7   Mirza, H. S. (1997). Introduction. In Mirza, H. S. (ed.), *Black British Feminism: A Reader* (pp. 1–28). London: Routledge.

8   Dyer, R. (1997). *White: Essays on Race and Culture*. London: Routledge.

9   Foutz, S. (1999). Ignorant Science: The Eighteenth Century's Development of a Scientific Racism. *Quodlibet* 1: 159–175.

10   Berne, E. (1959). The Mythology of Dark and Fair: Psychiatric Use of Folklore. *The Journal of American Folklore* 72(283): 1–13.

11   Essed, P. (2002). Everyday Racism. In Goldberg, T. and Solomos, J. (eds), *A Companion to Racial and Ethnic Studies* (pp. 202–216). Oxford: Blackwell Publishers, 204.

12   Ware, V. and Back, L. (2002). *Out of Whiteness: Colour, Politics and Culture*. Chicago: Chicago University Press.

13   Morrison, T. (1999). *Playing in the Dark: Whiteness and the Literary Imagination*. Cambridge, Mass: Harvard University Press.

14   Ibid.

15 Hartigan, J. (1997). Establishing the Fact of Whiteness. *American Anthropologist* 99(3): 495–505.
16 Ahmed, S. (2002). Racialised Bodies. In Evans, M. and Lee, E. (eds), *Real Bodies: A Sociological Introduction* (pp. 46–63). Basingstoke: Palgrave.
17 Barthes, R. (2000). *Mythologies*. London: Vintage Classics.
18 Lewis, A. E. (2004). 'What Group?': Studying Whites and Whiteness in the Era of Color-Blindness. *Sociological Theory* 22(4): 623–646.
19 Rawlings, A. V. (2005). Ethnic Skin Types: Are There Differences in Skin Structure and Function? *International Journal of Cosmetic Science* 28: 79–93.
20 Charmaz, K. (2003). Grounded Theory. In Smith, J. A. (eds), *Qualitative Psychology: A Practical Guide to Research Methods* (pp. 81–110). Thousand Oaks: Sage.
21 Poran, M. (2006). The Politics of Protection: Body Image, Social Pressures, and the Misrepresentation of Young Black Women. *Sex Roles* 55(11–12): 739–755.
22 Yancy, G. (2008). *Black Bodies, White Gazes: The Continuing Significance of Race*. New York: Rowman & Littlefield Publishers.
23 Tate, S. (2009). *Black Beauty: Aesthetics, Stylization, Politics*. Farnham: Ashgate Publishing.
24 Jeffreys, S. (2005). *Beauty and Misogyny: Harmful Cultural Practices in the West*. New York: Routledge.
25 West, C. (1995). Mammy, Sapphire, and Jezebel: Historical Images of Black Women and Their Implications for Psychotherapy. *Psychotherapy* 32(3): 458–466.
26 Hill Collins, P. (2004). *Black Sexual Politics: African Americans, Gender and the New Racism*. New York: Routledge.
27 hooks, b. (1992). *Black Looks: Race and Representation*. Boston: South End Press.
28 Truth, S. (1992), Ain't I a Woman? In Schneir, M. (ed.), *Feminism: The Essential Historical Writings* (pp. 93–95). New York: Vintage.

Chapter 9

1 Collins, P. H., (2002). *Black Feminist Thought: Knowledge, Consciousness, and the Politics of Empowerment*. New York: Routledge.
2 Emejulu, A. and Bassel, L., (2015). Minority Women, Austerity and Activism. *Race & Class* 57(2): 86–95.
3 Nash, J. C. (2011). Home Truths on Intersectionality. *Yale Journal of Law and Feminism* 23(2): 445–470.
4 Crenshaw, K. (1991). Mapping The Margins: Intersectionality, Identity Politics, and Violence against Women of Color. *Stanford Law Review* 43(6): 1241–1299.
5 Emejulu and Bassel, Minority Women, Austerity and Activism.

6   Women's Budget Group (2018). Intersecting Inequality: The Impact of Austerity on BME Women in the UK, 30 January. Available online at: https://wbg.org.uk/main-feature/intersecting-inequalities-impact-austerity-bme-women-uk/.

7   Reynolds, T. (2005). *Caribbean Mothers: Identity and Experience in the UK.* London: Tufnell Press.

8   Emejulu and Bassel, Minority Women, Austerity and Activism.

9   Reynolds, T., Erel, U. and Kaptani, E. (2018). Migrant Mothers: Performing Kin Work and Belonging Across Private and Public Boundaries. *Families, Relationships and Societies* 7(3): 365–382.

10   Vannoy, D. (2001). *Gender Mosaics: Social Perspectives.* Los Angeles: Roxbury.

11   Ibid.

12   Updating Ethnic Contrasts in Deaths Involving the Coronavirus (COVID-19), England and Wales: Deaths occurring 2 March to 28 July 2020, https://www.ons.gov.uk/peoplepopulationandcommunity/birthsdeathsandmarriages/deaths/articles/updatingethniccontrastsindeathsinvolvingthecoronaviruscovid19englandandwales/deathsoccurring2marchto28july2020

13   MBRRACE (2020). Saving Lives, Improving Mothers' Care. https://www.npeu.ox.ac.uk/assets/downloads/mbrrace-uk/reports/MBRRACE-UK%20Maternal%20Report%202019%20-%20WEB%20VERSION.pdf

14   Sowemimo, A. (2020). Why Are So Many Black Women Still Dying In Childbirth? *Independent*, 20 August. https://www.independent.co.uk/life-style/health-and-families/black-maternity-deaths-women-childbirth-mary-agyeiwaa-agyapong-a9625276.html

15   Ibid.

16   Braithwaite, C. (2020). *I Am Not Your Baby Mother.* London: Quercus Editions Ltd.

17   Tate, S. A. (2015). *Black Women's Bodies and the Nation: Race, Gender and Culture.* Basingstoke: Palgrave Macmillan.

18   Delgado, R. and Stefanic, J. (eds) (2000). *Critical Race Theory: The Cutting Edge* (2nd edn). Philadelphia, PA: Temple University Press; Delgado, R. and Stefanic, J. (eds) (2001). *Critical Race Theory: An Introduction.* New York: New York University Press.

19   Crenshaw, 1989, 1991.

20   Collins, P. H. (2002). *Black Feminist Thought: Knowledge, Consciousness, and the Politics of Empowerment.* New York: Routledge.

21   Ibid.

22   Marshall, A. (1995). From Sexual Denigration to Self-Respect: Resisting Images of Black Female Sexuality. In D. Jarret-Macauley (ed.), *Reconstructing Womanhood, Reconstructing Feminism: Writings on Black Women* (pp. 5–36). London, Routledge.

23 Guardian, Something Has to Be Done. *Guardian*, 20 October. https://www. theguardian.com/lifeandstyle/2020/oct/02/something-has-to-be-done-tackling-the-uks-black-maternal-health-problem

24 Hall, S. (2006). Stuart Hall and Cultural Studies: Decoding Cultural Oppression.

25 Cocchiara, F., Bell, M. P. and Berry, D. P. (2006). Latinas and Black Women: Key Factors for a Growing Proportion of the US Workforce. *Equal Opportunities International* 25(4): 272–82.

26 Bailey, M. (2016). Misogynoir in Medical Media: On Caster Semenya and R. Kelly. *Catalyst: Feminism, Theory, Technoscience* 2(2): 1–31.

27 Tyler, I. and Bennett, B. (2010). 'Celebrity Chav': Fame, Femininity and Social Class. *European Journal of Cultural Studies* 13(3): 375–393.

28 Women's Budget Group (2018). Intersecting Inequality: The Impact of Austerity on BME Women in the UK, 30 January. Available online at: https://wbg.org.uk/main-feature/intersecting-inequalities-impact-austerity-bme-women-uk/

29 Department for Work and Pensions (2020). Ethnicity Facts and Figures. https://www.ethnicity-facts-figures.service.gov.uk/work-pay-and-benefits/benefits/state-support/latest

30 Allen, K., Mendick, H., Harvey, L. and Ahmad, A. (2015). Welfare Queens, Thrifty Housewives, and Do-It-All Mums: Celebrity Motherhood and the Cultural Politics of Austerity. *Feminist Media Studies* 15(6): 907–925.

31 Bailey (2016).

32 In a recent analyses of Black women's bodies and nationality in the US and UK context, Tate (2015) discusses how Black British Supermodel Naomi Campbell – whose identity she describes as being made into a *'spectacle'* – adheres to many of the racialized, gendered and sexualized discourses of Black womanhood. Considered to be a *'diva'*, *'wild'* in adornments of hints of animality, *'hypersexualised'* and *'sexually deviant'*, are notable labels associated with her. Campbell's identity destabilizes notions of gendered and nationalized discourses which equate Englishness with purity and White femininity (Tate, 2015).

33 Robinson-Wood, T., Balogun-Mwangi, O., Fernandes, C., Popat-Jain, A., Boadi, N., Matsumoto, A. and Zhang, X. (2015). Worse than Blatant Racism: A Phenomenological Investigation of Microaggressions among Black Women. *Journal of Ethnographic & Qualitative Research* 9(3): 221–236.

34 Lewis, J. A., Mendenhall, R., Harwood, S. and Hunt, M. B. (2013). Coping with Racial Microaggressions among Black Women. *Journal of African American Studies* 17: 51–73; Pierce, C. M. (1985). Stress Analogs of Racism, Sexism: Terrorism, Torture, and Disaster. In C. V. Willie, P. P. Rieker, B. M. Kramer and B. S. Brown (eds), *Mental Health, Racism, and Sexism* (pp. 277–293). Pittsburgh, PA: University of Pittsburgh Press; Solórzano, D. G., Ceja, M. and Yosso, T. J. (2000). Critical Race Theory, Racial

Microaggressions, and Campus Racial Climate: The Experiences of African American College Students. *Journal of Negro Education* 69: 60–73.

35   As above.
36   Marshall, A., (1996). From Sexual Denigration to Self-Respect: Resisting Images of Black Female Sexuality. *Reconstructing Womanhood, Reconstructing Feminism: Writings On Black Women* (pp. 5–36). New York: Routledge, p. 18.
37   Adegoke, Y. and Uviebinené, E., (2018). *Slay in Your Lane: The Black Girl Bible*. London: HarperCollins UK.
38   Ibid.
39   Marshall (1996).
40   Gines, K. T. (2011). Black Feminism and Intersectional Analyses: A Defense of Intersectionality. *Philosophy Today* 55 (Supplement): 275–284.
41   Mirza, H. S. (2015, August). 'Harvesting Our Collective Intelligence': Black British Feminism in Post-Race Times. *Women's Studies International Forum* 51: 1–9.
42   Chen, K.H. and Morley, D. eds., 2006. Stuart Hall: Critical dialogues in cultural studies. Routledge.
43   Kim-Puri, H. J. (2005). Conceptualizing Gender-Sexuality-State-Nation: An Introduction. *Gender & Society* 19(2): 137–159.
44   Yuval-Davis, N. (1997). Women, Citizenship and Difference. *Feminist Review* 57(1): 4–27.
45   Reynolds, T. (2005). *Caribbean Mothers: Identity and Experience in the UK.* London: Tufnell Press.
46   Ibid., p. 45.
47   Settles, I. H., Pratt-Hyatt, J. S. and Buchanan, N. T. (2008). Through the Lens of Race: Black and White Women's Perceptions of Womanhood. *Psychology of Women Quarterly* 32(4): 454–468.
48   Emejulu, A. and Bassel, L. (2015). Minority Women, Austerity and Activism. *Race & Class* 57(2): 86–95.

Chapter 10

1   Ajamu (2017). Interviewed by Eddie Bruce-Jones in Brixton, London, 27 January. All direct quotations from Ajamu in this chapter are from the same interview.
2   Minott, Z. (2013). Fierce and That: Ponderings on the Work of Ajamu X, an Original Afro Punk. *Afropunk*, 27 March. Available at: http://afropunk.com/2013/03/fierce-and-that-ponderings-on-the-work-of-ajamu-x-an-original-afro-punk/ [Accessed 27 January 2019].
3   X, Z. (2014). What Is It To Be Fierce? The Photography of Ajamu. *OpenDemocracy*, 11 November. Available at: https://www.opendemocracy.

net/transformation/zia-x/what-is-it-to-be-fierce-photography-of-ajamu
[Accessed 27 January 2019].

4 Crenshaw, K. (1991). Mapping the Margins: Intersectionality, Identity
Politics, and Violence against Women of Color. *Stanford Law Review* 43(6):
1241–1299, 1299.

5 Ferguson, Roderick. A. (2004). *Aberrations in Black: Toward a Queer of
Color Critique*. Minneapolis: University of Minnesota Press.

6 El-Tayeb, F. F. (2011). *European Others: Queering Ethnicity in Postnational
Europe*. Minneapolis: University of Minnesota Press.

7 I owe the idea for this approach to the sensitive editorial review of earlier
drafts, offered by Crenshaw, Andrews and others.

8 Crenshaw (1991), p. 1283. Here, Crenshaw argues that 'the production of
images of women of color and the contestations over those images tend to
ignore the intersectional interests of women of color'. The representational
aspects of Black queers is the central form of engagement that Ajamu
pursues through his portraiture.

9 Jarrett, K. (2017). Psalm 139: The Last Time My Mouth Was Detained by
Customs. In K. Jarrett, *Selah*. Portishead: Burning Eye Books. A portrait of
Jarrett is featured in *Fierce*.

10 Emphasis added.

11 The Guild Hall website (2019). Available at: http://www.guildhall.
cityoflondon.gov.uk/history [Accessed 27 January 2019].

12 Williams, P. (1991). *The Alchemy of Race and Rights*. Cambridge, MA:
Harvard University Press.

13 Ajamu is referring to a concept, written about in a poem by Essex Hemphill
and captured in Marlon Riggs' influential 1989 film on Black, gay men in
New York, *Tongues Untied*.

14 Ferguson, Roderick. A. (2004). *Aberrations in Black: Toward a Queer of
Color Critique*. Minneapolis: University of Minnesota Press, p. 26.

15 Spade, D. (2012). *Against Equality: Queer Revolution, Not Mere Inclusion*.
Chico, CA: AK Press.

16 Lorde, A. (1984). The Uses of the Erotic: The Erotic as Power. In A. Lorde,
Sister Outsider: Essays and Speeches. Trumansburg, NY: Crossing Press.

17 For further recent works by Black queer writers, artists and thinkers in
the UK, see Opoku-Gyimah, P., Beadle-Blair, R. and Gordon, J. R. (eds)
(2018). *Sista!: An Anthology of Writings by Same Gender Loving Women of
African/Caribbean Descent with a UK Connection*. London: Team Angelica
Publishing; Alabanza, T. (2018). *Burgerz*. London: Oberon Books; Gordon,
J. R. and Beadle-Blair, R. (eds) (2014). *Black and Gay in the UK: An
Anthology*. London: Team Angelica Publishing.

Chapter 11

1   Byrd, W. C., Gilbert, K. L. and Richardson, J. B. Jr (2017). The Vitality of Social Media for Establishing a Research Agenda on Black Lives and the Movement. *Ethnic and Racial Studies* 40(11): 1872–1881. doi: 10.1080/01419870.2017.1334937.

2   Williams, R. A. Jr (1997). Vampires Anonymous and Critical Race Practice. *Michigan Law Review* 95: 741–765. Rpt. in Delgato R. and Stefancic, J. (eds) (2000), *Critical Race Theory: The Cutting Edge* (pp. 614–623). Philadelphia: Temple University Press.

3   For examples see Adewunmi (2014). Kimberlé Crenshaw (2014) on Intersectionality: 'I wanted to come up with an everyday metaphor that anyone could use'. *The New Statesman*, 2 April. Available at: http://www. newstatesman.com/lifestyle/2014/04/kimberl-crenshaw-intersectionality-i-wanted-come-everyday-metaphor-anyone-could [Accessed 2 June 2016]; Lewis, H. (2014). The Uses and Abuses of Intersectionality. *The New Statesman*, 20 February. Available at: http://www.newstatesman.com/helen-lewis/2014/02/uses-and-abuses-intersectionality [Accessed 2 June 2016].

4   Cullers, P. and Nguvu, N. (2017). From Africa to the US to Haiti, Climate Change Is a Race Issue. *Guardian*, 14 September. Available at: https://www. theguardian.com/commentisfree/2017/sep/14/africa-us-haiti-climate-change-black-lives-matter

5   Robertson, E. (2017). Intersectional-What? Feminism's Problem With Jargon Is That Any Idiot Can Pick It Up and Have a Go. *Guardian*, 30 September. Available at: https://www.theguardian.com/world/2017/ sep/30/intersectional-feminism-jargon [Accessed 16 October 2018].

6   Hall, S. (1981). Notes on Deconstructing the Popular. In S. Raphael (ed.), *People's History and Socialist Theory*. London: Routledge & Kegan Paul.

7   Smith, A. (2014). *African Americans and Technology Use: A Demographic Portrait*. PEW Research Centre, pp. 1–10. Available at: http://www. pewinternet.org/files/2014/01/African-Americans-and-Technology-Use. pdf [Accessed 2 June 2016]. Although this is platform specific (Twitter, Tumblr), as some social media spaces like Reddit show higher engagement from White males.

8   Mogilevsky, M. (2014). A Brief History of the War between Reddit and Tumblr. *The Daily Dot*, 23 May. Available at: https://www.dailydot.com/via/ inside-war-between-reddit-tumblr/ [Accessed 18 November 2018].

9   Tumblr. (2017). Privacy Policy. https://www.tumblr.com/privacy/en. [Accessed 27 January 2019].

10 Toffler, A. (1980). *The Third Wave*. New York: Morrow.

11 Fiske, J. (1994). *Understanding Popular Culture*. London: Routledge, 35.

12 O'Reilly, T. (2007). What is Web 2.0: Design Patterns and Business Models for the Next Generation of Software. *Communications & Strategies* 65 (Q1): 17–37.

13 Taylor, T. (2018). Digital Space and *Walking Dead* Fandom's Team Delusional. In Tumblr and Fandom, edited by Lori Morimoto and Louisa Ellen Stein, special issue, *Transformative Works and Cultures*, 27. Available online: http://dx.doi.org/10.3983/twc2018.1180 [Accessed 1 December 2018].

14 A few examples are 'contagiousqueer.tumblr.com', 'neilsociology' (tagline: 'Sociology 101') and 'fayonyx.tumblr.com' (tagline: 'Intersectional Social Justice').

15 Lorde, A. (1984). The Master's Tools will Never Dismantle the Master's House. In *Sister Outsider: Essays and Speeches* (pp. 110–113). Freedom, CA: The Crossing Press Feminist Series.pp.

16 Kludt, T. and Stettler, B. (2018). White Anxiety Finds a Home at Fox News'. CNN.com, 28 September. Available at: https://edition.cnn.com/2018/09/28/media/fox-news-laura-ingraham-tucker-carlson-white-nationalism/index.html.

17 ITV requires a British postcode to view the segment after its airing.

18 Amnesty International. (2018). Toxic Twitter: A Toxic Place for Women. Available at: https://www.amnesty.org/en/latest/research/2018/03/online-violence-against-women-chapter-1/.

19 De Certeau, M. and Rendall, S. (1984). *The Practice of Everyday Life*. Berkeley: University of California Press.

20 Hall, S. (1980). Encoding/Decoding. In S. Hall, D. Hobson, A. Lowe and P. Willis (eds), *Culture, Media, Language* (1st edn, pp. 128–139). London: Hutchinson.

21 Jenkins, H. (1992). *Textual Poachers*. New York: Routledge, 26.

22 Gray, J., Sandvoss, C. and Harrington, C. L. (2017). *Fandom: Identities and Communities in a Mediated World* (2nd edn). New York: New York University Press.

23 Guillard, J. (2016). Is Feminism Trending? Pedagogical Approaches to Countering (Sl)activism. *Gender and Education* 28(5): 609–626.

24 Manovich, L. (2001). *The Language of New Media*. Cambridge, MA: MIT Press.

25 Sorapure, M. (2006). Five Principles of New Media, Or Playing Lev Manovich. *Kairos*. Available at: http://kairos.technorhetoric.net/8.2/coverweb/sorapure/five.pdf [Accessed 18 April 2018].

26 Caldwell, P. (2000). A Hair Piece: Perspectives on the Intersection of Race and Gender. In Delgato, R. and Stefancic, J. (eds), *Critical Race Theory: The Cutting Edge* (pp. 275–285). Philadelphia: Temple University Press.

27 Mahr, K. (2016). Protests Over Black Girls' Hair Rekindle Debate about Racism in South Africa. *The Washington Post*, 9 February. Available at: https://www.washingtonpost.com/world/africa/protests-over-black-girls-hair-rekindle-debate-about-racism-in-south-africa/2016/09/02/27f445da-6ef4-11e6-993f-73c693a89820_story.html?noredirect=on&utm_term=.6a119b796aaf [Accessed 27 January 2019].

28   Tate, S. A. (2009). *Black Beauty: Aesthetics, Stylization, Politics*. Abingdon: Routledge.

29   Jenkins (1992), 19.

30   Yampolskiy, R. V. and Spellchecker, M. S. (2016). *Artificial Intelligence Safety and Cybersecurity: A Timeline of AI Failures*. arXiv preprint arXiv:1610.07997

31   Dolcourt, J. (2018). Tumblr Outs 84 Accounts It Says Are Trying to Game You. *Cnet.com*, 23 March. Available at: https://www.cnet.com/news/tumblr-outs-84-accounts-it-says-are-trying-to-game-you-propaganda/ [Accessed 20 April 2018].

32   Tumblr (2018). Account Security. https://tumblr.zendesk.com/hc/en-us/articles/360002280214 [Accessed 20 April 2018].

33   Not all of the eighty-four blogs that Tumblr identified as propaganda sites specifically targeted Black voters, but those who did had 'Black' in the title of their blogs. African Americans are among the most reliable voting block of the Democratic party. Hohmann, J. (2018). The Daily 202: Russian Efforts to Manipulate African Americans Show Sophistication of Disinformation Campaign. *Washington Post*, 17 December. Available at: https://www.washingtonpost.com/news/powerpost/paloma/daily-202/2018/12/17/daily-202-russian-efforts-to-manipulate-african-americans-show-sophistication-of-disinformation-campaign/5c1739291b326b2d6629d4c6/?utm_term=.2ad2c533c38e.

34   Chatman, D. (2017). Black Twitter and the Politics of Viewing *Scandal*. In Gray, J., Sandvoss, C. and Lee Harrington, C. (eds), *Fandom: Identities and Communities in a Mediated World* (2nd edn). New York: New York University Press., p. 30.

35   Marwick, A. E. (2013). *Status Update: Celebrity, Publicity, and Branding in the Social Media Age*. New Haven, NJ: Yale University Press.

Chapter 12

1   Runneymede Trust (2010). David Lammy on Fatherhood: Fact sheet. Available at https://www.runnymedetrust.org/projects-and-publications/parliament/past-participation-and-politics/david-lammy-on-fatherhood/fact-sheet.html [Accessed 18 April 2018].

2   Clarke, E. (1999). *My Mother Who Fathered Me* (2nd edn). London: George Allen Unwin.

3   Patterson, S. (1965). *Dark Strangers*. Penguin: London.

4   Moynihan (1965). *The Negro Family: The Case for National Action*. Washington, DC: U.S. Department of Labour. Available at: https://web.stanford.edu/~mrosenfe/Moynihan%27s%20The%20Negro%20Family.pdf [Accessed 18 April 2018].

5 Cabinet Office (2011). PM's speech on the fightback after the riots. Available at https://www.gov.uk/government/speeches/pms-speech-on-the-fightback-after-the-riots [Accessed 18 April 2018].
6 Lammy, D. (2011). *Out of the Ashes*. London: Guardian Books.
7 Cecil, N. and Bryant, M. (2012). Absent Fathers Are Key Cause of Knife Crime, Says David Lammy. *Evening Standard*. Available at: https://www.standard.co.uk/news/absent-fathers-are-key-cause-of-knife-crime-says-david-lammy-8193990.html [Accessed 18 April 2018].
8 Liddle, R. (2019). Half of Black Children Do Not Live With Their Father. And We Wonder Why They're Dying. *The Times*. Available at: https://www.thetimes.co.uk/article/half-of-black-children-do-not-live-with-their-father-and-we-wonder-why-they-re-dying-pj0n3th6g [Accessed 24 January 2019].
9 Lewis, G. (1993). Black Women's Employment and the British Economy. In James, W. and Harris, C. (eds), *Inside Babylon*. London: Verso, pp. 73–96; Bryan, B., Dadzie, S. and Scafe, S. (1985). *The Heart of the Race*. London: Virago.
10 Phoenix, A. (1996). Social Construction of Lone Motherhood: A Case of Competing Discourses. In Silva, E. B. (ed.), *Good Enough Mothering? Feminist Perspectives on Lone Motherhood*. London: Routledge, pp. 167–190.
11 Reynolds, T. (2005). *Caribbean Mothers: Identity and Experience in the UK*. London: Tufnell Press.
12 Lawrence, E. (1986). In Abundance of Water the Fool Is Thirsty: Sociology and Black Pathology. In Centre for Contemporary Culture Studies (ed.), *The Empire Strikes Back: Race and Racism in 70s Britain*. London: Hutchinson, pp. 95–142.
13 Duell, M. (2018). Absentee Fathers Are to Blame for Rise in Gang Killings and Explosion in Violent Crime Says Ex-Ofsted Chief to the Fury of Single Mothers. *Daily Mail*. Available at: https://www.dailymail.co.uk/news/article-5681849/Single-mothers-react-fury-Ofsted-chiefs-comments.html [Accessed 12 May 2018].
14 Reynolds, T. (2009). Exploring the Absent/Present Dilemma: Black Fathers, Family Relationships, and Social Capital in Britain. *The ANNALS of the American Academy of Political and Social Science* 624(1): 12–28.
15 Sewell, T. (2018). Let's Talk About Gang Culture's Elephant in the Room: Absent Black Fathers. *Telegraph*. Available at: https://www.telegraph.co.uk/news/2018/08/29/talk-gang-cultures-elephant-room-absent-black-fathers/ [Accessed 1 September 2018].
16 Rollock, N., Vincent, C., Gillborn, S. and Ball, S. J. (2015). *The Colour of Class*. London: Routledge.
17 Pattillo, M. (1999). *Black Picket Fences* (2nd edn). Chicago: University of Chicago.
18 Byfield, C. (2008). *Black Boys Can Make It*. Trentham: Staffordshire.
19 Randolph, S. M. (1995). African American Children in Single-Mother Families. In Dickerson, J. D. (ed.), *African American Single Mothers*. Thousand Oaks: Sage, pp. 117–145.

20 Bowling, B. and Coretta, P. (2007). Disproportionate and Discriminatory: Reviewing the Evidence on Police Stop and Search. *Modern Law Review* 70(6): 936–961.

Chapter 13

1   Malcolm X. (1962). Speech in Los Angeles. 5 May.
2   Johnson, U. (2012*). Psycho-Academic Holocaust: The Special Education and ADHD Wars against Black Boys*. Philadelphia: Prince of Pan-Africanism Publishing.
3   Malcolm X. (1964). The Ballot or the Bullet. Speech at Cory Methodist Church in Cleveland, Ohio, 3 April.
4   Andrews, K. (2014). From the Bad Nigger to the Good Nigga: An Unintended Consequence of Black Power. *Race and Class* 55(3): 22–37.
5   Nas (2002). Get Down. *God's Son*. Columbia.
6   Seale, B. (1970). *Seize the Time: The Story of the Black Panther Party*. New York: Random House, 18.
7   Cleaver, E. (1972). On Lumpen Ideology. *The Black Scholar* 4(2–10): 2.
8   Ogbar, J. (2004). *Black Power: Radical Politics and African American Identity*. Baltimore: John Hopkins University Press.
9   Olusoga, D. (2016). *Black and British: A Forgotten History*. London: Macmillan.
10 Wolfers, J., Leonhardt, D. and Quealy, K. (2015). 1.5 Million Missing Black Men. The Upshot, *The New York Times*, April 20. Available at: https://www.nytimes.com/interactive/2015/04/20/upshot/missing-Black-men.html?mtrref=www.ecosia.org&assetType=REGIWALL
11 Higher Education Statistics Agency (2019). HE Academic Staff by Ethnicity and Academic Employment Function (2018/9). *Who's Working in HE?: Personal Characteristics*. Available at https://www.hesa.ac.uk/data-and-analysis/staff/working-in-he/characteristics
12 Rollock, N. (2019). *Staying Power: The Career Experiences and Strategies of UK Black Female Professors*. London: University College Union.
13 Solanke, I. (2017) Black Female Professors in the UK. Runnymede Trust. Available at: https://www.runnymedetrust.org/blog/black-female-professors-in-the-uk
14 Black Female Professors Forum. Available at: http://Blackfemaleprofessorsforum.org
15 Oakley, A. (1974). *Housewife*. London: Allen Lane.
16 Taylor, B. (2017). Color and Class: The Promulgation of Elitist Attitudes at Black Colleges. In Gasman, M. and Tudico, C. (eds), *Historically Black Colleges and Universities: Triumphs, Troubles, and Taboos* (pp. 189–206). New York: Palgrave Macmillan.
17 Hare, N. (1972). The Battle for Black Studies. *The Black Scholar* 3(9): 32–47.

18 Malcolm X. (1964) The Ballot or the Bullet. Speech at Cory Methodist Church in Cleveland, Ohio, 3 April.
19 Kohl, H. and Brown, C. (2005). *She Would Not be Moved: How We Tell the Story of Rosa Parks and the Montgomery Bus Boycott*. New York: The New Press.
20 Law, I. and Tate, S. A. (2015). *Caribbean Racisms: Connections and Complexities in the Racialization of the Caribbean Region*. London: Routledge.
21 Anderson, E. (2012). The Iconic Ghetto. *The Annals of the American Academy of Political and Social Science* 642(1): 8–24.
22 Crenshaw, K. (1992). Whose Story Is It, Anyway? Feminist and Antiracist Appropriations of Anita Hill. In Morrison, T. (ed.), *Race-ing Justice: En-gendering Power* (pp. 402–440). New York: Pantheon Books.
23 Sewell, T. (2010). Black Boys Are Too Feminised. *The Guardian*, 15 March.
24 Crenshaw, K. (2014). The Girls Obama Forgot: My Brother's Keeper Ignores Young Black Women. *New York Times*, 29 July.
25 Wells, I. (2014). *The Light of Truth: Writing of an Anti-Lynching Campaigner*. London: Penguin.
26 Bunce, R. and Field, P. (2017). *Renegade: The Life and Times of Darcus Howe*. London: Bloomsbury.
27 See Blain, K. (2018). *Set the World on Fire: Black Nationalist Women and the Global Struggle for Freedom*. Philadelphia: University of Pennsylvania Press; Farmer, A. (2016). *Remaking Black Power: How Black Women Transformed an Era*. Chapel Hill: University of North Carolina Press; Spencer, R. (2016). *The Revolution Has Come: Black Power, Gender, and the Black Panther Party in Oakland*. Durham: Duke University Press.
28 Khan-Cullors, P. and Bandele, A. (2017). *When They Call You a Terrorist: A Black Lives Matter Memoir*. New York: St Martins.
29 Hanisch, C. (1978). The Personal Is Political. In Redstockings of the Women's Liberation Movement (ed.), *Feminist Revolution* (pp. 204–215). New York: Random House.
30 Young, D. (2019). *What Doesn't Kill You Makes You Blacker: A Memoir in Essays*. New York: Harper Collins.
31 Hill Collins, P. (2000). *Black Feminist Thought: Knowledge, Consciousness, and the Politics of Empowerment*. London: Routledge.

Chapter 14

1 Crenshaw, K. (1989). Demarginalizing the Intersection of Race and Sex: A Black Feminist Critique of Antidiscrimination Doctrine, Feminist Theory and Antiracist Politics. *University of Chicago Legal Forum* 1(8): 139–167, 149.

Bibliography

Abernethy, G. (2010). 'Not Just an American Problem': Malcolm X. in Britain. *Atlantic Studies* 7(3): 285–307.

Acciari, L. (2021). Practicing Intersectionality: Brazilian Domestic Workers' Strategies of Building Alliances and Mobilizing Identity. *Latin American Research Review* 56(1): 67–81. doi: https://doi.org/10.25222/larr.594

Ahmed, S. (2004). *The Cultural Politics of Emotion* (2nd edn). Available at: https://mronline.org/wp-content/uploads/2018/10/Ahmed-Intro_Ch-7.pdf

Ahmed, S. (2017). *Living a Feminist Life*. Durham, NC: Duke University Press.

Ahmet, A. (2020). Who Is Worthy of a Place on These Walls? Postgraduate Students, UK Universities, and Institutional Racism. *Area* 52(4): 678–686.

Alabanza, T. (2018). *Burgerz*. London: Oberon Books.

Andrews, K. (2021). *The New Age of Empire: How Racism and Colonialism Still Rule the World*. London: Penguin UK.

Andrews, K. (2020). Blackness, Empire and Migration: How Black Studies Transforms the Curriculum. *Area* 52(4): 701–707.

Andrews, K. (2018). *Back to Black: Retelling Black Radicalism for the 21st Century*. Farnham: Bloomsbury Publishing.

Arday, J. & Mirza, H. S. (eds) (2018). *Dismantling Race in Higher Education: Racism, Whiteness and Decolonising the Academy*. London: Palgrave Macmillan.

Bell, D. (1992). *Faces at the Bottom of the Well*. New York: Basic Books.

Benston, K. W. (2000). *Performing Blackness: Enactments of African-American Modernism*. London: Routledge.

Berne, E. (1959). The Mythology of Dark and Fair: Psychiatric Use of Folklore. *The Journal of American Folklore* 72(283): 1–13.

Blain, K. (2018). *Set the World on Fire: Black Nationalist Women and the Global Struggle for Freedom*. Philadelphia: University of Pennsylvania Press.

Bordo, S. (2003). *Unbearable Weight: Feminism, Western Culture and the Body* (10th anniversary edition). California: University of California Press.

Carbado, D., Crenshaw, K., Mays, V. and Tomlinson, B. (2013). Intersectionality: Mapping the Movements of a Theory. *Du Bois Review* 10(2): 303–312.

Charmaz, K. (2003). Grounded Theory. In Smith, J. A. (ed.), *Qualitative Psychology: A Practical Guide to Research Methods*. Thousand Oaks: Sage, pp. 81–110.

Clarke, E. (1999). *My Mother Who Fathered Me* (2nd edn). London: George Allen Unwin.

Crenshaw, K. W. (ed.). (2019). *Seeing Race Again: Countering Colorblindness across the Disciplines*. Berkeley: University of California Press.

Crenshaw, K. (2011). 'Postscript': Framing Intersectionality: Debates on a Multi-faceted Concept. In *Gender Studies*. Farnham, VT: Ashgate, pp. 221–233.

Crenshaw, K. (2002). Background Paper for the Expert Meeting on the Gender-Related Aspects of Race Discrimination. *Rev. Estud. Fem.* 10(1): 171–188. Brown v. Board of Education, 347 U.S. 483.

Crenshaw, K. (1992). Whose Story Is It, Anyway? Feminist and Antiracist Appropriations of Anita Hill. In Morrison, T. (ed.), *Race-ing Justice: En-gendering Power* (pp. 402–40). New York: Pantheon Books.

Crenshaw, K. (1991). Mapping the Margins: Intersectionality, Identity Politics, and Violence against Women of Color. *Stanford Law Review* 43(6): 1241–1299.

Crenshaw, K. (1989). Demarginalizing the Intersection of Race and Sex: A Black Feminist Critique of Antidiscrimination Doctrine, Feminist Theory and Antiracist Politics. *University of Chicago Legal Forum* 12: 139–167.

Delgado, R. and Stefanic, J. (eds) (2001). *Critical Race Theory: An Introduction*. New York: New York University Press.

Dumangane, C., Jr (2020). Cufflinks, Photos and YouTube: The Benefits of Third Object Prompts When Researching Race and Discrimination in Elite Higher Education. *Qualitative Research* 53(2): 1468794120972607.

Dyer, R. (1997). *White: Essays on Race and Culture*. London: Routledge.

Emejulu, A. and Bassel, L. (2015). Minority Women, Austerity and Activism. *Race & Class* 57(2): 86–95.

Emejulu, A. and Sobande, F. (2019). *To Exist Is to Resist: Black Feminism in Europe*. London: Pluto Press.

Erevelles, N. (2011). *Disability and Difference in Global Contexts: Enabling a Transformative Body Politic*. New York: Palgrave Macmillan.

Farmer, A. (2016). *Remaking Black Power: How Black Women Transformed an Era*. Chapel Hill: University of North Carolina Press.

Ferguson, Roderick (2004). *Aberrations in Black: Towards a Queer of Color Critique*. Minneapolis: University of Minnesota Press.

Frankenberg, R. (1993). *White Women, Race Matters: The Social Construction of Whiteness*. Minneapolis: University of Minnesota Press.

Gillborn, David, Warmington, Paul and Demack, Sean (2018). QuantCrit: Education, Policy, 'Big Data' and Principles for a Critical Race Theory of Statistics. *Race, Ethnicity and Education* 21(2): 158–179.

Gilmore, R. W., Gilroy, P. and Hall, S. (2021). *Stuart Hall: Selected Writings on Race and Difference*. Durham: Duke University Press.

Gordon, J. R. and Beadle-Blair, R. (eds)) (2014). *Black and Gay in the UK: An Anthology*. London: Team Angelica Publishing.

Hall, S. (1997). *Race: The Floating Signifier*. Sut Jhally. Available from http://www.mediaed.org/cgi-bin/commerce.cgi?preadd=action&key=407 [Accessed 24 May 2016].

Hare, N. (1972). The Battle for Black Studies. *The Black Scholar* 3(9): 32–47.

Harris-Perry, M. V. (2011). *Sister Citizen: Shame, Stereotypes, and Black Women in America*. New Haven: Yale University Press.

Hill-Collins, P. (2009). *Black Feminist Thought*. Oxon: Routledge.

hooks, b. and West, C. (1991). *Breaking Bread: Insurgent Black Intellectual Life*. Boston: South End Press.

hooks, bell. (1989). *Talking Back: Thinking Feminist, Thinking Black*. Cambridge: South End Press.

Jackson, V. (2003). In Our Own Voice: African-American Stories of Oppression, Survival and Recovery. *Off Our Backs* 33(7/8): 19–21.

Jenkins, H. (1992). *Textual Poachers: Television Fans and Participatory Culture*. New York: Routledge.

Lawrence, E. (1986). In Abundance of Water the Fool Is Thirsty: Sociology and Black Pathology. In Centre for Contemporary Culture Studies (eds), *The Empire Strikes Back: Race and Racism in 70s Britain*. London: Hutchinson, pp. 95–142.

Levine, E. (ed.) (2012). *Cupcakes, Pinterest, and Ladyporn: Feminized Popular Culture in the Early Twenty-First Century*. Chicago: University of Illinois Press.

Lewis, G. (2013). Unsafe Travel: Experiencing Intersectionality and Feminist Displacements. *Signs* 38(4): 869–892. doi: https://doi.org/10.1086/669609

Lorde, A. (1984). *Sister Outsider: Essays and Speeches*. New York: Crossing Press.

Marshall, A. (1995). From Sexual Denigration to Self-Respect: Resisting Images of Black Female Sexuality. In D. Jarret-Macauley (ed.), *Reconstructing Womanhood, Reconstructing Feminism: Writings on Black Women* (pp. 5–36). London: Routledge.

Miller, P. (2020). Race Discrimination, the Politics of Knowledge, and Cultural Inequality in England. *Handbook on Promoting Social Justice in Education*, 1913–1934.

Mirza, H. S (1997). Introduction. In Mirza, H. S. (ed.), *Black British Feminism: A Reader*. London: Routledge, pp. 1–28.

Moynihan (1965). *The Negro Family: The Case for National Action*. Washington, DC: U.S. Department of Labour. Available at: https://web.stanford. edu/~mrosenfe/Moynihan%27s%20The%20Negro%20Family.pdf [Accessed 18 April 2018].

Nash, J. C. (2018). *Black Feminism Reimagined after Intersectionality*. Durham: Duke University Press.

Nayak, S. and Robbins, R. (eds). (2018). *Intersectionality in Social Work: Activism and Practice in Context* (1st edn). London: Routledge. https://doi. org/10.4324/9781315210810

Nayak, S. (2021). Black Feminist Intersectionality Is Vital to Group Analysis: Can Group Analysis Allow Outsider Ideas In? *Group Analysis* 54(3): 337–353. doi: 10.1177/0533316421997767

Opoku-Gyimah, P., Beadle-Blair, R., and Gordon, J. R. (eds) (2018). *Sista!: An Anthology of Writings by Same Gender Loving Women of African/Caribbean Descent with a UK Connection*. London: Team Angelica Publishing.

Phoenix, A. (1996). Social Construction of Lone Motherhood: A Case of Competing Discourses. In Silva, E. B. (ed.), *Good Enough Mothering? Feminist Perspectives on Lone Motherhood*. London: Routledge, pp. 167–190.

Pilkington, A. (2018). The Rise and Fall in the Salience of Race Equality in Higher Education. In *Dismantling Race in Higher Education* (pp. 27–45). Cham: Palgrave Macmillan.

Puar, J. (2017). *The Right to Maim: Debility, Capacity, Disability*. Durham: Duke University Press.

Reynolds, T. (2009). Exploring the Absent/Present Dilemma: Black Fathers, Family Relationships, and Social Capital in Britain. *The Annals of the American Academy of Political and Social Science* 624(1): 12–28.

Reynolds, T. (2005). *Caribbean Mothers: Identity and Experience in the UK*. London: Tufnell Press.

Rollock, N. (2019). *Staying Power: The Career Experiences and Strategies of UK Black Female Professors*. London: University College Union.

Rhodes, M. A. (2016). Placing Paul Robeson in History: Understanding His Philosophical Framework. *Journal of Black Studies* 47(3): 235–257.

Shilliam, R. (2019). Behind the Rhodes Statue: Black Competency and the Imperial Academy. *History of the Human Sciences* 32(5): 3–27.

Sobande, F. (2021). Screening Black Lives Matter: On-Screen Discourses, Distortions, and Depictions of Black Lives Matter. *Feminist Media Studies* 21(5): 853–856.

Spencer, R. (2016). *The Revolution Has Come: Black Power, Gender, and the Black Panther Party in Oakland*. Durham: Duke University Press.

Tate, S. (2015). Are We All Creoles? 'Sable-Saffron' Venus, Rachel Christie and Aesthetic Creolization. In Tate, S. and Rodríguez, E. G. R. (eds), *Creolizing Europe: Legacies and Transformations*. Liverpool: Liverpool University Press.

Tate, S. (2015). *Black Women's Bodies and the Nation: Race, Gender and Culture*. Basingstoke: Palgrave Macmillan.

University College London (2018). Legacies of British Slave-ownership (Legacies). Available at: http://www.ucl.ac.uk/lbs/

Wanzo, R. (2015). African American Acafandom and Other Strangers: New Genealogies of Fan Studies. *Transformative Works and Cultures*, 20.

Warmington, Paul, (2020). Critical Race Theory in England: Impact and Opposition. *Identities: Global Studies in Culture and Power* 27(1): 20–37.

Weems, C. (1987). Mirror Mirror, http://www.nathanielturner.com/carriemaeweems.htm

Wells, I. (2014). *The Light of Truth: Writing of an Anti-Lynching Campaigner*. London: Penguin.

X., M. (1964). The Ballot or the Bullet. Speech at Cory Methodist Church in Cleveland, Ohio, 3 April.

Index